8/73

D1499755

# A PICTORIAL HISTORY OF
# AMERICAN LABOR

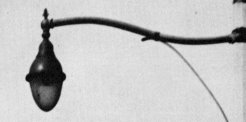

# A PICTORIAL HISTORY OF
# AMERICAN LABOR

## BY **William Cahn**

CROWN PUBLISHERS, INC., NEW YORK

BOOKS BY WILLIAM CAHN

*A Pictorial History of American Labor*

*Einstein*, a pictorial biography

*The Story of Writing*, from cave art to computer (with Rhoda Cahn)

*Milltown*, a pictorial narrative of an industrial town

*Van Cliburn*, the story of a new American hero

*The Jazz Age*, based on NBC Project 20 Program (with Marvin Barrett)

*No Time for School, No Time for Play*, the story of child labor in **America**
(with Rhoda Cahn)

*Labor, USA*, the story of American labor

*A Matter of Life and Death:* The Connecticut Mutual Story

*Out of the Cracker Barrel:* The Nabisco Story

*The Story of Pitney-Bowes*

*Harold Lloyd's World of Comedy*

*Good Night, Mrs. Calabash:* The Secret of Jimmy Durante

*A Pictorial History of the Great Comedians*

*Library of Congress Catalog Card Number: 70–185099*

*ISBN: 0–517–50040x*

*Designed by Ruth Smerechniak*

*Manufactured in the United States of America*

*Published simultaneously in Canada by General Publishing Company Limited*

COMPOSITION BY SPARTAN TYPOGRAPHERS

*I am the people—the mob—the crowd—the mass.*
*Do you know that all the great work of the world is*
    *done through me?*
*I am the workingman, the inventor, the maker of the*
    *world's food and clothes.*

—CARL SANDBURG

# CONTENTS

# A PICTORIAL HISTORY OF
# AMERICAN LABOR

# INTRODUCTION

The history of America has been largely created by the deeds of its working people and their organizations. Nor has this contribution been confined to raising wages and bettering work conditions; it has been fundamental to almost every effort to extend and strengthen our democracy.

We are informed at length about our statesmen and captains of industry, who did, indeed, contribute much to our nation's growth. But we are inadequately acquainted with the men and women whose physical and mental labor cleared the wilderness, built the roads, bridges, levees, railroads, dams, factories, and whatever else helped create our civilization. Their hands and heads did it. But too much of history is written as if they did not exist.

Labor and its organizations have been, from the nation's start, part of the developing democratic process. Seeking redress of grievances and bargaining collectively are as much an element of democratic involvement as voting or seeking public office.

More accurate knowledge of the role of the worker can assist in introducing needed realism in our study of history. The part working people play in developing democracy was pointed out early by Walt Whitman:

See, mechanics, busy at their benches, with tools—See from among them, superior judges, philosophers, Presidents, emerge, drest in working dresses . . .

1

Labor, usually reflecting the society about it, has spoken out and acted for more rather than less democracy; for more rather than less public education; for more rather than less security for the poor and underprivileged. When working people have rallied to a common cause, they have usually succeeded in influencing the nation in the direction of a more humanistic society.

The test of our progress, Franklin D. Roosevelt once said, is "not whether we add more to the abundance of those who have too much, it is whether we provide enough for those who have too little." In such

a test, labor certainly has made a contribution worthy of study.

Today, we must prepare for a different kind of heroics than that to which we have grown accustomed: not the role of "the great man" or the "leader," but the influence of masses of ordinary mortals.

Working people have come a long way since 1791 when journeymen carpenters of Philadelphia bravely announced they "mean hereafter . . . to protect each other." Union membership now extends to crafts, trades, and occupations throughout the nation including mailmen, teachers, basketball players, hair-

OSCEOLA.

dressers, nurses, policemen, and insurance agents, as well as miners, mechanics, and carpenters.

Ours is the story of *all* labor, organized and unorganized, skilled and unskilled, young and old, men and women, white and black, native and foreign born.

The story of American labor—particularly authenticated through photographs, woodcuts, drawings, letters, and documents—is dramatically relevant to today's society. There is scarcely an issue that has not been, and is not, influenced by labor's organized efforts or lack of them.

We have attempted in this work to follow a middle road, avoiding use of extremely partial data, even when its credibility appeared unquestioned. This was done because the subject of labor history has been so surrounded by myths that even a restrained recounting of events sometimes seems partisan.

As we survey labor from its early beginnings to its present complex development (necessarily incomplete in a single volume), certain conditions remain dramatically constant. The historic need for struggle, without which, as Frederick Douglass stated, "there is no progress," remains as valid today as ever.

The fact is that a machine civilization is constantly

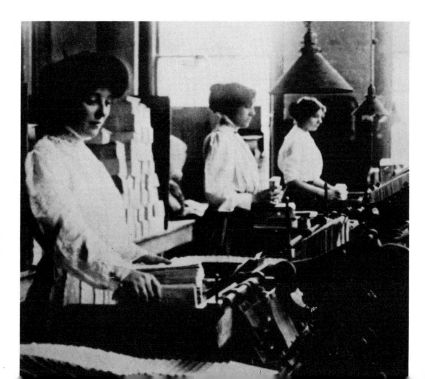

making inroads into human values. Without organized resistance to the exploitation of our human and natural resources, the welfare of all is placed in jeopardy. Labor has been the focus of this resistance, and the study of the history of working people—both in defeat as well as in victory—provides a basis for optimism and courage. We have much to learn from the men and women and even children whose faith in their nation and in themselves never flagged under trial and duress that is scarcely equaled anywhere.

—WILLIAM CAHN

# ONE

# 1607-1760

# A NATION IS FOUNDED
# ON HARD WORK

*"In this country,*
*is no living*
*without hard labour."*

All that stood between life and disaster for the first settlers of America was their ability to labor. They had arrived well equipped with dreams: of riches beyond description; of free, untired land. But they were not prepared for the inexorably hard work that needed doing. So the "Knights, Gentlemen, Merchants, and other Adventurers" wrote home for help.

"When you send again," Captain John Smith wrote from Virginia Colony to his sponsors, "I entreat you rather send but thirty carpenters, husbandmen, gardiners, blacksmiths, masons and diggers of trees, roots, well provided, than a thousand of such as we have . . ."

Captain Smith was impatient with the arrival of a "perfumer" and six tailors rather than essential workingmen. Incentives were set up in some of the colonies to encourage the sending of needed people. Those who dispatched even a single laborer to Virginia were rewarded with substantial land grants, at first one hundred acres per worker, later reduced to fifty.

The iron ore industry in Virginia provides an example of the problems colonies faced in obtaining and maintaining labor. Shortly after the settlement of Jamestown Colony in 1607, a report by Sir Thomas Gates in London stated that there were diverse minerals in the New World, especially "iron oare." A

Indians fishing.

"Declaration of the State of Virginia" published in 1620 declared that among those recently sent to the colony there were "out of Sussex about 40, all famed to iron workes."

In his *History and Present State of Virginia*, Robert Beverley wrote of an "iron work at Falling Creek in Jamestown River, where they made proof of good iron ore, and brought the whole works so near a perfection, that they writ word to the company in London that they did not doubt but to finish the work and have plentiful provision of iron for them by the next Easter."

But there were troubles ahead. In the following year, three of the master iron workmen died. The company, therefore, sent over twenty more experienced ironworkers. But the entire group was soon attacked by Indians and killed. Thus, the manufacture of iron temporarily stopped and was not revived in the Virginia area until many years later.

Meanwhile, from other colonies also came pleas for workers. The Province of Pennsylvania expressed need for "Carpenters, Masons, Smiths, Weavers, Taylors, Tanners, Shoemakers, Shipwrights . . ." The need for workers contributed to Massachusetts passing a law proclaiming idleness a crime. Agricultural labor was encouraged by allotments of land, with their cultivation compulsory. By 1640, each family was ordered to sow at least one spoonful of English hemp

The settlement of Jamestown.

seed, and cultivate it in a "husbandly manner" for the future supply.

The Fathers also fixed by law the rate of wages for labor. The number of hours for a working day was set at eleven in the summer and nine in the winter. The law also fixed the price of commodities. No advantage was to be taken of new settlers, or of the scarcity of laborers.

In response to the plea, a carpenter and a salt maker arrived at Plymouth in 1642, sent by the London Company. Governor Bradford recorded tragically in his history that the new worker "quickly builds two very good and strong shallops, with a great and strong lighter, and had hewn timber for catches, but this spoilt; for at the heat of the season, he falls into a fever and dies, to our great loss and sorrow."

There was some attempt made to solve the labor shortage by use of the native Americans without whose help the early settlers could not have survived. Some Indians were skilled craftsmen, after their fashion; they built dwellings, farmed, fished, hunted, traded, wove, made canoes, tools, weapons. Other American Indians also worked crude copper mines before the white man arrived, particularly in the Lake Superior region.

Indians were often amazed by innovations brought by the settlers. Although a plow was a simple instrument, it seemed complicated to the natives of the new land. They were astonished to see that it tore up more ground in a day than they, with their clamshells, scraped up in a month.

But there were not many plows in the early settlements of the New World. In 1637, there were as few as thirty-seven plows in the entire colony of Massachusetts. Twelve years after the landing of the Pilgrims, the farmers of Boston had no plows at all and were compelled to break up the bushes and prepare for cultivation with their hands and with crude, clumsy hoes.

From the beginning, Indian labor proved unsatisfactory to the settlers. There were fundamental cultural differences. To the eyes of William Bradford, the land was "full of willd beasts and willd men."

Early American Indians working copper mines in the Lake Superior area.

The limitation of wages to two shillings a day in Massachusetts Bay Colony, 1630. The law was amended a few years later.

*Att a Court of Assistants, holden att Boston, March 22ᵗʰ, 1630–31.*

IT is ordered, (that whereas the wages of carpentᵣˢ, joyners, & other artificers & workemen, were by order of Court restrayned to pticulʳ somes) shall nowe be lefte free & att libertie as men shall reasonably agree./

*A Court of Assistants, holden att Charlton, 28ᵗʰ of Septembʳ, 1630.*

It is ordered, that noe maister carpenter, mason, joyner, or brickelayer shall take aboue 16ᵈ a day for their worke, if they haue meate and drinke, & the second sort not aboue 12ᵈ aday, vnder payne of xˢ both to giuer & receauer./

Indians at work in the field.

Indians making a canoe.

Smithing, one of the oldest crafts known to man.

From the viewpoint of the arrivals, Indian culture and customs were odd or barbaric or both. The work habits of Indian women often conflicted with the white man's traditional patterns of social organization.

An account written in 1644 described how Indian women "are obliged to . . . do everything. . . . The men do nothing but hunt, fish, and make war . . ." While more or less accurate, it did not tell the whole story. Except in certain areas, such as what became Arizona and New Mexico, where young and middle-aged men worked the fields, most Indian males served as hunters—usually of big game. Since Indians were primarily meat eaters, it was often full-time employment, especially since Indians had few if any domesticated beef animals.

One of the few locales where men did not spend most of their time in the strenuous work of big game hunting was the Puget Sound area. There fishing was common; but elsewhere, save for raiding and war pursuits, Indian men worked at hunting.

If men's work was thus specialized, women performed a wider variety of tasks. General housekeeping engaged much of their time—preparing food, clothes, house building and house repairing, setting up the new home after moving, making furniture, utensils, tools. The woman, rather than the man, was usually the practical laborer and mechanic.

It appears that most Indian women accepted their role as necessary to their people's way of life. The man's wife, according to one authority, "took up her share of the burden cheerfully, and would have scorned as effeminate the husband who took any other view of the situation . . ."

The majority of the Pilgrims who settled at Plymouth were not gentlemen or merchants with money to buy slaves or servants. On the contrary, they were for the most part artisans, small farmers, and laborers, accustomed to hardship. Men, women, and children were accustomed to long hours of toil. When a few did try to enslave the Indian and use Negro slaves to work in the fields, such assistance proved impractical. Large estates supervised by a handful of owners were not possible in the New England terrain. Slavery was not a practical means of solving the labor problem.

Furthermore, during much of the colonial era, Indians were just too strong a force to be enslaved. The Iroquois Six Nations actually held a balance of power between the French and British. Because of this and the fact that they were masters of statesmanship, colonial authorities dealt with them as equals, and were well aware of the need for maintaining such tribal friendships.

The practical solution to the labor problem, in general, obviously lay in the Old World, crowded as it was with men, women, and children eager to escape hunger, poverty, and persecution of various kinds. Glowing tales were spread there of the opportunities in far-off America.

Occasionally such tales were fully based on fact. For example, an early glassmaking factory in America

The manufacture of glass bottles.

was founded in 1739 in New Jersey. Caspar Wistar, the owner, enticed skilled glassblowers over from Holland by entering into an unusual contract with them, providing for the payment of ten shillings a day and sharing one-third of all the profits. Interestingly, the descendants of these early Wistar glassblowers, a century later, organized the first glassblowers' labor union in America.

Many laborers of the Old World willingly bound themselves out for periods of years. They signed contracts with shipmasters in Europe to do "any work in which the employer shall employ them." About half of those who emigrated to America were indentured servants, who sold their services for stated periods to finance their trip. Almost two-thirds of the residents of Virginia in the early days were indentured. Agents dispatched to countries abroad, especially western Germany and northern Ireland, enthusiastically encouraged people to make the trip under such conditions.

But the voyages were often dreadful experiences; the food was inadequate; the holds were filthy; one out of every three who made the trip during the early eighteenth century, it is estimated, died en route.

One individual who came to America in 1750 recalled his trip with horror: "To keep from starving, we had to eat rats and mice. We paid from eight pence to two shillings for a mouse, four pence for a quart of water."

These indentured wage workers, or "servants," as they were called, were of two kinds: voluntary and involuntary. The first were most numerous and consisted of redemptioners and apprentices. Redemptioners were those who paid for their passage from Europe for a stipulated period of service as a bond servant in America.

Apprentices were often children of the poor, under twenty-one years, shipped to the colonies by local governments from their homes.

Gottlieb Mittelburger's journey to Pennsylvania in 1750 gives us this vivid insight:

When the ships have landed at Philadelphia after their long voyage, no one is permitted to leave them except those who pay for their passage or can give good security; the others, who cannot pay, must remain on board the ships till they are purchased and are released from the ships by their purchasers. The sick always fare the worst, for the healthy are naturally preferred and purchased first; and so the sick and wretched must often remain on board in front of the city for two or three weeks, and fre-

When they have come to an agreement, it happens that *adult persons bind themselves in writing* to serve three, four, five, or six years for the amount due by them, according to their age and strength. But very young people, from ten to fifteen years, must serve till they are twenty-one years old.

Many parents must sell and trade away their children like so many head of cattle, for if their children take the debt upon themselves, the parents can leave the ship free and unrestrained; but as the parents often do not know where and to what people their children are going, it often happens that such parents and children, after leaving the ship, do not see each other again for many years, perhaps no more in all their lives . . .

quently die, whereas many a one, if he could pay his debt and were permitted to leave the ship immediately, might recover and remain alive.

The sale of human beings in the market on board the ship is carried on thus: Every day Englishmen, Dutchmen, and High German people come from the city of Philadelphia and other places in part from a great distance, say twenty, thirty, or forty hours away, and go on board the newly-arrived ship that has brought and offers *for sale passengers* from Europe, and select among the healthy persons such as they deem suitable for their business, and bargain with them how long they will serve for their passage money, which most of them are still in debt for.

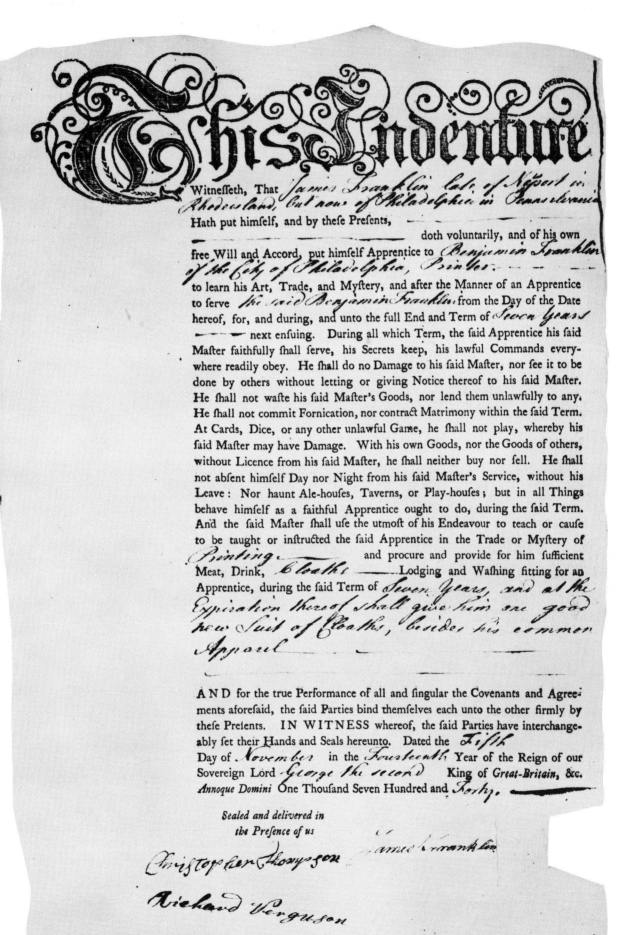

# This Indenture

Witnesseth, That *James Franklin late of Newport in Rhodeisland, but now of Philadelphia in Pennsylvania* Hath put himself, and by these Presents, ———————— ———————— doth voluntarily, and of his own free Will and Accord, put himself Apprentice to *Benjamin Franklin of the City of Philadelphia, Printer.* ———— to learn his Art, Trade, and Mystery, and after the Manner of an Apprentice to serve *the said Benjamin Franklin* from the Day of the Date hereof, for, and during, and unto the full End and Term of *Seven Years* ————— next ensuing. During all which Term, the said Apprentice his said Master faithfully shall serve, his Secrets keep, his lawful Commands everywhere readily obey. He shall do no Damage to his said Master, nor see it to be done by others without letting or giving Notice thereof to his said Master. He shall not waste his said Master's Goods, nor lend them unlawfully to any. He shall not commit Fornication, nor contract Matrimony within the said Term. At Cards, Dice, or any other unlawful Game, he shall not play, whereby his said Master may have Damage. With his own Goods, nor the Goods of others, without Licence from his said Master, he shall neither buy nor sell. He shall not absent himself Day nor Night from his said Master's Service, without his Leave: Nor haunt Ale-houses, Taverns, or Play-houses; but in all Things behave himself as a faithful Apprentice ought to do, during the said Term. And the said Master shall use the utmost of his Endeavour to teach or cause to be taught or instructed the said Apprentice in the Trade or Mystery of *Printing* ———————— and procure and provide for him sufficient Meat, Drink, *Cloaths* ————Lodging and Washing fitting for an Apprentice, during the said Term of *Seven Years, and at the Expiration thereof shall give him one good new Suit of Cloaths, besides his common Apparel*

AND for the true Performance of all and singular the Covenants and Agreements aforesaid, the said Parties bind themselves each unto the other firmly by these Presents. IN WITNESS whereof, the said Parties have interchangeably set their Hands and Seals hereunto. Dated the *Fifth* Day of *November* in the *Fourteenth* Year of the Reign of our Sovereign Lord *George the second* King of Great-Britain, &c. Annoque Domini One Thousand Seven Hundred and *Forty.* ————

Sealed and delivered in
the Presence of us

*Christopher Thompson*

*Richard Ferguson*

*James Franklin*

A typical apprentice contract. At the age of twelve Benjamin Franklin was "bound out" to learn the printer's craft.

The attitude toward servants varied within the colonies. "In general, the master was not permitted to discharge a servant for an incurable illness," says Richard B. Morris in his valuable study of government and labor in early America.

While the setting of wage levels was not continued for long, nevertheless, in many colonial communities, the authorities usually set the wages for certain semi-public functions such as millers, car men, porters, chimney sweepers, grave diggers, etc. Such authorities also habitually regulated the prices of certain products and services. Not only was it illegal for working people to organize to protect or advance their conditions of employment, but workmen were usually forbidden to leave their jobs until the end of an agreed term. Often when a workman would be seeking a new place of employment, it was necessary for him to show letters testifying that he was free to hire himself out. The one all-pervasive characteristic of colonial America was need for work.

"In this Country, is no living without hard labour," one labor overseer stated. Because of the need, there was an effort to increase the amount of immigration to America. In addition, every member of the household was a potential recruit for work. Before the Revolution, in New York City, Governor Moore stated that "every house swarms with children, who are set to work as soon as they are able to spin and card; and as every family is furnished with a Loom, the Itinerant Weavers who travel about the Country, put the finishing hand to the work."

Involuntary indentured servants, less numerous, were frequently people whose labor replaced imprisonment, perhaps for the "crime" of indebtedness.

Terms of the indenture were specific. One indenture, from the year 1763 in Connecticut, stated that the child was bound until she was eighteen years old,

during all of which term [she] . . . her said master faithfully shall serve, his secrits keep, his lawful commands gladly, every where obey, she shall do no damage to her said master or see it to be done of others without letting or giveing notis thereof to her sd. master. She shall not wast her said master's goods nor lend them unlawfully to any. She shall not commit fornication nor contract matrimony within said terms."

The employment contract between master and servant often had interesting clauses. Usually liquor was provided as a part of the contract. This was particularly so when the servants were involved in out-of-door occupations such as farming or fishing. Often free board and lodging was included in the contract. A source of frequent friction between master and

ONE CENT REWARD.

RAN away from the subscriber in Coventry, a few days since, an indented Apprentice, named Amos Brand. He was 13 years old in July last, is small of his age, has light hair and complexion, and dark eyes. Had on when he went away, a pair of dark cotton trowsers.— Whoever will return said runaway, or secure him so he can be taken by the subscriber, shall receive the above reward, but no charges paid. All persons are forbid harbouring or trusting said Brand, under the penalty of the law.
WANTON BRIGGS.
Coventry, August 2.

servant was the amount and quality of the food. On one occasion, a master in 1662 accused his servant of stealing flour and meat. The servant contended before authorities that he was refused food and tried to procure it, but there was little or no food for sale.

The development of the colonies in many ways was the result of the overpopulation of sixteenth- and seventeenth-century England. Many settlers were "pety theves" from British prisons. Various countries were happy to rid themselves of problem people.

As for nonproblem people, while many volunteered for the trip to the New World, others were kidnapped, or "spirited" away. Kidnapping became a sizable industry. Sometimes the victim was given liquor or knocked unconscious and carried on board ship, which set sail soon after. Sometimes unemployed workingmen would be taken by force on board ship— whether they wanted to go to America or not.

Upon arrival, the "servant" usually was marched to the center of town. There he was auctioned off for a sum that depended upon his skills. If he was not sold immediately, he might be turned over to what was called a "soul driver," who placed him in chains and led him around the country, looking for a buyer.

Many newly arrived indentures were disappointed with what they found, discovering "worse plagues than those . . . left behind." It was not unusual for servants to attempt to run away from a master. When captured, they were often whipped, sometimes even branded. Their time of indenture was often extended as punishment.

The first group of child workers, about a hundred from the slums of London, arrived at Virginia in 1619. The arrangement must have been successful because the demand for children—for colonies from Virginia to New York—increased. Frequently alm houses were emptied of adolescents to be sent to the colonies. At

Workers were in demand everywhere.

Woodworking

Papermaking by hand

Chimney sweeps

Leather currying

Making felt hats

Gathering
sugarcane

Pegging boots by hand

Fishing

# AN
# ORDINANCE OF THE
## Lords and Commons Affembled in Parliament,

For the Apprehending and bringing to condigne punifhment, all fuch lewd perfons as fhall fteale, fell, buy, inveigle, purloyne, convey, or receive any little Children. And for the ftrict and diligent fearch of all Ships and other Veffels on the River, or at the Downes.

### Die Veneris, 9 Maii. 1645.

Hereas the Houfes of Parliament are informed, that divers lewd Perfons doe goe up and downe the City of London, and elfewhere, and in a moft barbarous and wicked manner fteale away many little Children, It is ordered by the Lords and Commons in Parliament affembled, That all Officers and Minifters of Juftice be hereby ftreightly charged and required to be very diligent in apprehending all fuch perfons as are faulty in this kind, either in ftealing, felling, buying, inveigling, purloyning, conveying, or receiving Children fo ftolne, and to keepe them in fafe imprifonment, till they may be brought to fevere and exemplary punifhment.

It is further ordered, That the Marfhals of the Admiralty, and the Cinque-ports, doe immediately make ftrict and diligent fearch in all Ships and Veffels upon the River, and at the Downes, for all fuch Children, according to fuch directions as they have or fhall receive from the Committee of the Admiralty, and Cinque-ports.

It is further ordered, That this Ordinance be forthwith publifhed in Print, and Proclaimed in the ufuall manner as other Proclamations, in all parts of the City of London, within the Lines of communication, and in all Parifhes within the Bils of mortality, prefently: And in all Churches and Chappels by the Minifters, within the Line of communication, and Bils of mortality, on the next Lords day: And in all other Churches and Chappels elfewhere refpectively, the next Lords day after the recept hereof, that it may appeare to the World, how carefull the Parliament is to prevent fuch mifchiefes, and how farre they doe deteft a crime of fo much villany.

Mr. Spurftow, Mr. Vaffall, and Collonell Venn, (Members of the Houfe of Commons) are defired to goe to the Lord Mayor, and to acquaint him with this Order, and to take care that it may be Proclaimed prefently, and Publifhed according to the directions, on the next Lords day.

### Die Veneris, 9 Maii. 1645.

Ordered by the Lords and Commons affembled in Parliament, that this Ordinance fhall be forthwith Printed and publifhed prefently, and read in all Parifh Churches and Chappels within the Line of Communication and Bills of mortality, the next Lords day: and in all other Churches and Chappels elfewhere refpectively, the next Lords day after the receipt hereof.

J. Brown Cler. Parliamentorum.

London, Printed for John Wright at the figne of the Kings-head in the Old-baily May 9. 1645

the time, London had many poverty-stricken children, either roaming the streets or in charitable institutions.

A hysteria over incidents of "spiriting" developed in England. Unruly children were threatened with being sent across the ocean if they did not behave. Parents worried about their youngsters when they were out at play lest they be kidnapped and mysteriously disappear.

Government officials at one time countenanced the practice of luring children with candy, dragging them on board ships that quickly set sail.

The outcry against this type of kidnapping became so loud, however, that Parliament passed laws in the 1620s punishing such kidnapping by death.

There was dire need for women in the colonies. The men let this emphatically be known. As a result, the directors of the Virginia Company in London decided that "a fitt hundreth might be sent of women, maids young and uncorrupt, to make wives to the inhabitants and by that means to make the men there more settled and lesse movable . . ."

There was some concern about the welfare of the ladies. A letter was sent in 1621 from London to Virginia:

In case they cannot be presently married, we desire that they may be put with several householders that have wives, until they can be provided with husbands. . . . Every man that marries them gives 120 pounds of best leaf tobacco for each of them. We desire that the marriage be free, according to nature. . . . We pray you, therefore, to be fathers of them in this business, not enforcing them to marry against their wills.

Under the indenture system, girls were generally bound until sixteen or eighteen, or until they were wed. Types of instruction for girls under the apprenticeship system included plain sewing and "housewifery," as well as reading and writing. The early education of women included some emphasis on instruction in "spinning, weaving, sewing, knitting." Girls were apprenticed in such trades as stay and dressmaking, millinery, pastry cooking, confectionery, laundering, and so on.

With the demand for women in all the colonies, a widow with a number of children was more desirable than a woman without children. Such was the demand that women, like children, were often induced, on one pretext or another, to board a ship that quickly set sail. Once the ship arrived in the colonies, the women were then sold to the highest bidder.

Some of the reasons why women were needed come down to us in this description of a sixteenth-century housewife's tasks:

First sweep the house, dress up the dishboard, and set all things in good order within the house. Milk the kine, suckle the calves, strain the milk, take up and dress the children, provide breakfast, dinner and supper for the family and servants; arrange for sending corn and malt to the mill for baking and brewing when necessary. Measure it to and from the mill and see that you have full measure returned. Make butter and cheese when you can. Feed the swine morning and evening, and the poultry in the morning. Look after the hen and goose eggs and making sittings of them when the fowls are broody; and take care of the chickens.

In early March get the garden in order and then keep it weeded; sow flax and hemp. The housewife must know all about the treatment of

In Massachusetts fifteen shillings was the usual price for a wife.

Arrival of the women, who were often sold to planters.

Women's work in the colonies.

flax and hemp for sheets, board cloths, towels, shirts, smocks, and such other necessaries; . . . her distaff should be always at hand for a pastime, it stops an idle gap. . . . She should have part of the wool of the farm for clothes, blankets and coverlets; while other duties that may fall to her lot are winnowing corn, making malt, washing, haymaking, harvesting, spreading manure, plow driving, loading hay or corn; going to market to sell dairy produce, poultry or corn, and to buy all the household requisites . . .

The female immigrants, in colonial times, were often disappointed with conditions in the new land. One girl wrote home plaintively:

> *I have played in my part*
> *Both to plow and cart*
> *In the land of Virginny O*
> *Billets from the wood*
> *Upon my back they load*
> *When that I was weary, O.*

In 1656, the first compulsory labor law affecting women was passed by the Massachusetts General Court. "Fearing that it will not be so easy to import clothes as it was in past years, thereby necessitating more home manufacture," it was stated, ". . . all hands not necessarily employed on other occasions as women, girls and boyes shall . . . spin according to their skill and ability, and the selectman in every town, do consider the condition and capacity of every family, and accordingly do assess them at one or more spinners."

In 1620, the year that the Pilgrims landed at Plymouth, a Dutch vessel containing a cargo of twenty African men and women landed at Jamestown, the first black slaves brought to American shores. A few decades later, slavery became a recognized institution, not only in southern areas but to some degree in the North as well.

At first Virginia tended to discourage slavery. But the lure of profit from tobacco raising stimulated the development of the slave system. There was, however, some opposition to tobacco cultivation in the colony of Jamestown. Attempts were made to discourage the practice by diversifying the industries of the colony.

The London Company helped in this by sending over "husbandmen, gardners, brewers, bakers, sawyers, carpenters, joyners, shipwrights, boatwrights, ploughwrights, millwrights, masons, turners, smiths of all sorts, coopers of all sorts, weavers, tanners, pot-

Enroute to America, slaves were packed in the holds of slave ships. "It was impossible," one naval officer said, "for them to turn or shift with any degree of ease." Faces in drawings were often deliberately distorted.

ters, fowlers, fishhook makers, net makers, shoe makers, rope makers, tile makers, edge tool makers, brick makers, brick layers, dressers of hemp and flax, lime burners, lether dressers, men skillful in vines, men for iron works, men skillful in mines."

"The men lately sent have been, most of them, choice men, born and bred up to labor and industry," it was stated. Nevertheless, the culture of tobacco maintained its growing position as the chief industry with black slaves as the means of production.

Cultivation of cotton and sugar under slavery was also highly profitable to the landowners. The idea of a system of wageless labor increasingly appealed to them. With much work to be done, and labor scarce, there was a tendency for wages to rise. Slave labor presented no such problem.

About 125,000 Negroes were captured and brought to the new land from 1715 to 1760 alone. Before the slave trade was to end, the number was to grow to fifteen million blacks transported alive to the West-

Iron mining

gro, who now had become "tamed," assigning him to a special task of plantation work along with the other seasoned hands, who had long since learned to obey orders, to arise when the conch blew at "day clean," to handle a hoe . . . to stand still when a white man spoke.

ern Hemisphere. For every black who arrived alive, approximately five died on the way.

The black man coming to America was one of the first great migratory waves. Arriving, often branded and in chains, slaves were immediately put up for sale. Families were divided without heed. There were those who sought to encourage the revolt of such servants who were mistreated or whipped, a dangerous occupation. Punishment for those who encouraged others to run away or revolt was severe.

The process of introducing newly arrived blacks into the rigors of slave labor in South Carolina was described by an eyewitness:

> When a gang of fresh Africans were purchased, they were assigned in groups to certain reliable slaves, who initiated them into the ways of the plantation. These drivers, as they were called, had the right of issuing or withholding rations to the raw recruits and of inflicting minor punishments.
>
> They taught the new slaves to speak the broken English which they knew and to do the plantation work which required little skill. . . . At the end of a year, the master or overseer for the first time directed the work of the new Ne-

An early glass furnace.

Iron ore sent from the colonies to England in the 1600s.

Making iron in an earth oven, Jamestown, about 1610.

Dyeing

Bell making

Carriage making

Candlemaking

Wig making

Baking

Techniques for many trades were imported from abroad.

Joining

# 1630-1790

# BUILDING
# A DEMOCRATIC FOUNDATION

*". . . foundation
of civil power lies
in the people."*

Most early colonial settlers—more than 90 percent—depended upon agriculture for an existence. In the North, the farmer and his sons would work the field, herd the cattle, do carpentry, tanning, repairing, tool making, shoemaking. In the South, such work was increasingly demanded of slave labor.

"Work and labor in this new and wild land are very hard and manifold," one early settler wrote.

Work mostly consists in cutting wood, felling oak trees, rooting out, or as they say there, clearing large tracts of forest. Such forests, being cleared, are then laid out for fields and meadows. From the best hewn wood, fences are made around the new fields; for there all meadows, orchards, and fruit fields are surrounded and fenced in with planks made of thickly-split wood, laid one above the other, as in zigzag lines, and within such inclosures horses, cattle, and sheep are permitted to graze.

Our Europeans who are purchased must always work hard, for new fields are constantly laid out; and so they learn that stumps of oak trees are in America certainly as hard as in Germany.

As the settlements expanded—both in population

Clearing the woods

Early lumbermen

Goblet making

and area—the needs of the people grew. Every household wanted cabinets, benches, tools, chairs, bedsteads, kitchen utensils, buckets, churns, fireplaces, tableware, brooms, candles, whale-oil lamps, nails, textiles, knives, glass, spinning wheels, looms. Gradually, a working population developed to provide these materials and services.

Virgin forests covered most of the United States providing, it seemed, an inexhaustible supply of raw materials. Primitive sawmills were built in New England, New York, and elsewhere for the manufacture of the lumber needed for domestic uses, as well as for export trade to England.

One of the earliest groups of skilled working people in America was, of course, the carpenters. The original carpenter was a traveling worker who went from one frontier settlement to another working under contract. He supplied his tools and his skills and settled for brief periods in those areas in which they could be used to advantage. All materials as well as board and lodging was supplied by the carpenter's customers.

Glassblowing

But there was much more involved in being a carpenter in those early days. Not only did he build buildings but he actually had to select and fell the timber that was to be used. Like so many other skilled craftsmen, the carpenters gradually began to settle down as towns and cities were founded and grew. An apprentice system developed, and the experienced carpenter trained young workers who con-

Hauling logs

Ropemaking

Papermaking

tracted with him for three or four years, seeking the chance to become a master craftsman themselves.

Papermaking in the earlier days was not well organized. Newspapers scarcely existed prior to 1700 and there were not many books made. Hence, the demand for paper in substantial quantities was not urgent. The first paper mill in the land, built in 1690 in Philadelphia, seemed to provide an ample supply. As printing increased, so did the making of paper. In 1724, a paper mill was built in New York Colony and later another in New Jersey. Most employees of the mills were indentured servants learning the new trade.

One paper mill was built in the 1730s in Ephrata, Lancaster County, an early utopian-type community that was settled by Germans who came to Pennsylvania in the eighteenth century. The mill prospered to such a point, in fact, that its proprietors were expelled from the ascetic-minded community for becoming too materialistic. Despite change of management, the mill continued to prosper, and Ephrata paper became widely known.

Paper mills employed children as well as adults.

There was need for experienced papermakers as was indicated in 1789 when a paper-mill owner in Andover, Massachusetts, wrote home, saying he wished he had English workmen available "for good ones, used to writing paper in every stage, we would give fifteen shillings a week and board . . ."

Ropemaking was another essential craft. The wild hemp of New England, which the Indians used in making their nets and lines, attracted the attention of the Puritan settlers who used it for the same purpose. In 1629, hemp seed was received from England.

Cordage for ship rigging was particularly important to the early settlers. Ropemaking required, in addition to a building that contained the material and machinery, a rope walk of twelve hundred or thirteen hundred feet in length. This was indeed a walk, because workers walked from one end to the other and back again, weaving rope strands. By 1698, there were several rope walks in Philadelphia, Providence, and Newport. Maryland also entered the cordage business to keep up with the rapidly advancing manufacture of sailing vessels.

Among the most demanding trades in the new

Wheelwright's work

Anchor making

An early printer reading proof. . . and setting type.

land was printing, a craft requiring ability to read and spell, good eyesight, and a steady hand. Printing jobs were scarce in early America. One journeyman printer reported his experiences accepting a position in a New York printing shop:

It was the composition of a very small [32mo] New Testament, in double columns, of Agate type, each column barely 12 ems wide, the text thickly studded with references by Greek and superior letters to the notes, which of course were preceded and discriminated by corresponding indices, with prefatory and supplemental remarks on each Book, set in Pearl, and only paid for as Agate.

The type was considerably smaller than any to which I had been accustomed; the narrow measure and thickly sown Italics of the text, with the strange characters employed as indices, rendered it the slowest, and by far the most difficult, work I had ever undertaken; while the making up, proving, and correcting twice, and even thrice over, preparatory to stereotyping, nearly doubled the time required for ordinary composition.

I was never a swift type-setter; I aimed to be an assiduous and correct one; but my proofs on this work at first looked as though they had caught the chicken-pox, and were in the worst stage of a profuse eruption. For the first two or three weeks, being sometimes kept waiting for

letter, I scarcely made my board; while, by diligent type-sticking through twelve to fourteen hours per day, I was able, at my best, to earn but five to six dollars per week.

As scarcely another compositor could be induced to work on it more than two days, I had this job in good part to myself; and I persevered to the end of it.

But, other than farming, the occupation involving the most people was shipbuilding and other maritime pursuits such as fishing and whaling. There was a steady demand in the shipping centers of Philadelphia, Boston, and New York for skilled workers: shipwrights, caulkers, carpenters, joiners, smiths, ropemakers, sailmakers.

The boom in shipbuilding spread. Shipyards sprang up along the coast and were scenes of frenzied activity. Some seventy vessels a year were being launched by the 1750s in New England alone. With almost one hundred additional ships being built annually in other colonial ports, London shipbuilders began to suffer from declining trade. Many of their workmen left home to seek work in the colonies.

Fishing from American-built ships became, next to tobacco raising in the South, one of the most important branches of the American economy with Yankee fishermen active from the earliest days. Both men and women participated in the search for cod, mackerel, and other fish. The food supply of entire communities depended on the catch. The potential of the

COD FISHERY.

fishing trade thus realized an early prediction of John Smith, who wrote: "Let not the meanness of the word fish distaste you for it will afford as good gold as the mines of Guiana and Potassie."

Whale fishery particularly absorbed the energies and interests of New England people. Whaling provided oil so useful for the lamps of the early settlers.

American whaling vessels and seamen sailed waters throughout the world.

Life aboard a whaler, which sometimes did not touch land for several years at a time, called for persistence and courage. Seamen often did not work for wages but obtained shares of the profits, if any. These shares depended on the seaman's position: the owner

Whaling

would receive one-half of the profits, the master one-fifteenth, each able-bodied seaman one-fiftieth, and so on.

The joys of the whaleman were dramatically recounted by Walt Whitman:

*O the whaleman's joys! O I cruise my old cruise again!*
*I feel the ship's motion under me, I feel the Atlantic breezes*
*    fanning me,*
*I hear the cry again sent down from the mast-head, There—*
*    she blows!*
*—Again I spring up the rigging to look with the rest—We*
*    see—we descend, wild with excitement,*
*I leap in the lower'd boat—We row toward our prey, where*
*    he lies,*
*We approach stealthy and silent—I see the mountainous*
*    mass, lethargic, basking,*
*I see the harpooner standing up—I see the weapon dart*
*    from his vigorous arm:*
*O swift, again, now, far out in the ocean, the wounded*
*    whale, settling, running to windward, tows me,*
*—Again I see him rise to breathe—We row close again,*
*I see a lance driven through his side, press'd deep, turn'd*
*    in the wound,*
*Again we back off—I see him settle again—the life is leaving*
*    him fast,*
*As he rises he spouts blood—I see him swim in circles*
*    narrower and narrower, swiftly cutting the water—I see*
*    him die;*
*He gives one convulsive leap in the centre of the circle, and*
*    then falls flat and still in the bloody foam.*

But the precarious life of the whaleman also had its critics. There were those who described whalemen as "the most oppressed class of men in existence." Mutinies among whalemen over substandard living conditions aboard ship were common. "Not a raw recruit, marching from the bosom of his wife," wrote Herman Melville, "into the fever heat of his first battle; not the dead man's ghost encountering the first unknown phantom in the other world—neither of these can feel stranger and stronger emotions than the man does who for the first time finds himself putting into the charmed, churned circle of the hunted sperm whale . . ."

For a number of years the sea and rivers were practically the only way the colonists had of getting about. It took many years to convert Indian trails into passable roads. In the meanwhile, goods between the colonies were carried on water. The sea was the highway, and in this coastwise trade the New Englanders were the leaders.

In 1643, an early settler returned to England with specimens of iron ore that he had taken from ponds

Casting ingots in early steel industry

near Lynn, Massachusetts. Together with others, he soon formed a "company of undertakers for the iron works." The sum of approximately one thousand pounds was subscribed, and, in 1643, the group, with a corps of workmen, returned to New England.

Some years later, the General Court of Massachusetts granted the company the exclusive privilege of making iron, provided that, within two years, they made enough for the colony for the manufacture of tools.

In order to encourage the production of iron, the stockholders were exempted from taxation on their stock, and their agents from public charges, and they and their workmen received other privileges. By the summer of 1648, Governor Winthrop wrote that "the iron work goeth on with more hope. It yields now about seven tons per week. . . . There is a grave man of good fashion come now over to see how things stand here. He is one who hath been exercised in iron works."

The "company of undertakers for the iron works" went out of existence in 1677. The chief importance of the company was that it introduced the industry to the New World and encouraged the coming to America of skillful mechanics and ironworkers.

Eventually, iron forges were built in New England, New Jersey, Virginia, and Pennsylvania. As a result, mills were established to manufacture nails, kettles, chains, hardware, guns, and a wide variety of other iron articles.

Paul Revere, silversmith

THE LAUNCH OF A PACKET SHIP.

The search for fuel for industrial and home-heating purposes did not become a problem until the wood supply in certain areas began to run short. The growing scarcity of firewood in regions of Pennsylvania was influential in the start of coal mining there.

The earliest record of commercial coal mining in the country indicates the use of Negro slaves as the first miners, near Richmond, Virginia, in 1750.

Coal was later supplied by slave labor to factories making ammunition for the Continental army. Gradually immigrant workers arriving in the New World were sent into the mines to supply coal, iron ore, copper, salt, and other essential products found beneath the earth's surface.

The Indians called salt "magic white sand." Wars were sometimes fought between tribes over the ownership of salt springs, so important was salt to human survival.

Windmills on Provincetown, Massachusetts, beach, whose machinery pumped ocean water into evaporation vats to make salt.

Salt was found in a number of localities, including springs and in mines beneath the ground. While salt licks, or rocks of salt, appeared aboveground, most salt, like coal, lay far below the surface of the earth. Workers went underground to mine salt in such states as Michigan, Ohio, and Louisiana.

The lure of the New World continued for decades to attract working people from nations abroad. Many indentured servants enjoyed the new life. "The servants of this province," one servant wrote in 1659 from his home in Maryland, " . . . live more like freemen than the most mechanical apprentices in London."

Benjamin Franklin, himself once an indentured apprentice, helped spread word among the nations of Europe about the advantages of America. He wrote that land was plentiful "and so cheap . . . that a laboring man that understands husbandry can in a short time save money enough to purchase a piece of land sufficient for a plantation . . ."

BENJAMIN FRANKLIN

Quarrying stone

So the people kept coming, voluntary and involuntary, men and women, children and adults. But, at the start, few skilled workers were wage earners. They were either indentured servants or they produced only for themselves and their families in their homes. However, household manufacturing gradually evolved into an early form of industrial production. Craftsmen increasingly administered to the needs of townspeople and became more specialized in their skills. Blacksmiths, tailors, hatmakers, weavers, wheel-

wrights all began to find new outlets for their products within their communities and beyond. They either set up small shops or else became wandering itinerant artisans or mechanics, providing their labor wherever they happened to be.

The itinerant worker usually walked from one house to another, carrying his tools on his back, providing services as he went. Season after season he would frequent the same homesteads, where his visits were eagerly awaited. Much work was performed on the spot by these itinerant artisans. A weaver, for example, would enter the home, install his loom, and perform the needed work. Often craftsmen were skilled in several crafts.

By the start of the eighteenth century, many such craftsmen established themselves in permanent locations. Customers came to them. Craftsmen, located in small centers or stores, included carpenters, blacksmiths, tailors, shoemakers, and hatters. Once an itinerant worker settled down, it was not unusual for him to purchase an indentured servant to help him in his work.

While in theory shortages of labor tend to raise wage levels, oftentimes workers encountered obstacles to increased earnings. High wages were considered a temptation to idleness and even vice. Low wages were advocated as a means of keeping laborers in their place. Too much money, it was said, tended to encourage "the insolence of servants," and there was constant emphasis on the necessity for working people to dress and act according to their status in life. One colonial regulation expressed "utter detestation and dislike that men and women of mean conditions should take upon themselves the garb of gentlemen."

In the New England area, where there were fewer indentured servants, laws were passed by property owners setting maximum wages. There were regulations, too, that outlawed changes in occupation. In

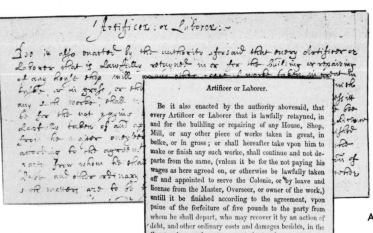

Artificer or Laborer.

Be it also enacted by the authority abovesaid, that every Artificer or Laborer that is lawfully retayned, in and for the building or repairing of any House, Shop, Mill, or any other piece of worke taken in great, in bulke, or in gross; or shall hereafter take vpon him to make or finish any such worke, shall continue and not departe from the same, (vnless it be for the not paying his wages as here agreed on, or otherwise be lawfully taken off and appointed to serve the Colonie, or by leave and license from the Master, Overseer, or owner of the work,) untill it be finished according to the agreement, vpon paine of the forfeiture of five pounds to the party from whom he shall depart, who may recover it by an action of debt, and other ordinary costs and damages besides, in the Courts where such matters are to be tryed.

A typical colonial labor code, from Rhode Island.

Spinning

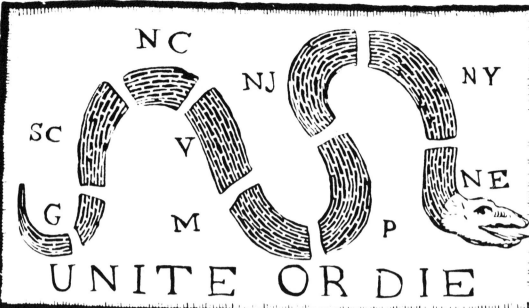

UNITE OR DIE

The spirit of union was born early.

Cotton press

1630, the Massachusetts General Court set a wage ceiling of two shillings a day for carpenters, joiners, sawyers, thatchers, bricklayers, and other skilled workers, and eighteen pence for all-day laborers, with the provision that "all workmen shall worke the whole day, alloweing convenient tyme for food and rest."

The court also announced that anyone who gave strong liquors to workmen would be fined twenty shillings for such offense. There were, in addition, price restrictions on basic commodities.

Occasionally voices spoke out for higher wage scales. "That community cannot be pronounced happy," one citizen stated, "in which from the lowness and insufficiency of wages, the laboring class procured . . . that [they] are reduced to beggary, whenever employment fails them, or age and sickness oblige them to give up work."

The founding of the nation, from the start, was based largely on commercial motives. The assignment of the Virginia Colony was specifically "to dig, mine and search for all Manner of Mines of Gold, Silver, and Copper . . ." Some who came to the new land were seeking freedom, economic and political. But commercial considerations were never unimportant.

In the eyes of England, America was primarily a financial investment. It was understandable, therefore, why in 1699 the mother country wanted to restrict competition by forbidding her colonies from manufacturing for export. This was followed by an interdict against the making of paper, hats, woolens, iron, and a variety of other products.

Resentment was aroused by a growing America whose people were engaged in a wide variety of productive pursuits, including the making of tools, furniture, paper, bricks, hats, glass, woolens, nails, iron, rum, shoes, linen, and ships.

In this mounting rivalry between commercial interests of Old and New Worlds, the American worker was, in many ways, a minor consideration. Property qualifications for the right to vote as well as to hold office were widespread. In some northern areas, ownership of a substantial number of acres of land was a qualification. In the South it was necessary, in some localities, to own at least ten slaves. In New Jersey, one qualification for becoming a legislator was ownership of one hundred acres of land.

According to one report: "When the son of a Boston bricklayer was elevated to the office of Justice of the Peace in 1759, his right to the office was attacked on the ground of his low social origin; and his defense was not the dignity of his calling, but a reply that the charge was false."

"A poor man," lamented a colonial resident of Philadelphia, "has rarely the honor of speaking to a gentleman on any terms and never with any familiarity, but for a few weeks before the election. How many poor men, common men, and mechanics have been made happy within this fortnight by a shake of the hand, a pleasing smile, and a little familiar chat with gentlemen who have not for these seven years

A
# JOURNAL
#### OF THE
# PROCEEDINGS
#### IN
## The Detection of the Confpiracy
##### FORMED BY
Some *White* People, in Conjunction with *Negro* and other *Slaves*,

FOR

Burning the City of *NEW-YORK* in AMERICA,
And Murdering the Inhabitants.

Which Confpiracy was partly put in Execution, by Burning His Majefty's Houfe in
Fort GEORGE, within the faid City, on Wednefday the Eighteenth of *March*, 1741. and
fetting Fire to feveral Dwelling and other Houfes there, within a few Days fucceeding.
And by another Attempt made in Profecution of the fame infernal Scheme, by putting
Fire between two other Dwelling-Houfes within the faid City, on the Fifteenth Day of
*February*, 1742 ; which was accidentally and timely difcovered and extinguifhed.

### CONTAINING,

I. A NARRATIVE of the Trials, Condemnations, Executions, and Behaviour of the
feveral Criminals, at the Gallows and Stake, with their *Speeches* and *Confeffions* ; with
Notes, Obfervations and Reflections occafionally interfperfed throughout the Whole.

II. AN APPENDIX, wherein is fet forth fome additional Evidence concerning the faid
Confpiracy and Confpirators, which has come to Light fince their Trials and
Executions.

II. LISTS of the feveral Perfons (Whites and Blacks) committed on Account of the
Confpiracy ; and of the feveral Criminals executed; and of thofe tranfported, with
the Places whereto.

*By the Recorder of the City of* NEW-YORK.

*Quid faciènt Dòmini, audent cum talia Furès?* Virg. Ecl.

NEW-YORK:
Printed by *James Parker*, at the New Printing-Office, 1744.

A report on the uprising of blacks and whites in New York, 1744.

30

Governor John Winthrop

past condescended to look at them. Blessed state
which brings all so nearly on a level. . . . Be freemen
then, and you will be companions for gentlemen annually."

Differences, usually based upon ownership of
property, increasingly separated the planters and the
developing merchant class from mechanics and small
farmers. And England did not help in this situation.
In an attempt to guarantee its commercial control of
the colonies, the Crown set up a system of royal administrators, or governors. The system proved ill
suited for colonies as far distant as those in America.
The royal governors were frequently lacking in di-
plomacy, taste, and tact, as well as in sympathy for
the common people. They often spent most of their
time trying to add to their private fortunes.

The most prominent royal governor, John Winthrop of Massachusetts, was convinced that democracy
was "among civill nations, accounted the meanest &
worst of all formes of governm't."

The Reverend John Cotton, a power in the Massachusetts Colony, also was skeptical about the propri-
ety of popular influence in government. He could not
conceive of a democracy being "a fitt government
eyther for a church or a commonwealth. . . . If the
people be governors," he asked, "who shall be gov-
erned?"

The Puritan philosophy held toil to be sacred and
idleness contrary to the will of God. Self-denial was
a virtue as were hard work and thrift. Early laws
punishing idleness and establishing compulsory labor
thus fit in with the needs of property owners. Labor
in the new land not only was essential, it was an end
in itself. Long hours and low wages not only helped
realize a profit, but also were sanctioned by religious
credo.

The New England character was thus marked
from the start by severe discipline for infringements

John Cotton

Whipping Quakers in New England.

The Reverend Roger Williams

of what was considered to be right conduct. A man was whipped for shooting fowl on Sunday. A swearer of oaths was forced to consider his sins by standing in a public place with his tongue in a cleft stick. Quakers were persecuted because they, particularly, rejected set forms of worship, refused to take oaths, and denounced ministers of the ruling group.

Other voices than Quakers were raised against the growing intolerance that had such a degrading influence on working people. Without the freedom to express their grievances, many found their conditions steadily growing worse. From the start, freedom of speech was thus closely bound with survival itself.

Among those who believed in basic rights was Mrs. Anne Hutchinson, a woman of independent mind and an early feminist, who insisted on her right to criticize the Massachusetts oligarchy. When her thoughts began to influence others, especially women, she was placed on trial. Governor Winthrop acted as both judge and prosecutor. The eventual sentence was banishment.

The Reverend Roger Williams of Salem also had independent ideas. He taught that "the sovereign and original foundation of civil power lies in the people." Massachusetts authorities did not agree. "Williams has broached . . . divers new and dangerous opinions against . . . authority," the court stated, and ordered him banished.

In faraway Jamestown the royal governor, William Berkeley, had little tolerance of opinions of other people and was grateful "there are no free schools or printing, and I hope we shall not have these hundred years; for learning has brought disobedience and heresy and sects into the world; printing has divulged them in libels against the best government. God keep us from both."

Obviously working people had little opportunity to better their conditions under such a philosophy. Indentured servants in Virginia were treated with brutality, severely punished for small offenses, sometimes half starved by their masters. There were numerous reports from the area of servants running away or rebelling in one way or another.

In 1676, their spokesman, Nathaniel Bacon, a twenty-eight-year-old Virginian, led an armed insurrection of frontier farmers, slaves, and servants against royal rule. "The poverty of the country," declared Bacon, "is such that all the power and sway is got into the hands of the rich, who by extortious advantages, having the common people in their debt, have always curbed and oppressed them in all manner of wayes."

Bacon led a march on Jamestown, which he captured. In the new government liberal laws were passed; taxes were equalized. Berkeley fled. But Bacon died shortly thereafter, and the revolt ended there. Its influence, however, was immeasurable, spreading to neighboring Maryland, South Carolina, and elsewhere.

To the north the royal governor who held sway over the dominion of New England was Sir Edmund Andros. His edicts annulling popular liberties were resisted strongly by the people. In 1689, they revolted, overthrew Andros, and imprisoned him.

In New York City in 1712, and again in 1741, black slaves revolted against their masters. Before the up-

Mrs. Anne Hutchinson

The confrontation of Governor Berkeley and Nathaniel Bacon.

The Sons of Liberty, largely made up of mechanics and artisans, demonstrated against the Stamp Act.

# The *American* CRISIS.

### NUMBER I.

## By the Author of COMMON SENSE.

THESE are the times that try men's souls: The summer soldier and the sunshine patriot will, in this crisis, shrink from the service of his country; but he that stands it NOW, deserves the love and thanks of man and woman. Tyranny, like hell, is not easily conquered; yet we have this consolation with us, that the harder the conflict, the more glorious the triumph. What we obtain too cheap, we esteem too lightly:---'Tis dearness only that gives every thing its value. Heaven knows how to set a proper price upon its goods; and it would be strange, indeed, if so celestial an article as FREEDOM should not be highly rated. Britain, with an army to enforce her tyranny, has declared, that she has a right (*not only to* TAX, but) "to " BIND *us in* ALL CASES WHATSOEVER," and if being *bound in that manner* is not slavery, then is there not such a thing as slavery upon earth. Even the expression is impious, for so unlimited a power can belong only to GOD.

WHETHER the Independence of the Continent was declared too soon, or delayed too long, I will not now enter into as an argument; my own simple opinion is, that had it been eight months earlier, it would have been much better. We did not make a proper use of last winter, neither could we, while we were in a dependent state. However, the fault, if it were one, was all our own; we have none to blame but ourselves*. But no great deal is lost yet; all that Howe has been doing for this month past is rather a ravage than a conquest, which the spirit of the Jersies a year ago would have quickly repulsed, and which time and a little resolution will soon recover.

I have as little superstition in me as any man living, but **my**

risings could be violently repressed, the slaves had burned large areas of the city and forcefully demonstrated against their bondage.

Property owners and those without property had their serious differences, but they were joined together by shared grievances against their common oppression from overseas. One of the results of mounting tensions was the formation in 1765 of the Sons of Liberty, largely a common man's patriotic association. The Sons of Liberty tended to focus mounting resentment through writings, demonstrations, and petitions.

The Sons of Liberty played a strategic role in organizing and rallying the American people against British rule. Mechanics' benevolent and protective associations of the era often collaborated with the Sons of Liberty. There was also functioning a kindred organization called the Daughters of Liberty. The Declaration of Independence reflected various influences including the ground swell of grievances from working people, yeomen, and small merchants.

By the opening days of the Revolution, working people were not only ready to serve their cause with guns in hand, but were also prepared to provide materials and supplies needed by the new nation. By then shipyards had been erected all along the coast and, by the time of the Revolution, about one-third of all British vessels were made in America. Despite British bans on manufacturing, in many parts of the colonies homespun garments were being made of cotton and wool in ever greater quantities.

The writing of Tom Paine inspired the nation.

Carpenters' Hall, Philadelphia, where the first Continental Congress met, was built in 1771 by the Carpenters' Company of Philadelphia, a trade guild or union.

In 1766, the Daughters of Liberty held all-day sessions of spinning at Providence, Rhode Island. As a result, the president and the first graduating class of Rhode Island College at commencement in 1769 were clothed in fabrics of American manufacture. The senior class in 1768 at Harvard College, Cambridge, was much commended for agreeing to graduate dressed wholly in native fabrics.

At the opening of the Revolution, New England was doing much to supply the demand for cheap clothing. Silk manufacture made a good start in Connecticut, Pennsylvania, Georgia, and South Carolina. "Silk culture was encouraged all over New England," one historian said, "and there is scarcely one of the New England cities that has not its Mulberry Street, named from the trees which were set out to furnish food for silkworms."

A rifle used in war.

A revolutionary soldier.

Sawmills, gristmills, and flax mills were commonplace in the New England countryside. "The improvement in power transmission and gearing that enabled several machines to be run from a single wheel-shaft," one chronicler of the times wrote, "was undoubtedly original in America, though possibly not first invented here; and minor laborsaving devices, such as log carriers in saw-mills and grain elevators in flour mills, were of American origin."

Iron-ore furnaces, rolling mills, foundries, forges, and tool shops were well established. Although the industrial revolution had not yet emerged in America, the colonies were demonstrating their own inventiveness at producing a wide range of iron goods. This served the colonies well in their revolutionary struggle, particularly in gunmaking.

Backwoodsmen from Virginia, Pennsylvania, and Maryland, often supplying their own rifles, became some of Washington's best soldiers. They were not only the most expert of all his marksmen, but also the best armed. "The worst of them," one Pennsylvania newspaper told the English, "will put a ball into a man's head at the distance of 150 or 200 yards, therefore, advise your officers who shall hereafter come out to America to settle their affairs in England before their departure."

Perfected by Swiss and Palatine German artisans and gunsmiths who settled in Pennsylvania around the Lancaster area, a new type of rifle contributed measurably to American success. The Pennsylvania rifle, or "long gun," was a product of the frontier culture of the Pennsylvania Dutch. The new weapon permitted a flatter trajectory of the ball; it thus went

A farm boy off to fight.

Thomas Paine

further and hit its target more frequently than British weapons. Using the technique of a rifled rather than a smooth bore, the Pennsylvania gunsmiths produced a long-barreled gun of amazing accuracy up to one hundred yards.

Pennsylvanians were of another help. Sulfur and saltpeter went into the making of gunpowder. These came in abundance from the German settlements along Codorus Creek in York County, where a song was sung: "Ohne Schweffel und Salzpeter gibt's keine Freiheit!" "Without sulfur and saltpeter, no freedom!" Canvas-covered wagons drawn by six-horse teams carried food and manufactured gunpowder and rifles to Coryell's Ferry on the Delaware, to Washington's army. So important was powder that workers in the powder mills were exempted from the draft.

So were workers in other essential industries. This practice followed an established precedent set a century or more before when Massachusetts exempted from military training fishermen during fishing seasons, ships' carpenters, and others. George Washington himself issued exemptions to many munition

Forging arms for the Minutemen.

Lieutenant Grosvenor and Peter Salem (his black servant) at the Battle of Bunker Hill.

Woodworking

workers whose craft outranked fighting in importance. In New York State, one miller was deferred for each grist mill; three powder makers for each powder-making plant; five steelworkers for each furnace.

Interestingly, four soldiers of the Revolutionary War were released from service because they had "attained so great a knowledge in the art of paper making," according to two Massachusetts paper man-ufacturers, "that their attendance on that business is absolutely necessary to its being carried out."

Ironworkers were generally exempted from mili-tary service. This was particularly necessary in the making of the giant iron chain that was stretched across the Hudson River near Fort Montgomery. The purpose of the eighteen-hundred-foot chain was, as the Secret Committee from the Provincial Convention of New York stated on July 16, 1776, "to obstruct navigation of the Hudson River so as to prevent any of the ships of the King of Great Britain coming up the same."

A number of ironworkers, blacksmiths, and car-penters were released from military duty to make the chain. Although it was well made, requiring more than twenty-two tons of iron, the chain actually failed in its purpose and was removed by the British.

It was traditional, too, during the war to impress skilled workers of one trade or another for military duty. Virginia and Maryland impressed carpenters and laborers during the Intercolonial Wars, years before the Revolution. Most colonies impressed driv-ers of horses and wagons to serve the military. This practice was also in use during the Revolution when required. The Continental army had use for a variety of workers for duties other than military. These in-cluded construction gangs, blacksmiths, tailors, car-penters, boatbuilders, harness makers, and so on.

But despite the use of trained workers, brought into the Continental army by impressment or as vol-unteers, much of the labor was performed by regular troops as fatigue duty. The bulk of the labor for the revolutionary army was performed by workers under

private contractors. Ironmaking took place in New Jersey, Virginia, and Pennsylvania; a clothing con-tractor in Maryland set up a factory with sixteen looms as well as a mill to process flax; a gunsmith in Mary-land hired nine employees to produce arms. In addi-tion to private contractors, there were also federal agencies involved in the manufacturing of iron, paint, clothes, leather, guns, and so on.

Most of the laboring people of the era served either in the Continental army, maintained by the Continental Congress, or were part of various bodies of militia recruited by individual colonies. While offi-cers in the Continental army were chosen by Con-gress, those in the militia were selected by the colony where the soldiers were recruited—sometimes being directly elected by the soldiers themselves.

After the fighting ended, there came, of course, the complex necessity of establishing the bases for

An incident in Shays's Rebellion.

building a new government. Most of those, however, entrusted with drafting the nation's Constitution were not convinced of the need for popular participation. As a matter of record, they feared it. Many were more concerned with establishing order than guaranteeing liberty.

Representatives attending the constitutional gatherings were almost unanimously from the ranks of the propertied class and the most well endowed: manufacturers, merchants, money lenders, slaveholders. There were no representatives among the fifty-five men attending from the mechanic or small farmer class.

A ground swell of apprehension that the Constitution lacked guarantees of liberties—without which people feared the settlement of their grievances would be impossible—influenced the Founding Fa-

thers. A series of amendments were proposed and approved, later known as the Bill of Rights, which went into effect in November 1791.

Just a decade after the signing of the Declaration of Independence, a veteran of the Battle of Bunker Hill, Captain Daniel Shays, led a six-month armed rebellion in Massachusetts against what he claimed were unfair taxes and foreclosures on the poor. Although troops were mustered to put the rebellion down, its repercussions were heard across the land.

"The ruling class trembled with fear lest the exploited masses rise and take away from them the wealth which they had accumulated during the War of Independence," said the historian John Bach McMaster. Commented Thomas Jefferson: "God forbid we should ever be twenty years without such a rebellion."

American troops at Valley Forge.

The Constitution

## 1790-1820

# LABOR FACES
# AN INDUSTRIAL REVOLUTION

*"Manufacturers are now
as necessary to our independence
as to our comfort."*

On April 30, 1789, George Washington—dressed in a coat, waistcoat, and breeches of dark brown cloth—was inaugurated as the first President of the United States.

For several reasons, it was an important event. In addition to political considerations, it also involved the display of home-manufactured clothing.

President Washington's apparel was made in the Hartford Woolen Manufactory, the first domestic woolen factory in which waterpower was used. "The cloth is of as fine a fabric," said one newspaper, "and so handsomely finished, that it is universally mistaken for a foreign manufactured superfine cloth."

In a letter to General Henry Knox, who sent him the suit, Washington wrote from Mount Vernon: "I beg of you to accept my acknowledgment of and thanks for . . . the trouble you have had in procuring and forwarding for use, a suit of the Hartford Manufacture. It is come safe and exceeds my expectation. I will take an early opportunity of paying the cost of it."

During the early years of the Republic, when Washington was President, the United States Congress and local state legislatures recommended to the people that greater attention be paid to the development of natural resources of the country and encour-

37

Thomas Jefferson

George Washington's diary entry of a visit to a factory.

Wednesday. 28.

"Wednesday 28th. Went, after an early breakfast, to visit the duck manufactory, which appeared to be carrying on with spirit, and in a prosperous way. They have manufactured 32 pieces of Duck of 30 or 40 yds. each in a week, and expect in a short time to increase it to . They have 28 looms at work, and 14 Girls spinning with Both hands, (the flax being fastened to their Waist.) Children (girls) turn the wheel for them, and with this assistance each spinner can turn out 14 lbs. of Thread pr. day when they stick to it, but as they are paid by the piece or work they do, there is no other restraint upon them but to come at 8 o'clock in the morning, and return at 6 in the evening. They are daughters of decayed families, and are girls of character—none others are admitted The number of hands now employed in the different parts of the work is but the Managers expect to increase them to . This is a work of public utility and private advantage. From hence I went to the Card Manufactory, where I was informed about 900 hands of one kind and for one purpose or another—all kinds of Cards are made; and there are Machines for executing every part of the work in a new and the teeth, wch.

aged many branches of manufacture by bounties for production. As American independence began to be reflected in its manufacturers, in 1785, the British Parliament prohibited, under severe penalties, the enticing of workmen skilled in the iron and steel manufactures from the British Kingdom. The law also forbade the exportation of tools used in manufacturing as well as machinery engines or parts, or models and plans.

The election to the Presidency in 1800 of Thomas Jefferson was a setback to those who still hoped the nation would move away from democracy and toward aristocracy. Jefferson's every follower, according to the historian John Bach McMaster, "was attacked as 'a Jacobin, a leveller, a socialist.'"

Jefferson's presence in the White House helped hurry along numerous democratic trends. The indenture system did not survive the Revolution. A growing number of states, too, were liberalizing regulations in connection with property qualifications for the right to vote. By 1800, slavery in the North had either ceased to exist or was on the way to legal abolition.

Jefferson had early placed his hopes for the future on an agrarian America. "Those who labored in the earth are the chosen people of God," he said, adding

*Pat Lyon at the Forge*, by John Neagle.

A canal boat pulled by a team of mules.

he would "never wish to see our citizens occupied at a work bench."

But the nation's needs were changing; and so were Jefferson's views. People were demanding an almost endless number of products, from ships to plows. The nation's transition from a farm economy to early industry was—whether Jefferson approved of it or not —already under way.

After the War of 1812 had cut off much of foreign trade and had stimulated even further the growth of independent American industry, Jefferson admitted in 1816 that "manufacturers are now as necessary to our independence as to our comfort. . . . We must now place the manufacturer by the side of the agriculturalist."

The domestic system, wherein goods were manufactured in the home by hand, was doomed. And of the crafts to move from the home to newly built factories, textile making was the first. The earliest factory of this kind was established in 1790 in Pawtucket, Rhode Island.

An early textile mill in Pawtucket, Rhode Island.

*April 11th 1808 This Day Wn Hoffman agrees & engages with Danl Focht present Manager of Greenwood Work, in manner & form following Witnesseth that he the said Hoffman will labour at Sundry Work, for the term of Two Months — Commencing as soon as his present Three Months is expired, & will do & perform all kind of work whatever may be requested of said Focht, — For the sum of Twenty Dollars & One pair of shoes for the term aforesaid as Witness Our Hands & seals the above Date —*

*Witness present*

*John Hoff*

*Danl Focht*

*Bill Zullman*

For two months' work, "Twenty Dollars one pair of shoes . . ."

One newspaper of the day described the working of an early Massachusetts cotton manufactory:

A plain three story building of brick, measuring about sixty by twenty-five feet with a pitching shingled roof, and a deep basement, in one end of which moved a heavy pair of horses to furnish rotary power. The horses were driven by a boy, Joshua Herrick, of Maine, who afterwards became a member of Congress.

When the horses went too fast, Mr. Somers would call out the window, "Hold on there! Not so fast! Slower!" and Herrick would slow up, but soon he would forget and speed up again, when again Somers would cry out, "Hold up!" and this continued most of the day . . .

While textile manufacturing spread, especially in New England, ironworks were established in New Jersey, Maryland, and Pennsylvania, including blast furnaces, forges, and stamping mills. Glassblowing shops were also established. Although in 1608 glassworkers had been sent by the London Company to build glass furnaces at Jamestown, it was not until later that glassworkers in New Jersey and Pennsyl-

A busy scene inside an early factory.

vania officially launched the industrial revolution in glassmaking.

The rise of industry followed closely the increase in the nation's population. From approximately four million people in 1790, the number rose to over five million by the turn of the century. By 1810, it had gone over seven million. A decade later the population was approaching ten million.

The demand was there, stimulating one's ingenuity to create new methods for doing almost everything: traveling, communicating, working. Steamers were no longer a novelty on the waterways. In 1825, the Erie Canal was ready for traffic. Railroads spanned vast segments of the country. Ideas poured into the United States Patent Office for doing things more easily, faster, and more efficiently.

For many workers—men, women, and children—the new industrialization presented opportunity. Sewing in the home, making shoes, or hammering out utensils in small shops began to disappear as factories attracted workers with the promise of a better livelihood. The man most directly responsible for speeding up this process was British-born Samuel Slater who carried in his head details of Richard Arkwright's machine for cotton spinning when he left home in 1789 for the New World.

Although there had been textile mills in America—in Massachusetts and Philadelphia particularly—it was Slater who put such establishments on an efficient

Famines in Ireland and other nations made people look hopefully to America.

business basis. Born in Derbyshire, Slater learned as an indentured apprentice how to manufacture cotton. He cleverly managed to outwit British authorities, who banned the export of manufacturing devices, by memorizing technical plans for the construction of a spinning frame. These ideas he put into concrete application in Pawtucket, Rhode Island, where he equipped a mill with a full set of machinery constructed from memory.

"The building in which Slater's new machines were

Agents were dispatched to nations overseas to recruit workers.

Samuel Slater

set up was the fulling mill of Ezekiel Carpenter, and stood on the southwest abutment of the Pawtucket bridge," according to an account by Perry Walton, an authority on the subject.

Slater at once began to build a water frame of twenty-four spindles, two carding machines, and the drawing and roping frames necessary for the spinners, and soon after added a frame of forty-eight spindles.

Great secrecy was maintained while the machinery was being made, shutters shielding the front windows and blinds covering the back windows. Sylvanus Brown cut out the parts of the spinning machines after Slater had chalked them out on the wood.

The building, which opened for operation in the winter of 1790, became the first modern factory in American history.

Later "the father of the American factory system," as President Jackson called him, organized the spread of factory production. His first textile mill employed only children—seven boys and two girls, all under twelve years of age. Slater mills multiplied rapidly and soon were located in more than a dozen locations throughout New England.

Slater developed the method of advertising in newspapers for entire families to work in his mills, men from the fields, women from the homes, children

The first factory workers were children.

RHODES & SMITH,
Mason's Buildings, Commercial-St. No. 1.
They wish to hire a WEAVER, capable
of taking charge of water-looms. Also, a
FAMILY, of from five to eight children,
capable of working in a Cotton Mill. None
need apply, unless well recommended.
April 20.

**FAMILY WANTED,**
*To work in a Thread-Mill:*

THE Mill is four miles and a half from
Providence, on the Turnpike road
leading from Providence to Chepachet,
and one fourth of a mile from Messrs.
Richard Anthony & Son's Cotton-Mill.
For particulars, enquire of ASA SAYLES, on
the premises.    A. SAYLES & Co.
*North-Providence, March 7.   tSW.*

as young as nine or ten years of age. One Connecticut ad read: "In collecting our help we are obliged to employ poor families and generally those having the greatest number of children."

Faced with insecurity and poverty, working people and farmers responded to such invitations in large numbers. Work on the farm was mercilessly hard, from sunup to sundown, with little laborsaving machinery. Monetary returns were meager. It was an isolated life with small opportunity for self-improvement. Educational opportunities were often nonexistent. So was social life. The lure of the city, romanticized in story and gossip, was hard to resist,

particularly for the young. Horace Greeley, the future New York newspaper editor who, as a New Hampshire farm boy, fled to the big city, later recalled:

Being the older son of a poor and hard-working farmer, struggling to pay off the debt he had incurred in buying his high-priced farm, and to support his increasing family, I was early made acquainted with labor. I well remember the cold summer [1816] when we rose on the eighth of June to find the earth covered with a good inch of newly fallen snow,—when there was frost every month, and corn did not fill till October. Plants grew very slowly that season, while burrowing insects fed and fattened on them. My task for a time was to precede my father as he hoed his corn, dig open the hills, and kill the wire-worms and grubs that were anticipating our dubious harvest.

To "ride horse to plough" soon became my more usual vocation; the horse preceding and guiding the oxen, save when furrowing for or tilling the planted crops. Occasionally, the plough would strike a fast stone, and bring up the team all standing, pitching me over the horse's head, and landing me three to five feet in front . . .

Burning charcoal in the woods south and southwest of us was a favorite, though very slow, method of earning money in those days. The growing wood, having then no commercial value, could usually be had for nothing; but the labor of cutting it down and reducing it to the proper length, piling it skillfully, covering the heap with sods, or with straw and earth, and then expelling every element but the carbon by smothered combustion, is rugged and tedious. I have known a pit of green wood to be nine days in burning; and every pit must be watched night and day till the process is complete . . .

Women went into factories by the thousands.

STRIVE TO EXCEL.

W. S. & C. H. THOMSON'S SKIRT MANUFACTORY.

Harvest

Making ready for cultivation

Corn husking

The slave was the basis of southern agriculture.

Picking stones is a never-ending labor on one of those rocky New England farms. Pick as closely as you may, the next ploughing turns up a fresh eruption of boulders and pebbles, from the size of a hickory-nut to that of a tea-kettle; and, as this work is mainly to be done in March or April, when the earth is saturated with ice-cold water, if not also whitened with falling snow, youngsters soon learn to regard it with detestation. I filially love the "Granite State," but could well excuse the absence of sundry subdivisions of her granite.

To return to the factories, particularly of cloth, that were recruiting people from the farms, the successful use of Arkwright's machines placed cotton manufacturing in the United States on a secure basis. By this time Slater had become interested in wool as well as cotton and was the leading textile manufacturer of his era. The War of 1812 greatly increased his prosperity, as cotton cloth sold at forty cents a yard and the demand was unlimited.

Slater was not the only refugee from abroad who came to America bearing secrets, either of machine construction or of worker techniques. Many more were to arrive. Industry was established at Ipswich

in 1818, with a number of knitters from Nottingham, England. The same year the first stocking machine was imported, secreted in the hold of a ship.

It was brought to Ipswich in 1822, where it was used to knit the first pair of stockings in the kitchen of a private dwelling. Other machines were also secretly imported.

All machines that helped speed industrialization in America were not by any means imported from abroad. Americans were also developing a talent for invention. Eli Whitney was born in Westboro, Massachusetts, and originally planned to be a lawyer. His mechanical aptitude, however, convinced him otherwise. In 1793, within ten days after addressing himself to the problem of separating the seed of cotton from the cotton itself, he produced a cotton gin that speeded up immeasurably the production of clean cotton.

Workers in factories often continued to farm on the side.

Road making

Eli Whitney

Separation of cotton from the seed and boll had been slow and tedious. The work was usually done by slave labor, largely the work of black women who separated the seed and cleaned the cotton from the boll with their fingernails.

It took a slave a day to pick a pound of cotton from the boll and separate it from the entangled seed. The invention of the cotton gin revolutionized the industry, as it enabled a worker to clean five thousand pounds of cotton a day, thereby greatly increasing the supply of American cotton, not to mention the profit.

This was just the start of Whitney's contribution to the country's rapid industrialization. Even more important was an idea that if all parts of a product being manufactured were standardized in size and shape, the completed item could be assembled at a later time. This for the first time in a practical way pro-

jected the idea of mass production.

Impressed, Thomas Jefferson wrote of Whitney: "He has invented moulds and machines for making all the pieces of his locks so exactly equal that take a hundred locks and mingle their parts, and a hundred locks may be put together as well by taking the first pieces that come to hand . . ."

This concept, increasingly used, was to alter the entire procedure of manufacturing. Standardization of parts came about through the creation of machines of a marvelously accurate caliber. An entire family of machine tools evolved, including milling, grinding, and boring machines. Contrivances thus evolved whose sole purpose was the making of other machines. From this an entire industry was to be born.

While the early factory made use of children as workers, by the 1830s the developing textile mill

The Morning Bell by Winslow Homer.

My general plan does not consist in one great complicated machine wherein if one small part is being out of order or not answering the purpose expected, the whole must stop & be rendered useless — If the mode in which I propose to make one part of the must should prove by experiment not to answer, it will in no way affect the mode of making any other part ____ One of my primary objects is to form the tools so the tools themselves shall fashion the work and give to every part its just proportion — which when once accomplished will give expedition uniformity and exactness to the whole — If the forgings are mere shapeless lumps of Iron out which the filler is to form and fashion the thing wanted — If each individual workman must form and fashion every part form the rude mass according to his own fancy & regulate the size & proportion by his own Eye or even by a measure of his own I should have as many varieties as there are numbers of each part & many of them would require an insertion upon them to point out the use for which they were designed — & it would require treble the number of hands to do the same work

A letter from Eli Whitney: "One of my primary objects is to form the tools so the tools themselves shall fashion the work and give to every part its just proportion . . ."

looked increasingly in the direction of young ladies as the most preferred type of "operative," as millworkers were known. Industrial managers in the newly created towns of Lowell and Lawrence, Massachusetts, sent agents throughout the rural areas of New England to visit farmhouses and recruit farm daughters to leave home and work in the new mills.

These "rosy cheeked maidens" entered the textile mills in large numbers, eager to leave dreary farm work behind them for the promise of a rewarding existence in mill towns. Their daily life in such communities as Lowell was, at first, carefully supervised. The girls were told when to arise in the morning, what to do on the job, when to have lunch, when the quitting time arrived, what to do for recreation, when to go to bed, where to go to church on Sunday.

In the beginning the girls found their new existence stimulating and intellectually exciting. They were encouraged to write poetry and read aloud to one another.

There were various opinions expressed in the *Lowell Offering*, a company publication for employees. Many articles sought to quiet discontent:

"I will not stay in Lowell any longer; I am determined to give my notice this very day," said Ellen Collins, as the earliest bell was tolling to remind us of the hour for labour.

"Why, what is the matter, Ellen? It seems to me you have dreamed out a new idea! Where do you think of going? and what for?"

"I am going home, where I shall not be obliged to rise so early in the morning, nor be dragged about by the ringing of a bell, nor confined in a close noisy room from morning till night. I will not stay here; I am determined to go home in a fortnight."

Such was our brief morning's conversation.

In the evening, as I sat alone reading, my companions having gone out to public lectures or social meetings, Ellen entered. I saw that she still wore the same gloomy expression of countenance, which had been manifested in the morning; and I was disposed to remove from her mind the evil influence, by a plain common-sense conversation.

"And so, Ellen," said I, "you think it unpleasant to rise so early in the morning, and be confined in the noisy mill so many hours during the day. And I think so, too. All this, and much more, is very annoying, no doubt. But we must not forget that there are advantages, as well as disadvantages, in this employment, as in every other. If we expect to find all sunshine and flowers in any station in life, we shall most surely be disappointed. We are very busily engaged during the day; but then we have the evening to ourselves, with no one to dictate to or control us . . .

"Ellen," said I, "do you remember what is

Francis C. Lowell: He was concerned with "the moral and religious instruction of the operatives."

Abbott Lawrence

said of the bee, that it gathers honey even in a poisonous flower? May we not, in like manner, if our hearts are rightly attuned, find many pleasures connected with our employment?

# HOUSE......No. 50.

The Spe
relati
subm

The
came fr
Quincy
"peace
Lowell.
thirteen
and are
tion, do
Legislat
stitute a
zen "sl
one set

The s
is signed
others.

for dinner. The air in the room she considered not to be wholesome. There were 293 small lamps and 61 large lamps lighted in the room in which she worked, when evening work is required. These lamps are also lighted sometimes in the morning.—About 130 females, 11 men, and 12 children (between the ages of 11 and 14.) work in the room with her. She thought the children enjoyed about as good health as children generally do. The children work but 9 months out of 12. The other 3 months they must attend school. Thinks that there is no day when there are less than six of the females out of the mill from sickness. Has known as many as thirty. She, herself, is out quite often, on account of sickness. There was more sickness in the Summer than in the Winter months; though in the Summer, lamps are not lighted. She thought there was a general desire among the females to work but ten hours, regardless of pay. Most of the girls are from the country, who work in the Lowell Mills. The average time which they remain there is about three years. She knew one girl who had worked there 14 years. Her health was poor when she left. Miss Hemmingway said her health was better where she now worked, than it was when she worked on the Hamilton Corporation.

She knew of one girl who last winter went into the mill at half past 4 o'clock, A. M. and worked till half past 7 o'clock, P. M. She did so to make more money. She earned from $25 to $30 per month. There is always a large number of girls at the gate wishing to get in before the bell rings. On the Middlesex Corporation one fourth part of the females go into the mill before they are obliged to. They do this to make more wages. A large number come to Lowell to make money to aid their parents who are poor. She knew of many cases where married women came to Lowell and worked in the mills to assist their [...] farms. The moral cha[...]

A group of women workers testified in 1845 before a committee of the Massachusetts legislature.

Why is it, then, that you so obstinately look altogether on the dark side of the factory life? I think you thought differently while you were at home, on a visit, last summer—for you were glad to come back to the mill in less than four weeks. Tell me, now—why were you so glad to return to the ringing of the bell, the clatter of the machinery, the early rising, the half-hour dinner, and so on?"

Numerous visitors praised the Lowell industrial system.

When Charles Dickens first came to America in the 1840s, included in his travels were visits to factories in Lowell, Massachusetts. "I solemnly declare," he wrote in his *American Notes*, "that I cannot recall or separate one young face that gave me a painful impression; not one young girl whom, assuming it to be a matter of necessity that she should gain her daily

# GENERAL REGULATIONS,

## TO BE OBSERVED BY PERSONS EMPLOYED BY THE

## LAWRENCE MANUFACTURING COMPANY, IN LOWELL.

1st. All persons in the employ of the Company, are required to attend assiduously to their various duties, or labor, during working hours; are expected to be fully competent, or to aspire to the utmost efficiency in the work or business they may engage to perform, and to evince on all occasions, in their deportment and conversation, a laudable regard for temperance, virtue, and their moral and social obligations ; and in which the Agent will endeavor to set a proper example. No persons can be employed by the Company, whose known habits are or shall be dissolute, indolent, dishonest, or intemperate, or who habitually absent themselves from public worship, and violate the Sabbath, or who may be addicted to gambling of any kind.

2d. All kinds of ardent spirit will be excluded from the Company's ground, except it be prescribed for medicine, or for washes, and external application. Every kind of gambling and card playing, is totally prohibited within the limits of the Company's ground and Boarding Houses.

3d. Smoking cannot be permitted in the Mills, or other buildings, or yards, and should not be carelessly indulged in the Boarding Houses and streets. The utmost vigilance must be exercised to prevent the ~~~~~~~~~~~~~ Mills, Pickers, Houses and other buildings, and proper arrangements being made for extinguish~~~~~~~~~~~~~~~~~~~~~~~~~~~~ld such an evil overtake ~~ by preparing

~~~~~~~~~~~~~~~~~~~~~~~~~~~~~~~~~~~~~

of their overseer, except ~~~~~~~~~~~~~~~~~~ emergency, when they w~~~~~~~~~~~~~~~~~~~~~~~~~ ~~~~~~~~~~~~ of the boarding houses in ed at labor, are required to board in one of the Company's boarding houses, and~~~~~~~~~~~~~~~~~~~~~~~~~~~~~~ which they live. All persons are required to attend public worship, at some regular place of worship, and to conform strictly to the rules of the Sabbath. Persons who do not comply with these regulations will not be employed by the Company. Persons entering the employ of the Company are considered as engaging to work one year, if the Company require their services so long. All persons intending to leave the employ of the Company are required to give notice of the same to their overseer at least two weeks previous to the time of leaving.

The above regulations are considered part of the contract with all persons in the employment of the Lawrence Manufacturing Company. All persons who shall have complied with them, on leaving the employment of the Company will be entitled to an honorable discharge.

14th. Persons in the employ of the Company will reflect, that it is their voluntary agreement to serve, and consequent mutual relations of the parties, which render it proper on their part to conform to regulations, or that warrants the Agent in promulgating rules for their observance, and which govern him as well as themselves. They will perceive that where objects are to be obtained, by the united efforts and labor of many individuals, that some must direct and many be directed. That their religious and political opinions need not however be influenced, nor their personal independence, or self respect, or conscious equality lost sight of or abandoned;—and the younger portion of them especially, are solicited and urged to appropriate their earnings and leisure hours to economical and useful purposes, and to the attainment of that knowledge and those qualifications in household economy, and other pursuits in life, necessary to a proper and faithful discharge of the various duties which may await them in all the relations of life; and it is no less desirable that all should be expert and cheerful at their business, and happy during hours of leisure or relaxation, in the participation of such rational amusements as shall please on reflection. They may apply with confidence to the Agent for advice; and such aid and counsel as he can afford them, will be cheerfully granted, especially to those who may be far from their parents and friends. It remains to encourage and cherish mutual respect, kindness and conciliation towards each other, and that peculiar instances of industrious and honest merit be rewarded, and which the Agent will reciprocate and aspire to accomplish.

WILLIAM AUSTIN, Agent.

Lowell, May 21, 1833.

Most early factories had regulations for employees that they strictly enforced. This is from a Lowell mill of 1833.

Charles Dickens

Harriet Martineau

The development of two New England mill towns: Woonsocket, Rhode Island, and

Lawrence, Massachusetts.

bread by the labor of her hands, I would have removed from those works if I had had the power. . . . It is their station to work. . . . And they do work. They labor in these mills, upon an average, twelve hours a day, which is unquestionably work and pretty tight work, too."

In 1834, Harriet Martineau, the British writer, visited a Massachusetts factory and noted:

Five hundred persons were employed at the time of my visit. The girls earn two, and sometimes three, dollars a week, besides their board. The little children earn one dollar a week. Most of the girls live in the houses provided by the corporation, which accommodate from six to eight each. When sisters come to the mill, it is a common practice for them to bring their mother to keep house for them and some of their companions, in a dwelling built by their own earnings. In this case, they save enough out of their board to clothe themselves, and have their two or three dollars a week to spare.

Some have thus cleared off mortgages from their fathers' farms; others have educated the hope of the family at college; and many are rapidly accumulating an independence. . . . The people work about seventy hours per week, on the average . . .

Kirk Boott: "He insisted on immediate obedience."

When President Jackson visited the textile center of Lowell in 1833, elaborate welcoming ceremonies were carefully arranged. Laboring men and women of the mills turned out to escort him. "Every woman carried a parasol and was dressed in white muslin, with a blue sash, save the women of the Hamilton corporation, who wore black sashes in respect for the memory of their agent [manager], who had just died," one eyewitness reported.

But gradually a change took place. And as far as factory employees were concerned, not for the better. Merchant capitalists who came into control of the mills had a way of instructing their managers to increase production. Most managers were eager to cooperate. "Gentlemen," answered Kirk Boott, the manager of Lowell plants, "give yourself no uneasiness about a deficit. We will take care of that."

The manner of "taking care of that" was usually increasing the number of looms that employees were required to tend. From one, the number might be increased to two or three or even four. Speeding up the machinery and increasing the number of looms was accompanied by the introduction of what was known as the premium system. Under this system, bonuses were paid to overseers, or managers, who succeeded in getting more work out of their operatives than before.

This premium system altered the relationship between employees and their superiors. Once there had been a friendly contact. Now this usually ceased. Once paternal supervision was a subject of pride. Now exploitation began to replace cooperation. Where once visitors praised the conditions under which the employees of Lowell and Lawrence worked, now there was increasing criticism. Speaking of the boardinghouse arrangement at the Lawrence mills, one newspaper correspondent addressed mill owner Abbott Lawrence, stating: "You furnish your operatives with no more healthy sleeping apartments than the cellars and garrets of the English poor. . . . You shut up the operatives two or three hours longer a day in your factory prisons than is done in Europe . . ."

A result of all this was disillusionment on the part of mill girls, and general demoralization. Writing about the ills attendant to those who continued to work in the mills, Benjamin F. Butler, later an outstanding Civil War general, stated: "I knew all their wants; knew their sicknesses and the causes thereof; saw the deterioration in their bodily health from year to year as they grew pallid and nervous . . ."

Major General Benjamin F. Butler

A woman textile worker.

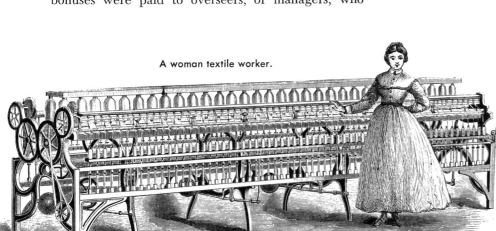

a connected page, opened at random, will be quoted, only with the same omission as before. The reader will notice the kind of offences recorded, and, from the dates, will be able to judge how frequently such cases occur.

"1838, *Dec*. 31. Ann ——. No. 4, weaving room; discharged for altering her looms and thinning her cloth.

1839, *Jan*. 2. Lydia ——. No. 1, spinning room; obtained an honorable discharge by false pretences. Her name has been sent round to the other Corporations as a thief and a liar.

*Jan*. 3. Harriet —— and Judith ——. From No. 4, spinning room, and No. 5, weaving room; discharged as worthless characters.

*Jan*. 9. Lydia ——. From No. 2, spinning room; left irregularly; name sent round.

*Feb*. 15. Hadassah ——. From No. 3, lower weaving room; discharged for improper conduct — stealing from Mrs. ——.

*March* 8. Abby ——. No. 2, spinning room; discharged for improper conduct.

*March* 14. Ann ——, No. 2, spinning room; discharged for reading in the mill; gave her a line stating the facts.

*March* 26. Harriet ——, No. 4, carding room; Laura ——, No. 4, spinning room; Ellen ——, No. 1, carding room; George ——, repair shop — all discharged for improper conduct.

*March* 29. Martha ——, No. 2, spinning room; Apphia ——, No. 2, spinning room; left irregularly, and names sent round.

*April* 3. Emily ——. No. 5, carding room; discharged for profanity, and sundry other misdemeanors. 'Name sent round."

It must be unnecessary to accompany the above quotations with any comment. The facts, selected with as much impartiality as is possible, speak for themselves. We have here sixteen honorable discharges given in sixteen

Rigorous rules for mill employees were reflected in a book devoted to subjects ranging from profanity to wages.

tution for Savings. Cases like the following, quoted from the discharge book, kept in one of the Corporation counting-rooms, might be presented in great numbers.

"*Sept*. 14, 1844. Eunice * * * worked twelve months, discharged to go home. She left home in * * * Me., just one year since, and promised to return in a year. She has clothed herself well, and carries with her seventy-five dollars, net savings of her year's work: has lost three days from all causes."

"*Oct*. 14. Mary * * * worked nine years, discharged to go on Lowell Corporation. She and her sister, who left a short time since to be married, and who had worked for us over ten years, have never lost so much time as they have made up by extra work. They are Irish. Their father died about nine years ago. They have since entirely supported their mother, having built her a house, costing six hundred dollars, in which they have kept

house together. They own a pew, which cost them one hundred and twenty-five dollars, and they have from one hundred to two hundred dollars each at interest."

"*June* 14, 1845. Harriet * * * one year, discharged to go home. This is her first visit to Lowell, has never worked in any factory before, was not well when she came, has lost considerable time, has clothed herself well, and carries home with her thirty dollars."

It may not be out of place to give here the pay days on the Corporations.

Appleton Co. week after last Saturday in each month.
Boott " " first "
Lowell Bleaching Co. Wed. after last Sat. each month.
Hamilton Co. week after last Sat. but one each month.
Lowell Co. week after last Saturday in each month.
Locks & Canals Co. Tues. after last Sat. each month.
Lawrence Co. week after second Sat. in each month.
Massachusetts Co. week after third Sat. in each month.
Merrimack Co. the Saturday before 16th of each month.
Middlesex Co. Friday and Saturday after the end of the month; but if the month ends on Tuesday, Wednesday or Thursday, then on the Friday and Saturday of the next week.

While such a group as the Lowell Female Reform Association was organized, it could not halt the steady disintegration of conditions in the mill towns. There was a growing fear of incurring the wrath of the manager. The names of girls who protested deteriorating work conditions were sent around to other companies.

This development of a blacklist spread widely and was greatly feared. So closely connected were the managements of various companies that any worker could be easily prevented from obtaining employment by any employer in the region if she incurred the displeasure of one.

What Norman Ware calls "the degradation of the operative" took place on an ever wider scale. In 1846, the Lowell *Voice of Industry* reported on observing a

singular-looking, long, low, black wagon passing along the street. We made inquiries respecting it, and were informed that it was what we term a "slaver." She makes regular trips to the

A maiden in a textile mill.

# REGULATIONS OF BOARDING HOUSES.

1. The boarding houses are erected and rented low for the accommodation of persons employed by the Company, and are subject to the supervision of the Agent, and must not therefore be occupied by persons not employed by the Company, nor let in any manner by those who may be admitted as tenants without the consent of said Agent. Rents must be paid punctually, at the close of each quarter, and board at the close of each month.

2. The tenants will consider themselves responsible for the order, punctuality of meals, cleanliness, and general arrangements for rendering their houses comfortable, tranquil scenes of moral deportment, and mutual good will.

They will report, if requested, the names and occupation of the boarders; also, give timely warning to the unwary, and report all cases of intemperance and dissolute manners.

3. The boarding houses must be closed at *ten o'clock*, in the evening—all persons in the employ of the Company, will therefore repair to their homes at that hour unless urgent circumstances prevent it, and it should be remembered that the tardy return of the boarders on such occasions takes from the needful rest of the tenant, and that we must give up some portion of what may be deemed our privileges, for the sake of enjoying the remainder in greater purity.

4. It follows therefore, that every kind of ardent spirit (except prescribed by a regular Physician) will be banished from the limits of the corporation, and that intemperate, immoral, and indolent persons, if they succeed in obtaining employment, or in being admitted as tenants, will be discharged or removed, unless they reform after due admonition. And it may well be remarked, that without some efforts to "please and be pleased," shall pervade the actions of all those employed by the Company, and those efforts shall be influenced by reasonable and justifiable objects, we shall forfeit our claims to individual and social prosperity. All persons employed by the Company, will duly observe and attend some place of public worship on the Sabbath, when practicable.

5. In order to promote health, the houses and cellars, in every part, sheds, yards, sinks, and sidewalks, *must* be kept clean, great care must be taken of the buildings, and if they shall be unnecessarily injured, the repairs will be charged to the occupants of the houses, or to those who thus injure them.

6. All persons in the employ of the Company, who have not been vaccinated and will submit to the operation, can be vaccinated gratis.

7. Some suitable provision must be made for the sick in each house, by setting apart, on such occasions and until further arrangements can be made, a retired and suitable room, where they can be properly attended.

8. Children not employed and of suitable age, should be sent to school, for which great facilities will be afforded.

WILLIAM AUSTIN, *Agent of Lawrence Man. Co., Lowell.*

Mill regulations extended to boarding-houses where mill operatives lived.

north of the state, cruising around in Vermont and New Hampshire, with a "commander" whose heart must be as black as his craft, who is paid a dollar a head for all he brings to the market, and more in proportion to the distance —if they bring them from such a distance that they cannot easily get back.

This is done by "hoisting false colors," and representing to the girls that they can tend more machinery than is possible, and that the work is so very neat, and the wages such, that they can dress in silks and spend half their time in reading. Now is this true? Let those girls who have been thus deceived answer.

Testifying before a state legislative committee in 1845, textile workers declared that they were confined "from thirteen to fourteen hours per day in unhealthy apartments" and were thereby "hastening through pain, disease and privation, down to a premature grave."

Urging legislation that "ten hours shall constitute a day's work," the petitioners were specific in their complaints. One weaver testified her wages averaged from sixteen to twenty-three dollars a month exclusive of board.

In the summer season, the work is commenced at five o'clock, A.M., and continued until seven o'clock P.M.

The air in the room she considered not to be wholesome . . . about 130 females, 11 men and 12 children [between the ages of 11 and 14] work in the room with her . . . The children work but 9 months out of 12. The other three months they must attend school.

Sarah Begley, a Lowell worker for over eight years, testified that "the chief evil, as far as health is concerned, is the shortness of time allowed for meals. The next evil is the length of time employed—not giving them time to cultivate their minds."

Contributing to such problems, in Lowell and elsewhere in the country, were reoccurring economic depressions, or "panics" as they were called. In 1819, one of these depressions caused much unemployment and suffering. A reporter for *The New York Times* commented: "Thousands of industrious mechanics who never before solicited alms, were brought to the humiliating condition of applying for assistance and with tears on their manly cheeks, confessed their inability to provide food or clothing for their families."

Working people and small businessmen in almost every area of endeavor felt the results of the rise of the merchant capitalist and the growing demand for higher profits from the machines and the people who tended them.

"There is no class of mechanics in New York who average so great an amount of work for so little money as the journeymen shoemakers," stated an article in the New York *Daily Tribune* in 1845.

*Bell Time*, by Winslow Homer.

The interior of an early machine shop.

The number of journeymen out of employment is also large. . . . There are hundreds of them in the city constantly wandering from shop to shop in search of work, while many of them have families in a state of absolute want. . . . We have been in more than fifty cellars in different parts of the city, each inhabited by a shoemaker and his family.

The floor is made of rough plank laid loosely down, the ceiling is not quite so high as a tall man. The walls are dark and damp, and a wide, desolate fireplace yawns in the center to the right of the entrance. There is no outlet back and of course no yard privileges of any kind. The miserable room is lighted only by a shallow sash, partly projecting above the surface of the ground and by the little light that struggles down the steep and rotting stairs.

In this . . . often live the man with his work-bench, his wife and five or six children of all ages, and perhaps a palsied grandfather or grandmother and often both. In one corner is a squalid bed and the room elsewhere is occupied by the work-bench, a cradle made from a dry-goods box, two or three broken, seatless chairs, a stew-pan and a kettle.

Loading a ship.

The industrialization of the new country, harsh as it was, provided the steel for the railroad tracks, the wheels for the wagons, the clothing for the burgeoning population; ships and plows and books, saddles and rifles and reapers; and such a variety of products as to prompt an elderly lady to exclaim: "I declare, I don't know what they'll be making next."

As mechanization proceeded, the skilled worker and mechanic—once proud of his artistry and craft—found himself increasingly without the opportunity to use his skills. Machines were able to do it better. He was becoming just another factory hand.

## NEW YORK, May 12.

*We have the satisfaction of announcing the arrival of the Ship Empress of China, Capt. Greene, commander, from the* EAST-INDIES, *at this port, yesterday, after a voyage of fourteen months and twenty-four days. She sailed from this port about the 15th of February, 1784, and arrived at Canton in August, having touched at the Cape de Verdes —she took her departure from China the first of last January, and in return touched at the Cape of Good Hope, from whence she made her passage here in about two months.—The crew during this long voyage have been remarkable healthy. The carpenter, who went out in a bad state of health, died on the homeward passage.*

*We learn that Captain Greene met with polite usage during his stay in Canton—the British Commodore was the first who saluted his flag on his arrival there.*

### HANNAH BINDING SHOES.

Poor lone Hannah,
Sitting at the window, binding shoes:
Faded, wrinkled,
Sitting, stitching, in a mournful muse.
Bright-eyed beauty once was she,
When the bloom was on the tree:
Spring and winter,
Hannah's at the window, binding shoes.

Lucy Larcom, Lowell poet and millworker, and one her poems.

---

Working people were not against the introduction of industrial machinery. But they were strongly opposed to being treated with less consideration than the machinery they operated. The loss of human values was the cause of continual frustration and even anger:

"I regard my work people," one factory agent stated, "just as I regard my machinery. So long as they can do my work for what I choose to pay them, I keep them, getting of them all I can. . . . When my machines get old and useless, I reject them and get new, and these people are part of my machinery . . ."

Hours of labor in industry in the early 1840s were usually from 6:00 A.M. to 10:00 P.M., six days a week. In Lowell, according to the study of John R. Commons, hours of work "varied from eleven hours and 24 minutes in December and January, to 13 hours and 31 minutes in April, the averages for the year being 12 hours and 13 minutes per day, or about 73 hours and 30 minutes per week."

Housing was bad. Urban health conditions were deplorable. Prisons were filled, according to Seth Luther, one of New England's leading spokesmen for the workingman in the 1830s, with "men guilty of no crime but being poor."

"No regard is paid to sex," one housing report put it, "men, women and children are huddled together in one disgusting mass. Without a breath of air from without, these holes are hotbeds of pestilence." A health officer reported: "Human life was nothing. The supremacy of property dominated all thought and laws."

The noisy, dusty, dangerous machine society—

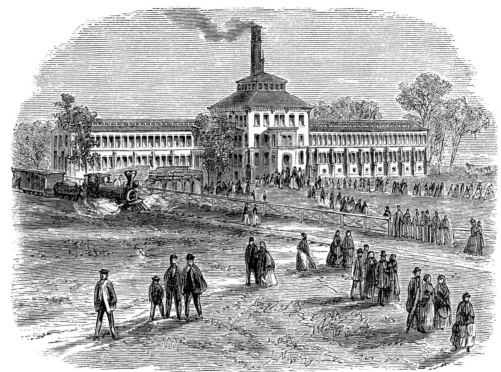

Change of factory shifts.

without safeguards of life or limb or security of any kind—offended and even frightened the fundamentally agrarian worker.

In the making of shoes, an early report stated that, at first,

Everything was done by hand, even to the cutting out of the soles, which was a slow process, and required the expenditure of a large amount of physical force. The introduction of sole-cutting and stripping machines, although used sparingly, was the first indication that a change was to take place in the business of shoemaking; but no one, even ten years ago, would have dared to prophesy that the change was to be so immediate and so great.

The rapid progress that has been made during that time . . . in the introduction of machinery in shoemaking, has been beyond all previous calculation. It may almost be said that handwork has already become the exception, and machinery the rule. The little shoemaker's shop and the shoemaker's bench are passing rapidly away, soon to be known no more among us; and the immense factory, with its laboring steam engine and its busy hum of whirling wheels, is rising up in their place to change the whole face of things in this ancient and honored metropolis of the "workers in the gentle craft of leather."

Change also reached out to the ships at sea. A new era in American maritime history was opened in 1817 when a fleet of packet boats operating out of New York announced that it would provide regular service across the Atlantic at "frequent and regular" intervals. The Black Ball Line provided square-rigged ships that were built for swift and safe operation. It turned

The demand increased for transportation on land . . .

and water.

out, as one writer put it, the ships "were captained by men who mercilessly used every ounce of their crew's endurance to keep to schedule."

Unbearable conditions and hard discipline on board ship caused much misery among seamen. Punishments inflicted on men who objected even mildly were severe and irrational. Many died of fevers and scurvy and from lack of even rudimentary sanitary safeguards. Desertions became common. In an effort to halt them, authorities frequently withheld wages for long periods, sometimes for years. But still the men deserted their ships.

Alternatives facing exploited seamen were dramatically summarized by Richard Henry Dana, Jr., in 1840:

> What is there for sailors to do? If they resist, it is mutiny; and if they succeed and take the vessel, it is piracy. If they ever yield again, their punishment must come; and if they do not yield, they are pirates for life. If a sailor resist his commander, he resists the law, and piracy or submission are his only alternatives. Bad as it was, it must be borne. It is what a sailor ships for.

Onshore, the transition from the farm to the factory had been an abrupt one for most employees. Many of those who had come from the farm returned there.

While farm life remained rugged and difficult, for many millworkers the relative peace and tranquillity of the rural scene—once disdained—was now preferred. If there was loneliness, there was less danger from accidents; if there were limited social contacts,

there was more time to enjoy what was available; if there were the all-consuming family chores, at least there was less chance to go hungry. Besides, farm machinery was making farm life somewhat less rigorous. The steel plow was coming into use; the Oliver plow with a chilled steel moldboard followed. The sickle was giving way to the "cradle," a kind of scythe with long curved wooden teeth parallel to it, the use of which, one farmer remarked, was "almost a trade in itself." By 1833, the first successful reaper was being introduced.

As the girl workers left the mills in Lowell and other mill towns, no longer "rosy cheeked," new recruits took their places—often from nations overseas.

The number of people arriving in America to seek their fortunes, or to avoid foreign persecutions, steadily mounted; from ten thousand during the year 1825, the number grew to seventy-six thousand a year scarcely more than a decade later. Fleeing famine and political and religious persecution, people sought the New World from Ireland, England, Germany, Norway, Scotland, and other nations.

The new American factories did not leave it to chance whether their supply of foreign workers was adequate. As the mills had once sent recruiting agents through rural New England, they now dispatched agents abroad to go through the provinces urging men, women, and children to come to the "new land of promise and plenty." Placards were distributed and posters placed on walls, frequently containing lurid exaggerations of the opportunities that existed in faraway America.

Many a native of a foreign country sold his last possession to pay for passage to the nation in which he hoped to find, as he was told, "the streets paved with gold and a fortune to be made by everyone."

FOUR

## 1820-1860

# EARLY EFFORTS
# AT LABOR ORGANIZATION

*"Why are you poor?*
*This is a question*
*you must ask yourself."*

It was inevitable that working people, confronted by common problems, would seek to unite their efforts for their own protection. But labor organization in the mid-nineteenth century was not new to America.

Even before the founding of the country itself, there were mutual aid or benevolent societies for masters, journeymen, and apprentices, founded usually to provide insurance against accidents and sickness. One early labor organization, the Society of Mechanics, announced that its purpose in 1801 was primarily for the "protecting and supporting [of] such . . . brothers who by sickness or accident may stand in need of assistance, and of relieving the widows and orphans of those who may die in indigent cir-

cumstances; and also providing the means of instruction for their children . . ." In their petition for organization the mechanics included the right to erect "a school house or place of instruction for the children of the members of the said corporation."

The original word for a *union* was "society" or "association," representing a local organization of journeymen within a single trade. Not until the 1830s did the term *trade union* come into use. Later came "national" and "international," meaning representing members in more than one country. And later still, in the 1860s, terms such as "trades assemblies" and "central labor unions."

Dr. Joseph A. Wytrwal believes that the first labor

59

*The New England Association of Working-men* adjourned their annual meeting on Saturday last, after a session of three days. Many important subjects were brought before the Association during its recent session, which were discussed in a manner that evinced an intelligence and ability highly creditable to the gentlemen who participated in the debate. Among others were the important subjects of Imprisonment for Debt, the Education of Mechanics' children, the treatment of children in Factories, the credit system, the organization of the Workingmen in every town and county in New England, a reform in the present Militia System, the effects of BANKING INSTITUTIONS, and other *monopolies*, the extension of the Right of Suffrage in those States where the people are now denied its essential privileges, the expediency of a LIEN LAW which shall protect the property of the actual laborers as well as their employers, the master workmen, &c. &c.

A report from the New England Association of Workingmen.

Draymen in New York participated in one of the earliest labor stoppages.

strike in America took place in Virginia Colony as early as 1619. At that time a group of Polish workers were employed in a glass factory and at other occupations. The workers refused to continue their labors "until accorded the same voting privileges as those enjoyed by the English settler; so they suspended operations in the glass factory, the tar distillery and the soap establishments."

Evidently their demand was achieved. Contributing to the effectiveness of this early job action was not only the shortage of labor but the fact that, as Captain John Smith tartly put it, they "were the only ones who knew what work was."

Thus, concludes Dr. Wytrwal, "Polish immigrants

to Jamestown were among the first champions of American civil liberties."

There is, however, a question as to this being a true strike, as strikes are generally understood. An authority on the subject, Richard B. Morris states that "a number of students of labor history called a printers' strike in Philadelphia in 1786, the first strike of wage earners in this country. . . . It is clear, however, that the New York printers' strike of 1778, the Salem, North Carolina, strike of the same year, the Philadelphia seamen's strike of 1779, and the shoemen's strike of 1785 take precedence." Philip S. Foner, labor historian, refers to a strike of chimney sweepers as early as 1763.

One of the more eloquent of early strikers were the Philadelphia carpenters who went on strike in 1791 for wages and hours—probably the first strike in American building trades. "'Tis one of the invaluable privileges of our nature," the carpenters declared, "that when we conceive ourselves aggrieved, there is an inherent right in us to complain . . ."

"Self preservation has induced us to enter into an indissoluble union with each other, in order to ward off the blows which are threatening us, by the insolent hand of pampered affluence. We mean hereafter, by a firm, independent mode of conduct, to protect each other."

Polish immigrants, recently arrived in Virginia in 1619, refused to work unless granted full equality.

. . . ght reasonable, if the qrter Co (as they doe not doubt) shall allow thereof.

Vpon some dispute of the Polonians resident in Virginia, it was now agreed (notw[th]standing any former order to the contrary) that they shalbe enfranchized, and made as free as any inhabitant there whatsoeuer: And because their skill in making pitch & tarr and sopeashees shall not dye w[th] them, it is agreed that some young men, shalbe put vnto them to learne their skill & knowledge therein for the benefitt of the Country hereafter. [33]

It was ordered vpon consideracon that many principall men depart the Court at or before . . .

*RECORDS OF THE VIRGINIA COMPANY*
*JULY 21, 1619*

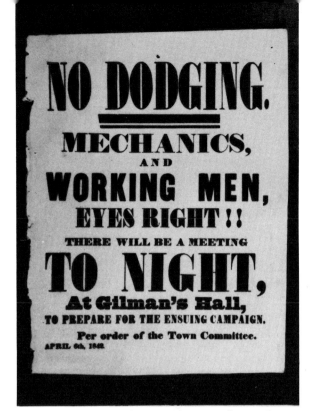

Efforts were made to bring working people together to discuss common problems.

The first permanent labor organization, it appears, was founded in 1792 when journeymen shoemakers of Philadelphia joined forces. Defending the right of labor to organize, one spokesman for working people said: "Men of property find no fault with combinations to extinguish fires, and protect their precious persons from danger. But if poor men ask *Justice,* it is a most *horrible combination.* The Declaration of Independence was the work of a combination . . ."

Early labor unions at first did not bargain collectively for their members. There were usually not even meetings between employees and employers. Union workers drew up their own proposed scale of prices and pledged to themselves "not to work for any employer who did not give the wages, nor beside any journeymen who did not get the wages."

The pioneer move in the direction of collective bargaining took place later when unionists sent a committee to present their price list to an employer. Unions, even in the earliest days, were fiercely antagonistic to fellow craftsmen who violated the agreed upon price lists. Such workers were called "rats," and various unions commonly exchanged "rat lists" so that those who had knowingly worked below the union standards could be exposed.

Inspired by the Declaration of Independence, working people repeatedly put forward their own grievances for the nation to see. "Let us awake," cried Seth Luther in an address to workingmen of New England in 1833 *on the state of education, and . . . the condition of the producing classes.*

Our Cause is the cause of truth—of justice and humanity. *It must prevail.* Let us be deter-

mined no longer to be deceived by the cry of those who produce *nothing* and who enjoy *all,* and who *insultingly* term us—the farmers, the mechanics, and laborers—the LOWER ORDERS—while the DECLARATION OF INDEPENDENCE—asserts that "ALL MEN ARE CREATED EQUAL."

It was not until 1827 that the first coordinated effort by a number of trades took place, the result of a strike of Philadelphia building-trades workers for a

Thomas W. Dorr led a popular rebellion in Rhode Island in 1841 to extend the franchise.

## BILL OF PRICES,

### AGREED ON BY THE

## BRICK-LAYERS OF CINCINNATI,

#### MARCH 1, 1814.

| | Dolls. Cts. |
|---|---|
| Brick laid (labor only) for brick & half walls, per thousand, | 3 00 |
| Do. for all exterior 9 inch walls, per thousand, | 3 50 |
| Do. for the 3d story of houses, per thousand, extra, | 1 00 |
| For finding lime, sand, loam and water, per thousand, | 1 00 |
| Outside arches, in front, common size, extra, | 1 50 |
| Back and side arches, outside, do. do. | 1 00 |
| For all inside arches, do. | 50 |
| Brick cornice, per foot, running, do. | 25 |
| Oiling and Penciling per yard, superficial, | 12 1-2 |
| For setting door sills, | 1 00 |
| For trimmers, common size, | 1 00 |
| For laying hearths, do. | 1 00 |
| Brick paved yard, superficial, | 18 3-4 |
| For filling-in with brick, do. | 18 3-4 |
| Ovens, 3 feet by 2 feet 6 inches, or under, each, | 3 00 |
| Do. larger, per foot in depth, | 2 00 |
| Chimneys to frame houses, per thousand, counted solid, | 4 00 |

Walls, laid Flemish bond, to be counted solid in all cases.
All other walls, doors and windows only, to be deducted.
The number of brick to be ascertained by counting them after they are laid.
Scaffold-boards and cords to be found by the employer.
We, the subscribers, have duly considered the above prices as low as can be worked for.

ISAAC STAGG,                    SAMUEL BROADWELL,
LOFTUS KEATING,              NATHAN DICKS,
JABEZ C. TUNIS,                  ELIAS FISHER,
JONATHAN PANCOAST,      JOSEPH PANCOAST,
HENRY CRAVEN,

CINCINNATI—PRINTED BY LOOKER AND WALLACE.

THE TRIAL

OF THE

*Journeymen*

BOOT & SHOEMAKERS

OF PHILADELPHIA,

ON AN INDICTMENT

*FOR A COMBINATION AND CONSPIRACY*

TO RAISE THEIR WAGES.

## THE TRIAL

OF THE

JOURNEYMEN BOOT & SHOEMAKERS

OF PHILADELPHIA.

### MAYOR'S COURT.

*PRESENT,*
LEVY, *Recorder ;* INNSKEEP, *Mayor ;*
AND
PETIT, DOUGLASS, and CARSWELL, *Aldermen.*
*The Commonwealth against George Pullis, et al.*
THE JURY.
1 Isa⁀ Watkins, Innkeeper,     7 John Livzey, Taylor,
2 Wn. Allibone, Merchant,      8 S. Kennedy, Innkeeper,
3 James Flamand, Grocer,       9 John Clark, Tavernkeeper,
4 John Kunius, Hatter,        10 Thos. M'Clean, Bottler,
5 W. Henderson, Tobacconist,  11 James Eccles, Grocer,
6 D. Lowndes, Watchmaker,     12 Neil Sweeney, Grocer
Jonathan Wharton, Shoemaker, was drawn as one of
the jurors, but objected to on account of his occupation.
*Counsel for the Prosecution.*
JARED INGERSOL AND JOSEPH HOPKINSON.
*Counsel for the Defendants.*
CAESAR A. RODNEY AND WALTER FRANKLIN.

MR. HOPKINSON.

May it please the court. The bill of indictment ex-
hibited before you, and which you, gentlemen of the
jury, are sworn to try, charges an offence not of every
day's production ; in order that you may fully comprehend the extent of the charges against the defendants ;
and although the bill is long, I will read the whole
of it to you, for your information. It is in these words :

▲

ten-hour workday. The protest helped bring about
the formation of the Mechanics Union of Trade Associations, the first effective city central organization
of wage earners in the world. This, in turn, set into
motion several other innovations including what is
believed to have been the first labor party in the
world—the Workingmen's party. This, in its turn, led
to the first industrial union in the country—the New
England Association of Farmers, Mechanics and other
Workmen.

From their beginning, unionists were subject to
bitter attacks and name-calling. "We are charged,"
said the Workingmen of Woodstock, Vermont, in
1830, "with being Deists and Infidels. On [the] one
hand it is alleged we are under Masonic influence—
on the other hand, it is said as confidently we are all
Anti-Masons. We are charged with being Agrarians
and Levellers, and that we intend to use the guillo-
tine."

In 1833, women shoemakers in Massachusetts
formed the Female Society of Lynn and Vicinity for
the Protection and Promotion of Female Industry.
Women leaders of the society insisted that "women
as well as men have certain inalienable rights." Among
these rights, the women stated, was obtaining fair
prices and "to form other salutary regulations . . .
relating to their common welfare."

By this time working people were realizing that
the factory system was here to stay. As industrial exploitation became more acute, organizations developed capable of uniting working people in support
of specific demands for the settlement of grievances.

The period from 1820 to 1840 has been described
as "the Awakening Period of the American Labor
Movement." And indeed it was. Labor organizations
prior to this period had been loosely organized, almost temporary in nature, often more like benevolent
societies than pragmatic organizations dedicated to
the economic advancement of their members.

As might be anticipated, there were those who
were not happy about the organizing activity of
working people. "We learned with surprise and re-
gret," a group of Boston employers stated in 1825
after six hundred of their journeymen had gone on
strike, that "a large number of those who are employed as journeymen in this city have entered into a
combination for the purpose of altering the time of
commencing and terminating their daily labor." The
employers expressed concern that their apprentices
might be seduced from "the course of industry and
economy . . . and would expose the journeymen
themselves to many temptations."

In 1806, when boot and shoemakers in Philadelphia organized
to better their conditions, they were arrested for "conspiracy."
"We find defendants guilty of a combination to raise wages" was
the verdict. "These masters . . . have their associations, their
meetings, and they pass their resolutions," the shoemakers said,
"but as they are rich and we are poor—they seem to think that
we are not protected by the Constitution in meeting peaceably
together and pursuing our own business . . ."

Hundreds of women shoemakers in Lynn, Massachusetts, demonstrated that "American ladies will not be slaves" in a Lynn, Massachusetts, "turnout," as strikes were called.

In his famous Plymouth oration, Daniel Webster upheld the dominance of property.

There were schools for the wealthy . . .

but there were few free public schools.

Commenting upon labor's early demands for shorter working hours, a Boston newspaper warned in 1832 that "to be idle several of the most useful hours of the morning and evening would surely lead to intemperance and ruin."

The rise of the business corporation brought a new relationship between employer and employee. People who lent money to corporations were frequently far removed, often uninterested in production except in the revenue returned. Such merchant capitalists frequently gained control of sources of raw materials and had little interest other than extracting profit from the processing of such materials. "The stockholders wanted large dividends, and they were having them," wrote Benjamin Butler. "The mills were exceedingly profitable."

Many children worked instead of attending school.

Cornelius Vanderbilt led the movement for combining railroads.

Daniel Drew, "the great bear," dominated stock speculation for almost a generation.

John Jacob Astor, fur merchant and shipowner.

While working people in the rapidly expanding cities faced insecurity and threats of poverty, they were not unaware of the developing wealth within their midst. "The rich are growing richer and the poor poorer, and Mammon is usurping sovereignty in all places," declared Baltimore mechanics in 1833. They went on to say that "a monied aristocracy hanging over us like a mighty avalanche, threatening annihilation to every man who dares to question their right to enslave and oppress the poor and the unfortunate." A newspaper of the era asked working people: "Why are you poor? This is a question you must ask yourself." While, in 1836, the National Typographical Society declared that there exists "perpetual antagonism between labor and capital."

The division was thus widening between the small employer and the "large, speculative capitalist builder," as one historian called him. "We would not be too severe on our employers," said the building mechanics of Boston in 1834, "they are the slaves to the capitalists as we are to them."

From almost the start of trade unions in America, one of the first demands was for free public education. "The most important and most frequently repeated demand of the working men," states historian John R. Commons, " . . . [was] for the general system of education. . . . Wherever the workingmen organized, public education was their first and foremost demand." In 1829, public education took its place distinctly and definitely at the head of the list of measures urged by the Workingmen's party, one of many such organizations that came into existence in the late 1820s and early 1830s.

The Mechanics and Workingmen of Philadelphia stated they "not only [were] interested in obtaining

Stephen Girard, shipper and banker.

free public education, but they had ideas of their own as to the type of schools that were needed . . ."

In demanding schools in New York, the *Working Man's Advocate* in 1830 said that the schools need be "not the most extravagantly expensive, not the most fashionable—but the best that the nation, in its wisdom, may be able to devise."

Those in debt, even for small amounts, were often imprisoned as criminals.

Candidates for the New York State legislature, nominated by the Workingmen's party in 1829, were pledged to favor "a general system of . . . education." "All history," the party stated a year later, "corroborates the melancholy fact that . . . as the mass of the people becomes ignorant, misrule and anarchy ensue . . ."

New England working people went on record in 1833 in favor of "manual labour schools, free for all, at the expense of each state."

But there was controversy. As the New England Workingmen's Association pointed out: "We have a powerful opposition to meet . . . talents and wealth, prejudice and ancient usage, are against us . . ."

Of course, there were other urgent issues in addition to public education raised by working people. The demand for a ten-hour day was one of them. Other matters of import included abolition of imprisonment for debt, wage increases, the end of child labor, reduction of qualifications for voting, direct election of public officials, free homesteads in the West, lowering of prices, factory legislation, and controlling competition from prison labor and women.

As realization of their demands was slow in coming, workers in increasing numbers entered unions. The issues raised were on their minds. They responded by joining together, and, where necessary, withholding their labor.

As a result of labor's activity, numerous gains were recorded. Strikes for higher wages and reduced hours were won. New York State abolished imprisonment for debt in the 1830s as did other states subsequently. Pennsylvania started a system of public education in 1834. In 1843, Massachusetts made it illegal to employ children under twelve for more than ten hours a day.

One of the earliest national labor organizations, the National Trades Union, came into existence in 1834 to "advance the moral and intellectual condition and pecuniary interests of the labouring classes . . ." The organization urged the formation of trade unions and took strong positions for education and improvement in hours, wages, and organization, and against child labor and factory exploitation. In 1837, a year of depression, the National Trades Union—which never became more than an agitational organization—passed from existence.

In 1840, in response to organized demands, President Martin Van Buren limited the workday to ten hours in all government employment.

But even while the ten-hour day was being sought, some workers were singing:

> *"We want to feel the sunshine*
> *And we want to smell the flowers;*
> *We are sure that God has willed it*
> *And we mean to have eight hours."*

By the time of Andrew Jackson, the young labor movement was on the move, especially in political activities. Gradually, some of the ideals of rule by the people were put into practice. Ownership of property became less influential. Increasingly, men were able to obtain voting rights based upon their manhood rather than their wealth.

This concept—that every man had a stake in the national government and its proper running—opened the way for support of a different kind of political officeholder. Governors were elected instead of being chosen by legislators. An increasing number of offices were made elective rather than appointive. Even popular election of judges became a reality in a number of states.

By the era of President Jackson, almost all states were committed to the principle of submitting their constitutions to the people for ratification. Such a procedure had been followed, during earlier days, by only a few. And with it all came a feeling that the people's judgment could be trusted more· than any other single grouping. There was a new wave of confidence in the wisdom of the ordinary man.

Still economic efforts to better conditions of working people were, at that time, opposed as "conspiracies" by the courts. Perhaps this is one reason why

President Martin Van Buren in 1836, responding to popular demand, issued an order establishing the ten-hour day on public works.

Richard M. Johnson, Van Buren's vice-president, was an opponent of imprisonment for debt, as well as a champion of religious liberty. Labor supported him for President.

Ely Moore, a New York union printer, was elected Labor's first congressman (1835–1839).

Josiah Warren, a militant labor spokesman in Philadelphia.

Mathew Carey was the first American to investigate women's work and champion working women (Philadelphia, 1830s).

Peter Force, president of the New York Typographical Society (1815), was elected mayor of Washington, D.C. (1836).

unions turned increasingly to independent political activity. With the gradual placing of voting rights in the hands of working people rather than just of those owning property, the ability of the workingman to participate in the activities of his government increased. The growth of cities brought about a closer relationship between working people that also made political activity possible and practical.

Such activity was not new. Probably the first political activity on the part of labor in the history of America dated back to the 1730s when the Popular party was developed in New York City and a number of candidates elected to the common council. The first real labor party in the history of America was formed in Philadelphia in 1828, comprising numerous independent working parties. In 1832, the reelection of Andrew Jackson was the result of a coalition between organized labor and small farmers and businessmen. In New York an Equal Rights party helped elect four candidates to Congress and a number of state officials.

In 1848, the "Friends of the Ten Hour System" organized the Workingmen's Association of Trenton. And six years later the Republican party emerged as a result of the needs of the day behind the slogan "Free soil, free labor."

New York workers bitterly fought the old political parties as being insensitive to their needs. In 1840, there developed what was called the Loco-Foco party, which received its name when lights were turned out at a workers' meeting and it was necessary to light friction matches, called loco-focos, in order to conduct the business. This organization, campaigning vigorously for a ten-hour day, included a New York City faction of the Democratic party, largely composed of working people.

## AN ADDRESS TO THE WORKING MEN OF NEW ENGLAND,

ON THE

### STATE OF EDUCATION,

AND

ON THE CONDITION OF THE PRODUCING CLASSES

IN

### EUROPE AND AMERICA.

WITH PARTICULAR REFERENCE TO THE EFFECT OF MANUFACTURING (AS NOW CONDUCTED) ON THE HEALTH AND HAPPINESS OF THE POOR,

AND

ON THE SAFETY OF OUR REPUBLIC.

DELIVERED

IN BOSTON, CHARLESTOWN, CAMBRIDGEPORT, WALTHAM, DORCHESTER, MASS., PORTLAND, SACO, ME., AND DOVER, N. H.

### BY SETH LUTHER.

"Who has not been delighted with the clock-work movements of a large cotton manufactory." *Hon. H. Clay, Speech in Senate.*
"They (Cotton Mills) are the principalities of the destitute, the palaces of the poor." *Hon. John Q. Adams, Report on Manufactures.*
"The poor must work or starve, the rich will take care of themselves." *Hon. John Whipple, Answer to Interrogatories from Sec'ry of Treasury.*
"Witness the SPLENDID EXAMPLE of England." *Hon. A. H. Everett, Report on Manufactures for N. Y. Central Committee.*

"'Tis yours to judge how wide the limits stand Between a splendid and a happy land."—*Goldsmith.*

SECOND EDITION.
CORRECTED BY THE AUTHOR.

NEW YORK.
PUBLISHED AT THE OFFICE OF THE WORKING MAN'S ADVOCATE,
BY GEORGE H. EVANS.
1833.

Ellis Lewis, a union printer, became Chief Justice of the Pennsylvania Supreme Court.

## GRAND RALLY!
### WORKING MEN ATTENTION!

There will be a meeting of the Working Men's Reform Political Party held at

## MUSICAL HALL,
### SUFFIELD,

On Saturday Evening, August 22d, 1857,

At 7 1-2 o'clock, P. M. All Working Men in favor of this Party are requested to attend.

N. B.—The Platform of the party will be presented at this Meeting.

Per Order of Committee.

Suffield, August 17, 1857.

An early political poster.

When the Workingmen's party was founded in New York, its organ, the *Working Man's Advocate*, issued stirring calls for action: "Your fathers of the Revolution secured for you a form of government which guarantees to you, almost universally, the elective franchise. . . . Awake, then, from your slumbers; and insult not the memories of the heroes of '76 . . ."

Although working people tried through their organizations—both political and economic—to secure a measure of security for themselves and their families, they were constantly frustrated in this effort. Somehow the promise of America, which seemed to be rewarding the wealthy with increased returns, eluded the propertyless man who worked with his hands. When it appeared that segments of the working population had gained some amelioration of their conditions, an economic panic or depression would deprive them of their jobs and reduce their earning power to nothing.

Writers, poets, editors, people of goodwill in general were deeply concerned by this social condition. As John Greenleaf Whittier, the poet, complained:

The merchants may agree upon their prices; the lawyers upon their fees; the physicians upon their charges; the manufacturers upon the wages given to their operatives; but the *laborer* shall not consult his interest and fix the price of his toil and skill. If this be the *law*, it is unjust, oppressive and wicked.

"Poverty in the midst of plenty," as it was put, appeared not only inhumane to the reformers but also unnecessary. There was an effort made to reform society, either partially or fundamentally, to eliminate the social ills seen on all sides.

As the depression of the 1840s devastated the country and created armies of unemployed, reformers increasingly sought solutions to this economic chaos. Community ownership of land and tools of production became a subject of common discussion. Brook Farm in Massachusetts was one of several experimental cooperative communities. Started in 1841, Brook Farm was supported by a number of prominent literary people including Nathaniel Hawthorne. Another such effort was New Harmony, a small, experimental community in Indiana that was created through the efforts of Robert Owen, the British reformer. Such was the attention paid to this utopian movement that Owen twice discussed its potential before the United States Congress.

The dream of the utopian was expressed by Louisa May Alcott in 1844.

Each member is to perform the work for which experience, strength, and taste best fit him. Thus drudgery and disorder will be avoided and harmony prevail. We shall rise at dawn, begin the day by bathing, followed by music, and then a chaste repast of fruit and bread. Each one finds congenial occupation till the meridian meal, when some deep-searching conversation gives rest to the body and development to the mind. Healthful labor again engages us till the last meal, when we assemble in social communion, prolonged till sunset, when we retire to sweet repose, ready for the next day's activity.

Walt Whitman, editor and poet.

John Greenleaf Whittier, poet.

Charles Fourier, early French utopian socialist.

Reformers of the era.

William Cullen Bryant, editor and poet.

Samuel Leggett, editor.

Robert Dale Owen, British utopian reformer.

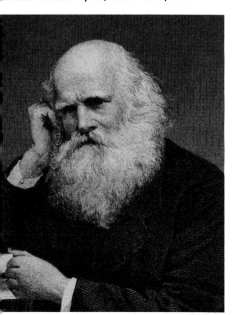

Albert Brisbane, utopian socialist.

Elihu Burritt, "the learned blacksmith."

Frances Wright, advocate of women's rights.

Reformers of the era.

Utopians had strong beliefs about social issues and injustices of the day.

"We declare," stated the Brook Farm Association, "that the imperative duty of this time and this country . . . lies in the reorganization of society . . ." Ralph Waldo Emerson wrote: "Not a reading man but has the draft of a new community in his waistcoat pocket."

Another voice of the era was that of George Bancroft, the historian, who stated: "The feud between the capitalists and the laborer, the House of Have and the House of Want, is as old as social union, and can never be entirely quieted."

The new thinking found its expression even in the courts. For years the United States Supreme Court,

under Chief Justice John Marshall, had placed emphasis on the rights of property. However, in 1837, the Charles River Bridge Company case came before the court involving the issue of property as opposed to community rights. Perhaps it was the democratic upsurge then going on. But this case provided the court with an opportunity to express a more liberal doctrine. Presided over by Chief Justice Roger B. Taney, a Jacksonian appointee, the court declared: "While the rights of property are sacredly guarded, we must not forget that the community also have rights . . ."

A dozen or more court convictions for "conspiracy" occurred before *Commonwealth v. Hunt* in 1842, a case involving the indictment of seven shoemakers that came before the Massachusetts Supreme Court.

The utopian community founded by Robert Owen, Sr., at New Harmony, Indiana.

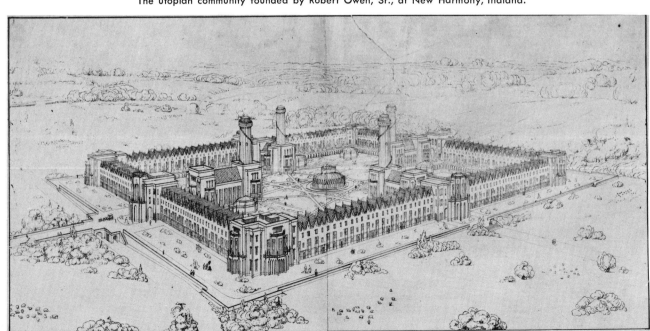

The claim was that they did "unlawfully, perniciously and deceitfully . . . unite themselves into an unlawful club, society and combination . . ."

In his finding, Chief Justice Lemuel Shaw of the Commonwealth of Massachusetts dismissed the indictment of conspiracy against the shoemakers stating, "Such an association might be used to afford each other assistance in times of poverty, sickness and distress. . . . We cannot perceive, that it is criminal for men to agree together to exercise their own acknowledged rights, in such a manner as best to subserve their own interests."

Hence the court found that "such agreement could not be pronounced a criminal conspiracy. We think, therefore," concluded Justice Shaw, "that the associations may be entered into, the object of which is to adopt measures that may have a tendency to impoverish another, that is, to diminish his gains and profits, and yet so far from being criminal or unlawful, the object may be highly meritorious and public spirited. The legality of such an association will, therefore, depend upon the means to be used for this accomplishment . . ."

By this finding, Justice Shaw thus established the right of working people to join organizations for their mutual protection and the "conspiracy" definition of labor organization was overruled.

Among the most effective reformers was Horace Greeley, the erratic but effective editor of the New York *Tribune*, who embraced almost every doctrine of social change as fast as it appeared.

"The earth, the air, the waters, the sunshine, with

Justice Roger B. Taney and Justice Lemuel Shaw issued judgments upholding the rights of the people.

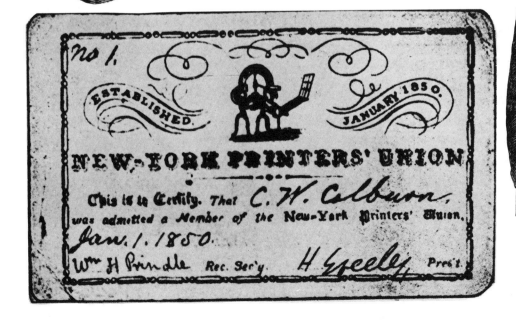

Horace Greeley, editor of the New York *Tribune* and first president of Typographical Union, No. 6, and his union's card.

their natural products, were divinely intended . . . for the enjoyment of the whole human family," stated Greeley. "But as society is now organized, this is not, and cannot be done . . ."

"The right of owning land is one thing," Greeley said. "The right to own thousands and even millions of acres of land is another. I condemn the system of land monopoly."

Greeley's voice, loud and shrill, was one of many being raised in the cause of "elevating the masses." As Emerson said: "Greeley does the thinking for the whole west." And indeed, the words of Bayard Taylor, the writer, were accurate when he said: "The *Tribune* comes next to the Bible all through the west."

Perhaps of all Greeley's many directives to his readers, the one most remembered was "Young man, go west and grow up with the nation."

The fact that there were available lands aplenty to the west theoretically permitted a method of escape for the industrial workers. A certain number of workingmen and women did go west to flee from industrial oppression. The land reform movement was led by the onetime editor of the *Working Man's Advocate*, George Henry Evans. A labor spokesman during the Jacksonian era, Evans crusaded strongly for free public land. "If a man has a right on the earth," Evans stated, "he has a right to land enough to raise a habitation."

Land reform, Evans believed, would restore independence to needy workers who were beaten down by the effects of the industrial revolution. The frontier beckoned all those in need of salvation.

The slogan, "Vote yourself a farm," was launched in 1845 in New York City. Handbills were distributed in which Evans stated: "Are you tired of slavery, of

The *Working Man's Advocate*, edited by the Evans brothers, was probably the first labor publication printed in the New World.

## Working Man's Advocate.

### NEW YORK:
### SATURDAY, OCTOBER 31, 1829.

### WORKING MEN'S TICKET.
#### ASSEMBLY.

ALEXANDER MING, senior, Printer,
FREDERICK FRIEND, Brass Founder,
THOMAS SKIDMORE, Machinist.
CORNELIUS C. BLATCHLEY, Physician.
ROBERT M. KERRISON, Whitesmith.
ALDEN POTTER, Machinist.
AMOS WILLIAMSON, Carpenter.
EBENEZER WHITING, Cooper.
SIMON CLANNON, Painter.
EBENEZER FORD, Carpenter.
[ ]N MOTT, Grocer.

#### SENATE.
[ ]. of Suffolk.

## THE TRIBUNE.
### MONDAY MORNING, MARCH 20, 1843.

#### The Wages of Labor.

We have received (and mislaid, or we should publish,) an appeal from one who maintains that the present prices of Labor are higher than employers can possibly afford, in the existing state of things, and entreating us to use our influence with the employed to persuade them to submit to a general reduction of wages. Having taken some little time to consider the matter, we shall say what we think of it:

1. The average of Wages is *already* reduced quite to the point from which it advanced in 1835-6. In Agriculture, Domestic Service, and most other capacities, the Wages now paid are, we think, quite as low as in 1832, and very much lower than in 1836.

2. There remain to be considered the rates of Wages in those vocations where an advance was acceded to in 1836, and has not since been abandoned. Of course, in all cases where the previous price was fair and adequate, this advance ought long since to have been abandoned, or ought now to be—the *reason* for it existing no longer.

But we think there are cases in which the previous rate was less than it ought to have been, and to which the reason for reduction does not fairly apply. These may be very few and exceptional, yet they ought to be considered. We believe, for instance, that the rates of journeymen's wages in our own trade, Printing, were less than they should have been prior to 1836. These rates were, and still are very clumsily constructed, enabling some workmen to earn $12 per week by less labor than others were re[ ]

[ ]dy together, we cannot hold back for [ ] he must work or starve.

It seems plain to us that the employer has no moral right to break over established rates of compensation, and say, ' I will pay you a reduced price; work for it or quit my employ!' Neither have the journeymen alone a right to raise the rates of their own compensation, and say to employers, ' We have raised our wages so much; pay it, or we will declare you infamous, and prevent any honorable man from working for you, even though he deem your price just and reasonable.' Both these are wrong. But the employers and journeymen in each trade ought severally to hold meetings and appoint delegates to a Joint Committee, who should be empowered to examine the whole ground, and fix the general rate of wages and the particular details as should to them appear just and proper, calling in an impartial umpire in case of irreconcilable variance; and the prices so fixed should be respected by every honorable employer and journeyman until, on due notice given, another general meeting of each class should appoint another Joint Committee to revise them again. We think each trade should in this manner revise its pri[ ] Spring, and again whenever an[ ]

A Greeley editorial on labor.

Covered wagons heading west.

drudging for others—of poverty and its attendant miseries? Then, vote yourself a farm."

What has been called "rounding out the continent" took place with breathless speed. Although plenty of workers found it impossible to escape from industrial exploitation by moving west, there were others—with property to sell that could finance their trip—who decided to become homesteaders or prospectors.

This movement west was pictured by a Kentuckian chronicler as

thousands of men, women and children . . . in successive caravans, forming continuous streams of human beings, horses, cattle, and other domestic animals, all moving onward along a lonely and houseless path to a wild and cheerless land . . . driving stock and leading pack horses, and the women, some walking with pails on their heads, others riding with children in their laps, and other children swung in baskets on horses, fastened to the tails of others going before.

A major task of the frontiersman was to clear the new land. The ax played a vital role in the development of the nation. It was one of the most necessary tools. The American ax has a famed coexistence with that of the American woodsman.

"While the American pioneer, axe in hand, boldly buries himself in the forest to clear and subdue it,"

Clearing the forest.

Fur Traders Descending the Missouri by George Caleb Bingham.

recorded one early historian, "the European keeps rather to the plains, as more easily managed. The experience in the use of the axe, and the various uses to which it is applied, have combined to produce great varieties, all of which have undergone continual improvement. Formerly, the operator depended upon the rude forges and limited skills of blacksmiths to supply axes. With the improvements that suggested themselves, special factories sprung up, and the largest factory of its kind in the world is in New England. There, 1200 tons of iron, and 200 tons of cast steel, are by machinery wrought annually into tools."

Americans became experts at the use of the ax. One English visitor remarked: "At cutting down trees or cutting them up, the Americans will do ten times as much in a day as any other man I ever saw. Let one of these men on upon a wood of timber trees, and his slaughter will astonish you."

Before the coming of the railroads, American pioneers had been basically a river people. Highways were waterways, and the traveler had to cope with river transportation. "It is estimated," one immigrant wrote in 1818, "that there are now in this village and in its vicinity, 300 families, besides single travellers, amounting in all to 1500 souls, waiting for a rise of the water to embark for the promised land."

Flatboats were often the means for travel. "I could not conceive what such large, square boxes could be, which seemed abandoned to the current," a French traveler described a trip down the Mississippi, "presenting alternately their ends, their sides, and even their angles. As they advanced, I heard a confused noise, without distinguishing anything on account of the height of the sides.

"On ascending the banks of the river, I perceived in these boats several families, bringing with them their horses, cows, fowl, carts, plows, harness, beds, instruments of husbandry; in short, all the furniture requisite for housekeeping, agriculture, and the management of a farm."

Handling a flatboat required skill and experience. Gradually, a professional river boatsman developed, of whom Mark Twain wrote:

Whoo-oop! I'm the old original iron jawed, brass mounted, copper bellied corpse maker from the wilds of Arkansas! Look at me! I'm the man they call Sudden Death and General Desolation! Sired by a hurricane, dam'd by an earthquake, half-brother to the cholera, nearly related to the smallpox on the mother's side! Look at me! I take nineteen alligators and a bar'l of whiskey for breakfast when I'm in robust health, and a bushel of rattlesnakes and a dead body when I'm ailing. I split the everlasting rocks with my glance, and I squench the thunder when I speak! Whoo-oop! Stand back and give me room according to my strength! Blood's my natural drink, and the wails of the dying is music to my ear. Cast your eye on me, gentlemen! and lay low and hold your breath, for I'm 'bout to turn myself loose! . . . Whoo-oop! I'm the bloodiest son of a wildcat that lives.

River transportation in the 1840s.

Flatboats were a frequent means of travel.

Many believed free land on the frontier was the answer to the workingman's problems.

Most women workers of the era were employed in the garment-making trades. They sewed children's clothes, shirts, pantaloons, and other ready-made clothes that were in demand. Many female workers hired out as seamstresses and tailoresses. Women not only were confronted with such duties as well as domestic chores, but there were other problems. Journeymen sometimes revealed prevailing discrimination against women, expressing their opposition to working for those who employed women. Such bias was fostered by the practice of paying women lower wages than men.

This practice of paying women less than men was common. For example, females working in their homes for a contractor earned on an average only $1.25 a week, while cotton factory workers in 1836 earned approximately twice that amount.

Efforts were made by women workers to improve their conditions. In the spring of 1836, the Female Improvement Society of the City and County of Philadelphia was organized. Next to the seamstresses, the women who were most interested in organizing were shoe binders. Often such women worked in their own homes, and next to seamstresses they were the poorest paid.

An early indication of the desire of women to organize took place in New York in 1831 when women tailoresses went on strike for higher wages. About one hundred women, members of the New York Association of Tailoresses, resolved that "the prices of Tailoresses ought to be advanced at least one-third, and some cases doubled." These militant women also resolved, whether they would win their fight or not, "We will not relax in our efforts to support and increase this Society. . . . This Society will prevent in future the like depression we now labour under."

Despite the efforts of women to achieve equality, antifemale propaganda handicapped their efforts. In September 1852, the influential editor of the New York *Herald*, James Gordon Bennett, wrote: "By her nature, her sex—[the woman] just as the Negro is and always will be to the end of time, inferior . . . and, therefore, doomed to subjection . . ."

Among the voices raised in the nation against such views was that, of course, of Horace Greeley. Once in disgust with Congress, Greeley wrote to a friend: "I wish the present Congress would go home and the members' wives left to legislate in their stead."

With the reform movement sweeping the nation, it was inevitable that women would increase their activities for redress of long-held grievances. In 1847, at Seneca Falls in New York, the first conference dedicated to the fight for women's rights took place to discuss "the social, civil and religious rights of women."

Although the conference was not dedicated specifically to assisting working women, nevertheless, the start of this civil-rights movement could not be separated from the struggle of working women. In addressing the meeting, Elizabeth Cady Stanton, who later was to participate actively in the labor movement, stated that the "time had come for the question of women's wrongs to be laid before the public. . . . Woman herself must do this work; for women alone can understand the height, the depth, the length and the breadth of her degradation." At the conclusion of the meeting, sixty-eight women and thirty-two men signed their names to a declaration of principles that officially gave birth to the movement for women's rights in America.

Mrs. Amelia Bloomer and Elizabeth Cady Stanton in the "reform dress" that was demonstrated in the early 1850s. "All the journals from Maine to Texas," said Mrs. Stanton, "seemed to strive with each other to see which would make our movement appear most ridiculous."

## RESOLUTIONS PASSED AT THE WOMAN'S RIGHTS CONVENTION HELD IN THIS VILLAGE ON THE 19TH AND 20TH INST.

Whereas, the great precept of nature is conceded to be "that man shall pursue his own true and substantial happiness;" Blackstone, in his commentaries, remarks, that this law of Nature being coeval with mankind, and dictated by God himself is, of course, superior in obligation to any other. It is binding over all the globe, in all countries, and at all times: no human laws are of any validity if contrary to this, and such of them as are valid, derive all their force, and all their validity, and all their authority, mediately and immediately from this original.

Therefore, *Resolved*, That such laws as conflict, in any way, with the true and substantial happiness of women, are contrary to the great precept of Nature, and of no validity, for this "is superior in obligation to any other."

*Resolved*, That all laws which prevent woman from occupying such a station in society as her conscience shall dictate, or which place her in a position inferior to that of man, are contrary to the great precept of Nature and therefore of no force or authority.

*Resolved*, That woman is man's equal, was intended to be so by her Creator, and the highest good of the race demands that she should be recognized as such.

*Resolved*, That the women of this country ought to be enlightened with regard to the laws under which they live, that they may no longer publish their degradation by declaring themselves satisfied with their present position, nor their ignorance by asserting they have all the rights they want.

*Resolved*, That inasmuch as man, while claiming for himself intellectual superiority, does accord to woman, moral superiority, it is pre-eminently his duty to encourage her to speak and teach as she has opportunity in all religious assemblies.

*Resolved*, That the same amount of virtue, delicacy, and refinement of behavior, that is required of woman in the social state, should be required of man, and the same transgressions should be visited with equal severity on both man and woman.

*Resolved*, That the objection of indelicacy and impropriety which is so often brought against woman when she addresses a public audience, comes with very ill grace from those who encourage by their attendance, her appearance on the stage in the concert, or in the

Statement from the first convention on women's rights, at Seneca Falls, New York.

# FIVE

# 1820-1865

# WORKING PEOPLE
# IN THE CIVIL WAR ERA

*"Whatever the pressure,*
*there is a point*
*where the working man may stop."*

The black slave, deprived of his cultural heritage, was taught one function thoroughly. That was how to pick cotton. In reporting in 1853, a onetime slave described his former labors:

About the first of July, when it is a foot high or thereabouts, it is hoed the fourth and last time. Now the whole space between the rows is ploughed, leaving a deep water furrow in the center. During all these hoeings the overseer or driver follows the slaves on horseback with a whip. . . . The fastest hoer takes the lead row. He is usually about a rod in advance of his companions. If one of them passes him, he is whipped. If one falls behind or is a moment idle, he is whipped. In fact, the lash is flying from morning until night, the whole day long. The hoeing season thus continues from April until July, a field having no sooner been finished once, than it is commenced again . . .

When a new hand, one unaccustomed to the business, is sent for the first time into the field, he is whipped up smartly and made for that day to pick as fast as he can possibly. At night it is weighed, so that his capability in cotton picking is known. He must bring in the same weight each night following. If it falls short, it is considered evidence that he has been laggard, and a greater or less number of lashes is the penalty . . .

The hands are required to be in the cotton field as soon as it is light in the morning, and, with the exception of ten or fifteen minutes, which is given them at noon to swallow their allowance of cold bacon, they are not permitted to be a moment idle until it is too dark to see and when the moon is full they often times labor till the middle of the night. They do not dare to stop even at dinner time, nor return to the quarters, however late it be, until the order to halt is given by the driver.

With passing years, the southern economy became increasingly dependent on the slave as a work force, not only as an unskilled field hand but for other labor as well. Black hands constructed the houses, streets, public buildings, docks, fences—much of what made up the southern town and city. Many blacks developed into skilled artisans and were often hired out profitably to others by their masters. Grandiose mansions, many still standing in New Orleans, Natchez, Vicksburg, and other centers, were financially practical because of the availability of unpaid labor. So were the various mills, factories, and railroads constructed. Slaves worked in early coal and gold mines; and the first fireman on the nation's first locomotive (1830), it is reported, was a black man.

"The whole machinery of slavery was so constructed as to cause labour, as a rule, to be looked upon as a badge of degradation, or inferiority," wrote Booker T. Washington, the famous black educator who was himself once a slave.

There were, of course, apologists for the slave system. One was quick to point out that nothing was wasted by slavery.

In other countries, a large part of the wages of labor is expended in strong drink; but the most stringent laws are everywhere passed against selling spirits to slaves. . . . Much time is lost in free countries in holidays and shows; in idleness and neglect of work; in seeking employment; in change from one place to another; but all this is saved in the south, for there are no idle hands about the plantation, and, excepting the week before Christmas and New Year's Day, when there is a general holiday, there is no time lost, except from sickness, in any part of the year.

Handbill (*reduced size*) of sale of livestock and other property

Branding a black woman slave.

Opponents of slavery were hooted and jeered. For years the subject was forbidden on the floor of Congress.

How free speech was denied on the floor of Congress.

Another apologist wrote:

The high wages of the north cannot be reduced by the labor of the slave. Instead of reduction, it causes an increase. His cheap toil is to their advantage. His labors, under the hot tropical sun, are for the benefit of every mechanic, and artisan, and workman, that now fears the competition of the northern free black. *As a slave, he benefits them, as a freeman he would be in their way.*

Slavery was supported as "a perfect labor system." Pro-slavery forces believed that the "laboring class was unfitted for self-government." One South Carolina newspaper said that "master and slave is a relation as necessary as that of parent and child, and the northern states will yet have to introduce it."

Contrary to some interpretations, slaves did not accept their serfdom willingly. Hundreds of revolts took place throughout the South. One of the few that was given publicity was a brief uprising in 1831 led by the clergyman Nat Turner, in which at least seventy-five people were killed. There were other forms of protest including strikes, mass suicides, mutilations, and runaways.

For the most part, labor before the Civil War was still too disorganized—economically and politically—to take part as an organized power in the antislavery movement. Besides, the slave power exerted a powerful, albeit often hidden, influence on much northern thought. "Slavery sat in the White House and made laws in the Capital," said the journalist George William Curtis.

Courts of justice were its ministers and legislatures were its lackeys. It silenced the preacher in the pulpit; it muzzled the editor at his desk and the professor in his lecture room. It set the price upon the heads of peaceful citizens; it robbed the mails and denounced the vital principles of the Declaration of Independence as treason . . .

The workingmen in the North, commented Russell B. Nye, perceived intuitively that their own liberties were at stake in the struggle.

Many working people opposed slavery in any form. Lowell workers, for example, represented by the Labor Reform League, were on record stating: "American slavery must be uprooted before the elevation sought by the laboring classes can be effected."

A petition to Congress for the abolition of slavery in the District of Columbia was circulated nearly every year among the mill girls of Lowell, and received thousands of signatures. A shoe worker in Lynn, Massachusetts, pointed out that slaves "can't vote, nor complain, and we can."

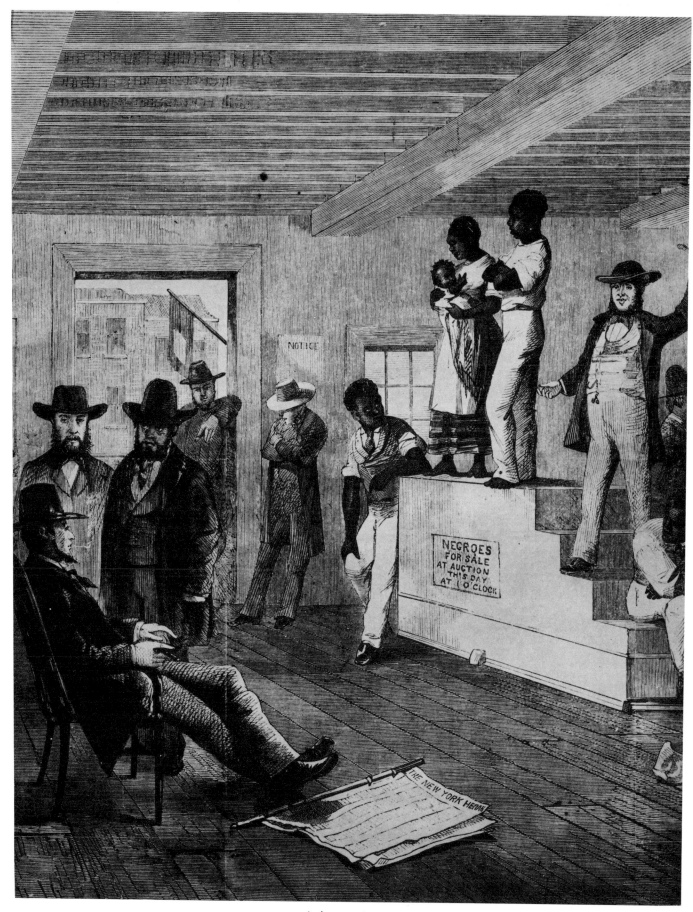

A slave auction.

THE FIRST COTTON-GIN.—Drawn by William L. Sheppard.

An antislavery poster.

But many white workers remained confused on the slavery issue. For one reason, there were abolition leaders who appeared unaware or uncaring of the semislave conditions under which much of northern labor toiled in the mills and mines.

When textile workers of Middlesex, Massachusetts, complained, they were often discharged. Some seventy girls left their jobs in protest against having to tend four looms instead of three. They were unable to find work elsewhere, being told that employers "wanted none of the turnouts from Middlesex." In Pennsylvania mining fields, a report of conditions described how "the worker is lucky if he escapes death on the job, since coal miners have a fatal accident rate much higher than that faced by men in any other occupation." The new railroads, just beginning to steam their way through frontier country, accumulated a horrifying record of deaths and injuries to workers, causing one writer to refer to the situation as "slaughter on rails."

Northern workers dreamed of going west to make their fortunes.

Two fighters against slavery: William Lloyd Garrison and Wendell Phillips. Phillips was to become an advocate of labor organization.

# CAUTION!!
## COLORED PEOPLE
### OF BOSTON, ONE & ALL,

You are hereby respectfully CAUTIONED and advised, to avoid conversing with the

## Watchmen and Police Officers
## of Boston,

For since the recent ORDER OF THE MAYOR & ALDERMEN, they are empowered to act as

# KIDNAPPERS
### AND
# Slave Catchers,

And they have already been actually employed in KIDNAPPING, CATCHING, AND KEEPING SLAVES. Therefore, if you value your LIBERTY, and the *Welfare of the Fugitives* among you, *Shun them* in every possible manner, as so many *HOUNDS* on the track of the most unfortunate of your race.

## Keep a Sharp Look Out for KIDNAPPERS, and have TOP EYE open.

*APRIL 24, 1851.*

OPERATIONS OF THE FUGITIVE-SLAVE LAW.

Nor were the abolitionists sensitive to the human havoc caused among the poor by reoccurring economic depressions. William Lloyd Garrison, perhaps the outstanding abolitionist of his day, wrote in the *Liberator* that "an attempt has been made . . . to inflame the minds of our working classes against the more opulent. . . . It is a miserable characteristic of human nature to look with an envious eye upon those who are more fortunate . . ."

While there were organizations of working people that spoke out against slavery, many unions did not. In the summer of 1859, iron molders launched a national strike. Examining the statements of the strike leadership, W. E. B. Du Bois observed: "There was not a word in this address about slavery and one would not dream that the United States was on the verge of the greatest labor revolution it had seen."

There was, too, widespread apprehension that emancipated slaves would compete for northern jobs. This fear—amounting to terror when jobs were scarce—was shrewdly stimulated by propaganda from those who profited from the slave system. The way in which racial prejudice acted to the detriment of trade unions was demonstrated in 1855 when New York longshoremen struck against a wage reduction. Black workers were hired and placed in their positions. "Of course, colored men can feel under no obligation," *Frederick Douglass's Paper* commented, "to hold out in a 'strike' with the whites, as the latter have never recognized them."

The symbolic workingman.

DIGNITY · OF · · LABOR·

The runaways

Discrimination in some unions reflected the shortcomings of the era. The bricklayers' union in Washington, D.C., forbade their members to work with black men. When four white union men were discovered working with blacks on government work, the union voted to expel them. A black printer, Louis H. Douglass, the son of Frederick Douglass, in 1869 was refused admission to the local union in Washington, D.C., in spite of the fact that the Constitution made no discrimination among members. An appeal was taken to the convention of the National Typographical Union, but was unsuccessful.

In the South, free workers had to produce as much as slaves to hold their own. This is a reason why national movements, such as that for the ten-hour day, never gained widespread support in the South. There were other problems. When Louisville bricklayers sought to win the ten-hour day, their efforts were defeated by the fact that black slaves were able to replace them. When painters and carpenters struck for higher wages, slaves were put in their jobs.

With the start of the Civil War, working people for the most part rallied to the support of the Union with dedication. Entire local unions enlisted at Abraham Lincoln's call. One of the first regiments to move to the defense of Washington was organized by a union iron molder, William H. Sylvis in Philadelphia. Tailors, clerks, shoemakers, carpenters, painters, millworkers, all joined. "It having been resolved to enlist with Uncle Sam for the war," one labor organization declared, "this union stands adjourned until either the Union is safe or we are whipped." The National Convention of Trade Unions, which met in Philadelphia

The first fatality of the war was Luther C. Ladd, a seventeen-year-old worker from a Lowell machine shop. His regiment was attacked by a mob when passing through Baltimore, and Ladd was killed.

N-YORK WEEKLY TRIBUNE

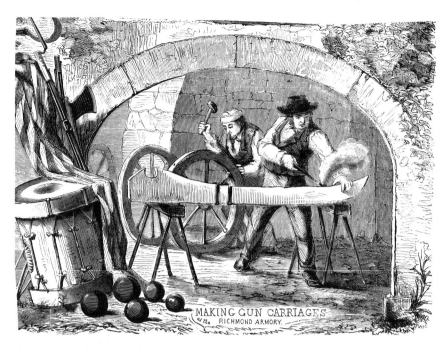

MAKING GUN CARRIAGES at the RICHMOND ARMORY.

in the winter of 1861, adopted a resolution supporting the northern cause. Many labor officials were commissioned into state regiments. Later investigations showed that a large percentage of northern soldiers were wage earners.

It was common to have notices posted on union bulletin boards: "Closed for the duration."

The most numerous groups in the Union army were farmers, who comprised nearly half the total, and common laborers. Well-represented categories were carpenters, shoemakers, clerks, blacksmiths, painters, soldiers, mechanics, sailors, machinists, masons, printers, teamsters, and teachers.

HOW SLAVERY HONORS OUR COUNTRY'S FLAG.

Workers on the home front making cartridges at the United States Arsenal, Watertown, Massachusetts.

"The varied accomplishment of the men in blue manifested itself in sundry and impressive ways," writes Bell Irvin Wiley. "When the colonel of the First Michigan Regiment at dress parade called for printers to run off some official papers, eight men stepped forward to offer their services." A Massachusetts colonel, whose mobility was seriously impeded by Rebel destruction of transportation facilities in Maryland early in the war, soon found that his men were equal to the emergency.

Walking up to the debris of a dismantled locomotive one of the soldiers coolly remarked: "I made this engine and I can put it together again." Others of section-gang background soon had the rails relaid; and when an engineer was requested to start the train rolling, nineteen Yanks from this one regiment avowed themselves capable of taking over the throttle.

Contributing to the participation of the black man

Women making munitions during the war.

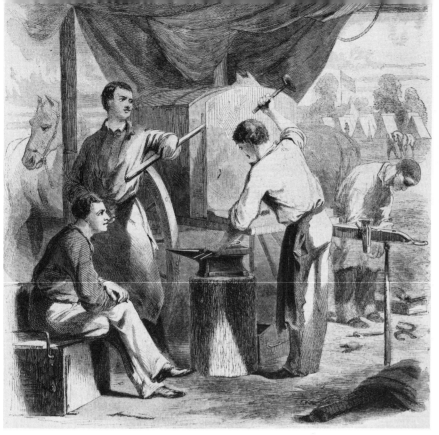

Civil War soldiers.

TURNING THE STOCK.

PLANING MACHINE.

PUTTING THE MUSKET TOGETHER

BORING MACHINE

RIFLING MACHINE

Gunmaking during the war.

An iron foundry in Paterson, New Jersey, active during the war.

Frederick Douglass, a runaway slave, was an effective advocate of abolition.

in the war for freedom was the call to arms by Frederick Douglass, a former slave and militant black leader:

> By every consideration which binds you to your enslaved fellow-countrymen, and the peace and welfare of your country; by every aspiration which you cherish for the freedom and equality of yourselves and your children; by all the ties of blood and identity which make us one with the brave black men now fighting our battles in Louisiana and in South Carolina, I urge you to fly to arms, and smite with death the power that would bury the government and your liberty in the same hopeless grave.

From the beginning, Douglass insisted that black people should be called into the Union army to fight for freedom. Before the war ended, one hundred eighty thousand Negro troops had served in Lincoln's army and thirty thousand in the navy. Another quarter of a million had helped the military as laborers, and some thirty-eight thousand black men had given up their lives in battle.

Abraham Lincoln had never lost touch with the common man. He was convinced that "the existing rebellion . . . is a war upon the rights of all working people." He did not hesitate, when he thought the time right, to speak out on controversial issues involving labor, if he thought it would help the cause of Union.

In a speech at Hartford, Connecticut, on March 5, 1860, Lincoln said: "Thank God that we have a sys-

During the war, many women entered factories.

About half-past eight o'clock near two thousand of the German Free Workingmen of the city marched in procession to the Burnet House, many of them bearing torches, and called upon the President elect. Mr. Lincoln was escorted to the balcony, and was greeted on behalf of the workingmen by Mr. Fred. Oberkleine, who formally presented the following brief address:

*To Abraham Lincoln, President elect of the United States:*

Sir—We, the German free workingmen of Cincinnati, avail ourselves of this opportunity to assure you, our chosen Chief Magistrate, of our sincere and heartfelt regard. You earned our votes as the champion of Free Labor and Free Homesteads. Our vanquished opponents have, in recent times, made frequent use of the terms "workingmen" and "workingmen's meetings," in order to create an impression, as if the mass of workingmen were in favor of compromises between the interests of free labor, and slave labor, by which the victory just won would be turned into a defeat. This is a despicable device of dishonest men. We spurn such compromises. We firmly adhere to the principles, which directed our votes in your favor. We trust, that you, the selfreliant because selfmade man, will uphold the Constitution and the laws against secret treachery and avowed treason. If to this end you should be in need of men, the German free workingmen, with others, will rise as one man at your call, ready to risk their lives in the effort to maintain the victory already won by freedom over slavery.

Willich's editorial, appearing in a Cincinnati newspaper, was read to Abraham Lincoln.

tem of labor where there can be a strike. Whatever the pressure, there is a point where the working man may stop." The next day in nearby New Haven he added:

I am glad to see that a system of labor prevails in New England under which laborers can strike when they want to, where they are not obliged to work under all circumstances and are not tied down and obliged to labor whether you pay them or not. I like the system which lets a man quit when he wants to, and wish it might prevail everywhere.

In Cincinnati, Lincoln was greeted by German-American workingmen who read an address written by August Willich, a labor leader who would rise to the position of general in the Union army: "We, the German free working men of Cincinnati, avail ourselves of this opportunity to assure you, our chief chosen magistrate, of our sincere and heartfelt regard. You earned our votes as a champion of Free Labor and Free Homesteads . . ." Lincoln responded: "The working men are the basis of all government, for the plain reason that they are the more numerous . . ."

In the spring of 1861, a committee of New York workingmen called upon Lincoln and notified him that their association had elected him an honorary member. "The honorary membership in your association," said Lincoln, " . . . is gratefully accepted. You

comprehend, as your address shows, that the existing rebellion means more, and tends to do more, than the perpetuation of African slavery—that it is, in fact, a war on the rights of all working people."

In his message shortly thereafter to Congress in December 1861, Lincoln called for unity of the people with such words as: "The strongest bond of human sympathy outside of the family relation, should be one uniting all working people, of all nations, and tongues and kindreds."

As the bloody war finally reached its conclusion, one labor leader stated:

I presume it is hardly necessary for me to enter into any arguments to prove that the working men, the great body of the people, the bone and muscle of the nation . . . are loyal; that, I take it, would be sheer mockery . . .; for the evidence of our loyalty one needs only point to the history of the war; . . . while armed treason and rebellion threaten our institutions with destruction, while the proud and the opulent of the land were plotting the downfall of our government, the toiling millions stood like a wall adamant between the country and all its foes.

Abraham Lincoln

According to Senator Benjamin F. Wade: "Abe Lincoln is the very incarnation of American labor."

August Willich, a labor leader, joined the Union army and rose to the rank of general.

# HIGHLY IMPORTANT.

## A Proclamation by the President of the United States.

The War Still to be Prosecuted for the Restoration of the Union.

## A DECREE OF EMANCIPATION

All Slaves in States in Rebellion on the First of January Next to be Free.

The Gradual Abolition and Colo'
Schemer A.''

## 1865-1873

# REBUILDING AFTER THE WAR

*"An injury to one is the
concern of all."*

While destruction of the United States had been predicted by the nation's enemies, the country emerged from the war, as James Russell Lowell wrote, with "amazing strength and no less amazing steadiness of democratic institutions."

There were, of course, monumental problems of reconstruction. How to bind up the wounds of the South? How to treat the freed men; how to parcel out the western lands; all these and more confronted the nation.

"Three-fourths of the people assume that the negro will not labor except on compulsion," a visitor to the South from the *Atlantic Monthly* wrote in 1866.

And the whole struggle between the whites on the one hand and the blacks on the other hand is a struggle for and against compulsion. The negro insists, very blindly perhaps, that he shall be free to come and go as he pleases; the white insists that he shall come and go only at the pleasure of his employer. The whites seem wholly unable to comprehend that freedom for the negro means the same thing as freedom for them . . .

By 1870, the Fifteenth Amendment established that the "right . . . to vote shall not be denied . . . on account of race, color, or previous condition of

Black war veterans at work in South Carolina.

"ONE VOTE LESS."—*Richmond Whig.*

**MISSISSIPPI KU-KLUX IN THE DISGUISES IN WHICH THEY WERE CAPTURED.**

servitude." However, Senator Carl Schurz reported that "although the freed man is no longer considered the property of the individual master, he is considered the slave of society . . ." The special restrictive "black codes," passed in southern states, were described as a "half way station back to slavery."

Four million black people had no land, no homes, no property. The complex process began of breaking up the big plantations into small farms and renting them to white people or Negroes. "They either paid their rental in cash or became share tenants or share croppers," one writer described it.

Share tenants furnished their own farm equipment and animals, and obtained the use of the land by agreeing to pay the owner a fixed share of the produce—one fourth or one third of the crop. The share croppers were much worse off.

They had neither equipment nor animals, nor, in many cases, even food for themselves and their families. They had nothing but their labor. The share the owner took from them was therefore larger—one half the crop or more.

The owner took out of the crop, too, what he had furnished his tenants and croppers in the way of seed, fertilizer, and food. The tenants and croppers, both white and black, were at the mercy of the landlord. He handled the sale of the crop; he kept the books; he charged what he liked for the food which he supplied out of his own commissary; he usually added an exorbitant interest charge plus a fee for "supervision." It was not surprising, therefore, that when the accounts were settled, the tenants and croppers often found that they were in debt to the owner —if they were lucky they might break even.

# WANTED!
# IMMEDIATELY!
## 3,000 LABORERS

To Work on Levees in Louisiana and Mississippi. Wages
$45 to $50 per Month, and Board. Steady Work
guaranteed all winter and spring.

## ALSO--500 WOOD CHOPPERS

For Michigan and Indiana. Highest wages paid. Steady
Employment all winter and spring.

## ALSO--250 MEN

For the **Pinery. Highest** wages paid and transportation
furnished.

### ALSO,

1,000 Rail Road Graders, Track-layers, Spikers, &c., with
good pay and board the year round.

For further information apply to

**OLMSTED & SNELL,**

No. 100 Madison Street, Room 4,          CHICAGO, ILL.

As such problems, and more, were confronting the nation, the momentum of industrial production—which had helped the Union forces win the war—now assisted the expansion of the nation as a whole. Soldiers of both contending forces shed their uniforms to help dig coal, build railroads, cut timber, drill for oil, build bridges and roads, clear forests, sail ships—and do the endless array of work that the developing nation demanded.

Railroads pushed their way across the frontier linking two oceans. "Forty miles of track for the Union Pacific," writes the historian Marshall B. Davidson, "were laid in 1866, two hundred and forty-five in 1867, four hundred and twenty-five in 1868, and the

*The Herring Net,* by Winslow Homer.

Workers in an India rubber mill.

remaining one hundred and five miles in the first few months of 1869."

"We found the workmen, with the regularity of machinery, dropping each rail in its place, spiking it down, and then seizing another," an eyewitness report stated. "Behind them, the locomotive; before, the tie-layers; beyond these the graders; and still further, in mountain recesses, the engineers. It was Civilization pressing westward—the Conquest of Nature moving toward the Pacific."

Hastily constructed steel mills provided the tracks on which the railroads ran. Newly dug coal mines provided their fuel. When these railroads first began to crisscross the country, firemen stood on small platforms in the locomotive and tossed logs into firepots to create the necessary steam to drive the wheels.

But greater demands for power continued to mount. A new technology was needed. Increasingly coal was used to provide this power. The mines were dug in coal outcroppings, particularly around the Pittsburgh and Midwest areas where water shipment was available. The mining industry grew as the use of coal began to become more familiar in the home and in the factory.

Factories still depended much on workers' skills. The art of glassblowing was a demanding one. Toward the end of the handcraft era glass bottles and jars were made by boiling away molten glass metal in big clay pots. Usually, there were some five pots to a single furnace. The glassworker was called a gatherer

The last spike is driven in Utah, May 10, 1869, where the Central Pacific and Union Pacific met.

An early train.

Unloading an ore vessel.

because he gathered the metal at the end of a long blowpipe by inserting the instrument into a hole in the furnace top.

The gatherer would reach his pipe into the pot and collect a mass of glass on its end. This was a difficult and skilled operation because the workers had to know just how much of the metal to collect at the end of the blowpipe. He also developed a marvel of skill in keeping it from rolling off.

The pipe would get white hot as the blower worked, and constantly had to be cooled with a stream of water. Otherwise, it could not be handled properly. The metal was worked by rolling it on a stone slab. Once this rolling process ceased, the hot-glass metal tended to lose its shape and even drop away.

While this operation was in process, the worker had to keep up a steady blowing into the pipe to maintain a bubble shape that eventually would become a bottle. As a result of long experience and acquired skill, the worker would know the exact moment when he would drop the hollow glass bubble into a cast-iron mold nearby. This mold determined the shape of the bottle or jar.

When the bubble of glass metal was placed in a mold, another workingman would appear with a knife or a pair of scissors to clip off the glass at the exact place necessary and at the exact moment. When the glass placed in the mold had cooled somewhat, another workman would lift out each piece with a pair of metal pincers, shape the top with a special tool, which he heated in a small furnace called a glory hole. Then the bottles were set aside and permitted to cool.

A good gatherer and his team, it was said, could make several hundred jars or bottles in a day's work. Work was based on the piecework system, and glassworkers were under daily tension to work as hard and as fast as possible with a minimum of breakage. It was considered not unusual for a man to work twelve hours a day, seven days a week.

News of the dramatically expanding nation—with its steadily increasing demand for labor—inevitably spread worldwide. So intense became the need for hands to do the work of the New World a-making that industry redoubled the number of its agents overseas, spreading the word about the opportunity that existed in industrial America. Special companies were now organized to import laborers, especially skilled laborers, from Great Britain, Belgium, France, Switzerland, Norway, and Sweden for manufacturers, railroad companies, and other employers in America.

Immigration was stimulated by posters and advertisements in the newspapers in this country and abroad. In 1871, a London newspaper printed the advertisment: "500 navvies wanted in New York and Pennsylvania to work on railroads. Wages from $1.75 to $2.50 a day. Single men preferred." In New York newspapers such advertisements as "200 men wanted to take contracts in the coal fields of Pennsylvania. Good wages guaranteed, and steady employment assured" were common.

Workers constructing a tunnel.

Danger ahead on the railroad.

Industrial America: Newark, New Jersey, and South Boston harbor.

Immigrants at an Omaha railroad depot.

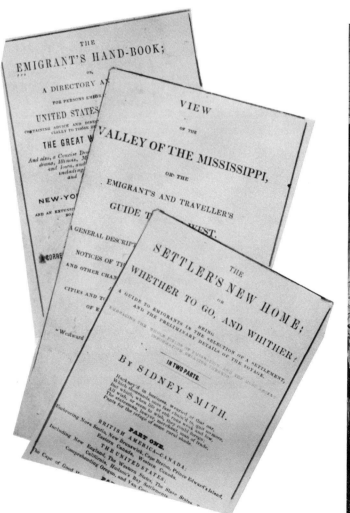

Manuals published to help recently arrived immigrants.

Testifying before a New York senate committee, the financier Jay Gould stated: "When I was in Europe, you couldn't go anywhere but you saw agents of American land grant companies."

"The greater the number of immigrants sent out from European countries to America," a labor spokesman commented, "the greater the profits of the agents who infested nearly every large city in Europe. . . . The agent in many cases was also in the pay of a steamship company, and never allowed his conscience to prevent him from holding out inducements of the most alluring character to every man, woman or child, who could rake, scrape, or borrow the passage money."

From 143,000 immigrants arriving in America from 1821 to 1830, the number swelled. From 1841 to 1850, there were 1,706,000 new arrivals. From 1851 to 1860, the number rose to 2,598,000. From 1871 to 1880, the number was 2,731,00. In sixty years from 1821 to 1881, there were some eleven million immigrants to the New World—and most of them eager to find work, of any kind, for any wage, and sometimes under any conditions.

Jay Gould

James Fisk, Jr.

Philip D. Armour

Panic on the floor of the New York Stock Exchange in 1873.

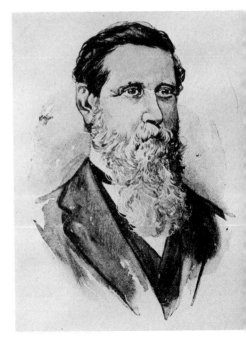

Jay Cooke

Although there were those enjoying prosperity in postwar America, periodic depressions still haunted the land and its people. The panic of 1867, followed six years later by even a more severe economic setback, threw tens of thousands of people out of work. Beyond charity, there was no place to seek assistance.

America was, at the same time, on its way to levels of progress never before possible. "What England had once accomplished in a hundred years," said Charles A. Beard, "the United States had accomplished in half the time." But to each decade the coming of a major depression was a stunning shock; the promise of prosperity in good times gave little warning to working people of what lay ahead.

The depression of 1873 occurred when the banking house of Jay Cooke & Company collapsed, bringing down with it scores of other banks and businesses. For reasons that seemed inexplicable to working people, doors of factories were closed and tens of thousands of people discharged.

"Thousands of homeless men and women are to be seen nightly sleeping in the seats in the public parks, or walking the streets. . . . The suffering next winter will be tremendous," one newspaper reported. In New York alone over a hundred thousand working people were without jobs. More than twenty thousand Chicago unemployed paraded, demanding "bread for the needy, clothing for the naked, and houses for the homeless."

According to the Chicago newspaper *Inter-Ocean*, there "never was a time in the history of the United States when a greater amount of misery, poverty and wretchedness existed."

The liberal newspaper editor John Swinton wrote:

We hear also that many of the recipients of relief are men who refused work at fair wages. You must judge whether it be just to say such things of our mechanics and laborers, or whether such men actually prefer the humiliation of idle pauperism to the pride of industrious independence. It is false to them, to human nature and to all our experience in the city, to say that they do.

When starving people sought to demonstrate their plight, they were frequently treated either with indifference or brutality. The human tragedy was described by a young New York cigar worker who personally observed conditions in 1873:

Next morning people began assembling early in the Square. I reached the Square a little after ten. . . . Soon the park was packed and all the avenues leading to it crowded. The people were quiet. There was nothing out of harmony with the spirit of friendly conferences between the chief public official and workless and breadless

Starving unemployed demonstrate at Tompkins Square in New York City.

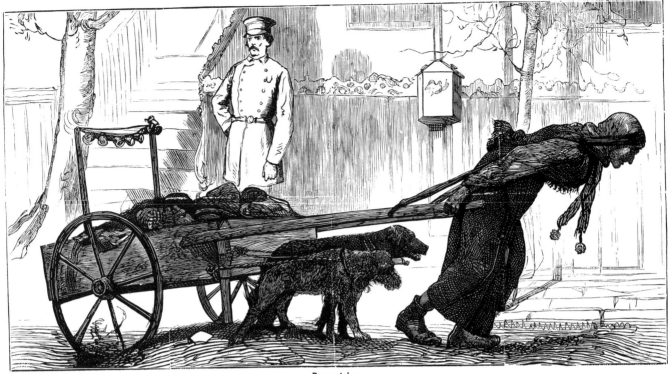

Rag picker

A poor family "turned out" of its home.

citizens. The gathering was planned as visible proof of suffering and destitution among New York unemployed . . .

It was about ten-thirty when a detachment of police surrounded the park. Hardly had they taken their position before a group of workers marched into the park from Avenue A. They carried a banner bearing the words, "TENTH WARD UNION LABOR." Just after they entered the park a police sergeant led an attack on them. He was followed by police mounted and on foot with drawn night sticks. Without a word of warning they swept down the defenseless workers, striking down the standard bearer and using their clubs right and left indiscriminately on the heads of all they could reach.

Shortly afterward the mounted police charged the crowd on Eighth Street, riding them down and attacking men, women, and children without discrimination. It was an orgy of brutality. I was caught in the crowd on the street and barely saved my head from being cracked by jumping down a cellarway. The attacks of the police kept up all day long—wherever the police saw a group of poorly dressed persons standing or moving together . . .

Between depressions, when there were jobs available, the speeding up of production to meet the needs of the market created a constant threat to a worker's safety. There were few safeguards. The responsibility for accidents was that of the worker, and long hours tended to create fatigue that made accidents in the fast-running machinery all too common.

Describing conditions among laboring people, one writer in Philadelphia stated:

Hundreds are most laboriously employed on turnpikes, working from morning to night at from half a dollar to three-quarters a day, exposed to the broiling sun in summer and all the inclemency of our severe winters. There was always a redundancy of wood pilers in our cities, whose wages are so low that their utmost efforts do not enable them to earn more than from 35¢ to 50¢ per day. . . . Finally, there is no employment whatever, how disagreeable or loathsome, or deleterious soever it may be, or however reduced the wages, that does not find persons willing to follow it rather than beg or steal.

The manpower problem of the nation was not that there were lacking those who were able to climb from the economic bottom to the top. Every field of endeavor had its talented or determined or lucky success stories. The problem lay in the percentage of those who made it. Despite publicity for the successful, the large majority of the poor stayed poor. Opportunity was there; but there was simply not enough

An eight-hour-day demonstration in New York City.

Pillars supporting the center of the Pemberton Mills (Lawrence, Massachusetts) buckled on January 10, 1860, bringing down the walls and roof. The huge building collapsed in sixty seconds, killing eighty-eight working men, women, and children, and injuring more than three hundred. A subsequent investigation found that the pillars had partially given way six years earlier, but the warning was not heeded.

Cowboys at work.

room at the top for more than a handful. The rich were fabulously rich; the poor shamefully poor.

Real-estate speculators often owned large numbers of urban tenements and slum dwellings, but were indifferent toward problems of the poor. "In a majority of cases, with the occupants of the poorer tenement houses of New York," one real-estate agent was quoted as saying, "it is a matter of choice with them. They are from the poverty stricken districts of the Old World, and therefore, not accustomed to much room; and as to the more perfect sanitary arrangements, they don't want them; and above all, they don't want to occupy quarters where they will be obliged to observe the ordinary rules of cleanliness."

Exploitation was not confined to industrial workers in urban centers. Others, including those working on the western frontier and the high seas, faced mounting economic oppression. Cattle breeders of the West, seeking to satisfy the growing demand for meat, were in constant need of cowhands to ride the range. The cowboy, who evolved into an international celebrity, actually had very little in common

with the romantic adventurer with pistols at his side and jingling spurs. The average cowhand was, in most instances, a laborer in the saddle whose daily job was long, difficult, and often dangerous.

As the demand for meat back east increased, the role of the cowhand grew in importance. It was he who drove the Texas longhorns on their seemingly endless journey to eastern stockyards. It was a dusty, dry, monotonous, lonely job, for which the cowhand received little pay and no security.

"A cowboy's life is not the joyous, adventurous existence shown in the moving pictures, read about in cheap novels, or to be seen in World's Exhibitions," a former cowboy wrote.

Cowboy's work begins at daybreak. If he is on the ranch, he rolls out of bed, slips on his pants, boots and hat, and goes to the barn to feed his saddle horses.

It is his greatest pride that he does not work on foot. Coming back, he washes his face and hands at the pump, takes his place at the long

Unskilled workers from the factory and rolling mill.

The uniform of an American sailor of a cargo crew.

table; the Chinese cook brings in piles of beef-steaks, potatoes, hot cakes, and "long butter" as the flour gravy is called, because on a big cattle ranch where there are thousands of cows, oft times, there will not be one milk cow, and no butter but what is hauled many miles from town to the ranch.

There are various kinds of work for the cowboy to do during the different seasons on a cow ranch. The cattle are not pastured or herded, but run wild on the mountains and sage brush flats. They are rounded up in the spring and fall . . .

One of the most dangerous occupations was logging and timber-making in the post-Civil War era. Injuries were a commonplace from the slipping of axes or from a misstep that sent a worker under rolling logs on a river to be either drowned or crushed to death. The day for the lumberjack was a long one, with Sunday being a welcome respite at which time he would repair his saw and grind his ax.

The work life of the lumberjack was a hard battle. Each worker expected that he would be in and out of the water as logs were floated down rivers in the spring thaw. Often the logs would develop huge jams, which could only be broken by a lumber worker

IN THE STOKE-HOLE.

using rare judgment by freeing the log that was causing the trouble and setting the rest rushing on their way.

According to one account, "when a near accident had passed and a jack had by a hair's breadth escaped disaster, he would laugh bitterly, prod the offending log . . . and shout after it 'Hell, no! You ain't got my name writ on your dastard bark. Get along with yer, scoundrel!' "

Another much glamorized worker of the era was the American seaman who continued to be ruthlessly exploited as he had been in colonial days. There had been an active merchant marine. However, after the Civil War, financial interests turned from shipbuilding to the building of railroads and the development of the frontier. American merchant vessels received less attention than prairie schooners heading west. American shipping was largely handled by foreign shipowners subsidized by the American government.

If popular attention was not focused on America's merchant marine, neither was it paying attention to the conditions facing American seamen. Carryovers from the days of slavery were common on board American ships. So difficult did it become to recruit seamen that the practice of shanghaiing developed. Under this system, men were kidnapped and spirited aboard ships, often after being drugged or intoxicated. Special agencies developed on land whose profession was to supply seamen, whether voluntary or involuntary.

Pennsylvania miners voting. Political action was an important part of the National Labor Union's program.

A federal proclamation ordering the eight-hour day without reduction of wages for government employees, 1869.

George E. McNeill, an eight-hour-day leader, and Jonathan Fincher, one of the early American labor journalists.

Sailors aloft.

Small farmers, too, were facing severe problems wherever they were located. Condemned by the vagaries of nature to constant insecurity, they encountered increasing hardships from high taxes, railroad freight rate discriminatory practices, and high prices on what they had to buy. In the South, the farmer— black and white—was particularly harassed following the Civil War, often being reduced almost to servitude by the town merchant.

Improvements in output were taking place on farms, particularly the larger ones. This resulted from betterment in seed brands and livestock breeding, in technological knowledge and, of course, in machinery available to do work once done by man or animal.

Such increase in productivity was of great value to the nation as a whole. But, increasingly, the small farmer found the products he now raised in abundance taxed by rising transportation costs before it could reach the market.

Particularly in the West, small farmers faced economic disaster. In Kansas, many had to surrender their farms and return east. One farmer put a sign on his horse and wagon: "Going Back East to the Wife's Folks." Another displayed a placard: "In God We Trusted—in Kansas We Busted!" Other bankrupt farmers, deprived of ownership of land, remained in farm country, serving as workers for hire.

Another frequently exploited category of working

*The strike and the family, a cartoon of the day, 1872.*

A farmer at work.

people were those who provided personal household services—usually for the affluent. With the passing of the indentured servant after the Revolution, property owners faced a servant problem that persisted for a lengthy period. The South had its slaves; but in other sectors of the nation, the independent tradition of the New World discouraged the development of a hired servant class. Many cooks, maids, butlers, nurses—when not obtained from slaves and families of slaves—were recruited from working people born or trained in other nations—Ireland, China, England, and so on.

In the days of horse-drawn vehicles, men, often without other skills, served as footman, coachman, porter, stableman. Such servants had other duties to perform such as taking care of the lawn, marketing for food, cleaning shoes, washing windows, repairing the house, waiting on table. The influence of men of property was reflected in privileges sometimes extended to servants.

However, as the democratic spirit spread through the nation, the concept of serving another as an obvious unequal became unpopular. It was difficult to find, and keep, servants—especially when they had to dress and act with a show of deference. Oftentimes Americans of wealth made efforts to steal servants who accompanied Europeans on visits to this country.

The spirit of independence of American servants was observed by Alexis de Tocqueville and other famed visitors to America. A French woman visitor remarked in 1859: "No American will receive an insulting word. . . . A common mode of resenting an imperious order is to quit the house without waiting or even asking for a reckoning."

The household domestic was to become rarer, except in the most affluent homes, as the years passed.

A new type of commercial "servant" developed as a service industry tended to replace the servant system: hotel busboys, elevator operators, professional chefs, commercial messengers, hotel maids, waiters, cooks, and dishwashers in public restaurants. Public taxi drivers were to replace the private coachman; the hotel chambermaid was to become more numerous than the house servant; and the gas-station attendant was to be the lineal descendant of the stable-boy.

During the post-Civil War era, the affluent did not appear to even notice the plight of the poor, whether in cities, on the frontier, on the high seas, or on farms. "I defy any man to show that there is pauperism in the United States," said Andrew Carnegie, the steel magnate, speaking before the Nineteenth Century Club. Learned professors would explain the misery in the midst of plenty by referring to "certain

Early servants

The U.S. Infantry attacking the Snake River Indians.

natural laws." "Too many are trying to live without labor . . .," said the industrialist Joseph Medill. "Too many squander their earnings on intoxicating drinks, cigars and amusements." Those in high positions did not seem to even notice, much less have compassion on the plight of the less fortunate.

Nor was there effort on the part of the wealthy to hide their opulence—even in the midst of mass unemployment and despair. "The old barons," in the words of Matthew Josephson, continued to flaunt their "private palace cars on rail, their imitation-Renaissance castles, and their pleasure yachts . . ."

During the Civil War a handful of financiers and speculators made enormous profits. This resulted in a growing concentration of wealth in the period following the conflict. With the nation expanding rapidly and markets for goods springing up everywhere, the opportunities to reap rich rewards were plentiful. Fortunes were piled upon fortunes almost overnight.

"Of course I have no other interest in life but my business," Philip D. Armour, the Chicago meat-packing pioneer, said, " . . . I do not love the money;

what I do love is the getting of it, the making of it. . . . I do not read, I do not take any part in politics . . . but in my counting house, I am in my element."

The new "captains of industry" applied the relentless logic of the new industrial age. The old competitive system with its wastefulness, its duplications, its squanderings of human energy and money, was given second place to the new system of "combination." Monopoly was so much simpler; so much more practical; so much more profitable. What Walt Whitman described as "this almost maniacal appetite for

The Brains, a cartoon by Thomas Nast.

wealth" held much of the nation in its grasp. Although the United States census showed in 1870 an average income of about four hundred dollars per person, nevertheless, it was an era when, in Chicago alone, more than two hundred men amassed private fortunes of a million dollars each.

The nation's first great monopoly—created by John D. Rockefeller—was described by the New York Senate: "The actual value of property in the trust control at the present time is not less than 148 millions of dollars. . . . This sum in the hands of nine men . . . possibly the most formidable monied power on this continent."

The need to combine was increasingly becoming apparent to exploited working people as it was to industrialists themselves. The Civil War may have paralyzed but did not destroy the young labor movement. While many union members were in the armed forces, and some locals shut up shop for the duration, many continued to maintain their organization. In the winter of 1863, there were some twenty trades organized into unions, which number increased to fifty-three a year later and to sixty-nine by the end of the war.

The Knights of St. Crispin was an early labor organization in the shoe industry about 1867.

Unions that were organized during and after the war included the American Miners' Association, 1861; United Sons of Vulcan (ironworkers), 1862; cigar makers, ship carpenters, plasterers, and couriers, 1864; carpenters, bricklayers, painters, tailors, heaters, coachmakers, 1865; silk and fur hat finishers, 1866;

spinners, 1867; Knights of St. Crispin (shoe workers), 1868; wool hat finishers, Daughters of St. Crispin, 1869. There were also those who had been organized before the Civil War that included molders, machinists, blacksmiths, hat finishers, and the typographical union.

Unprecedented railroad expansion brought about the formation of unions of railroad workers organized among the various crafts: Locomotive Engineers (1863); Railway Conductors (1868); Locomotive Firemen (1873); and others. Later they were to unite into a federation called the Railroad Brotherhood.

The new machines sometimes incurred the anger of frustrated workers. Occasionally, strikes were called to show their disapproval of the new technology. In a vain effort to stop the coming of the machines, the Grainmen's Protective Union of New York went on strike, not for higher wages, but that "we still be allowed to work as we have heretofore, industriously, peacefully, usefully to ourselves, our families, and the whole mercantile community." But the effort was in vain. There was no turning back the coming of the machines. Working people simply had to adjust. One voice of organized labor was that of Jonathan Fincher, national secretary of the Machinists and Blacksmiths Union, who became editor of a labor newspaper, *Fincher's Trades' Review.* "Organize! Organize!" Fincher wrote. ". . . At no time in the history of labor, perhaps, have passing events placed before workmen so many advantages. There are few idle—work is plenty. . . . Organize in every village and hamlet."

Evidently such appeals were heeded by William H. Sylvis, a Philadelphia molder and an officer of the

Richard F. Trevellick,
president of the Ship Carpenter's Union.

William H. Sylvis,
founder of the National Labor Union.

"The design of the founders of the Republic," the union's preamble stated, "was to institute a government upon the principle of absolute inherent sovereignty of the people . . . that when the laws are enacted destructive of these ends, they are without moral binding force, and it is the right and duty of the people to alter, amend or abolish them . . ."

Behind these broad words were certain specific plans on such issues as the shorter work week. There was a growing national movement, headed by a Boston machinist, Ira Stewart, for the eight-hour day. Stewart lost his twelve-hour-a-day job for supporting the eight-hour movement. From that time on, he dedicated himself completely to the eight-hour crusade. He claimed that long working hours dulled the sensibility of working people. "How can they be so stimulated to demand higher wages," he asked, "when they have little or no time or strength to use the advantages which higher wages can buy or procure."

Sylvis was elected to the presidency of the NLU, and he and Stewart worked together to strengthen the eight-hour-day movement. "The ignorance of the masses," Sylvis agreed, "was a direct and inevitable result of overwork."

The widely supported National Labor Union viewed all working people as equal with full rights to membership. This included women who, the NLU believed, were entitled to equal pay with men. Similarly, the National Labor Union spoke out in favor of equality for black workers. "When the shackles fell from the limbs of four million blacks," said Sylvis, "it did not make them free men. .. . The labor movement is a second Emancipation Proclamation . . ."

Sylvis dedicated literally all his time to the National Labor Union. "I love this union cause," he said, "I hold it more dear than I do my family or my life. I am willing to devote to it all that I am or have or hope for in this world." But despite his leadership and the warm support received from working people, the National Labor Union was not destined to last long.

The death of Sylvis in 1869 was a blow to the union he helped build to a size of five hundred thousand members. Moreover, there were other reasons for the decline of the organization. Leaders of the NLU tended to become more deeply involved in reformism than in serving the day-to-day economic interests of their members. The support of greenbackism, a movement advocating increased issues of paper currency, tended to divide the organization. Black workers, for example, maintained their allegiance to the Republican party, which had been instrumental in abolishing slavery. With the NLU supporting greenbackism on the political field, black workers tended to become alienated.

Shortly thereafter, supporting "free land for freedmen," a new labor organization, the National Colored Labor Union, was established, led by Isaac Myers, a Baltimore Caulkers' Union officer, and Frederick

International Molders' Union. As the war came to an end, Sylvis, described as "the first great figure in the American labor movement," noted the growth of industry to national proportions. Observing the conditions of working people, he came to the conclusion that there was need for a national labor organization as well. "If working men and capitalists are equal copartners," he wrote, ". . . why do they not share equally in the profits? Why does capital take to itself the whole loaf, while labor is left to gather up the crumbs? . . . If the workingmen have learned anything," said Sylvis, "it is that there can be no success but in union—the union of all who labor . . . the whole united power of labor is necessary . . ."

In 1866, more than seventy-seven delegates from local unions, city-trade assemblies, national unions, and "eight-hour leagues" convened in Baltimore to discuss organizing a national labor federation. A banner on display outside the meeting hall welcomed the delegates with the words: "Welcome to the Sons of Toil, from the North, South, East and West."

From the deliberations of this conference came the nation's first genuine national labor federation, the National Labor Union.

Douglass. However, this organization was not to survive for long. It, too, tended to favor over much political activity and ignore daily grievances of its membership.

The coming of the 1873 depression assisted in the disintegration of these organizations and they soon ceased to contribute further to the labor movement.

In 1874, the "Sovereigns of Industry" organized, largely in New England, in an effort to establish an association "of the industrial laboring classes, without regard to race, sex, color, nationality or occupation." But this organization proved to be more a mutual assistance group than an active union.

However, a new federation, of an entirely different kind, was already under way. In 1869, a small group of Philadelphia garment cutters had decided to establish an organization called the Noble and Holy Order of the Knights of Labor. Such by then was the fear of reprisals against union activity that utmost secrecy was written into the permanent bylaws; the very name of the organization was kept

secret and in its place five asterisks, * * * * *, substituted.

"An injury to one is the concern of all," the order's motto, was to be a rallying cry among working people for decades.

"When that beautiful watchword . . . resounded through my life," stated Martin Irons, a railroad worker who joined the Knights of Labor and became a militant leader, "when I learned that knighthood embraced every grade of honest toil . . . then I felt I had reached a field in which I was ready to spend the remaining energies of my life."

The Knights of Labor enunciated its guiding principles: "Mutual assistance among workers . . . the lightening of the exhaustiveness of toil . . . solidarity among working people . . . universal brotherhood . . . education in reading and writing for working people."

The Knights declared that their organization "will include men and women of every craft, creed and color . . ." Also included were the skilled and the nonskilled, the citizen as well as the noncitizen.

The order looked with alarm upon the massing of

Workers in Australia pioneered in the fight for the eight-hour day. The Australian spirit was reflected in the quatrain: "Eight hours to sleep, Eight hours to play, Eight hours to work, And eight bob a day."

THE FIRST EIGHT HOUR BANNER USED IN VICTORIA, AUSTRALIA, APRIL 10, 1856.

The Knights of Labor welcomed black workers. Isaac Myers, a ship's carpenter, was the leading black unionist of the era. Peter H. Clark, of the Colored Teachers Co-operative Association, "Cincinnati's most famous colored citizen," and Frederick Douglass, former abolitionist and co-founder with Myers of the National Colored Labor Union.

Two anti-Negro cartoons.

*Founders of the Knights of Labor*

Officers of the Knights of Labor holding a picture of Uriah S. Stephens, founder.

The seal of the Knights of Labor contained the inscription: "That is the most perfect government in which an injury to one is the concern of all." A union officer stated: "The Grand Officers . . . studied carefully and well before adopting that motto."

great wealth: accumulation of "aggregated wealth, which, unless checked, will invariably lead to the pauperization and hopeless degradation of the toiling masses, render it imperative . . . that a check should be placed upon its power and upon unjust accumulation and a system adopted which will secure to the laborer the fruits of his toil . . ."

Leaders of the Knights spoke of "the greatest good to the greatest number," and were particularly in favor of "the reserving of the public lands—the heritage of the people—for the actual settler; not another acre for railroads or speculators."

The order was, in its early days, a fighting organization, demanding justice for all humankind. Its members lustily sang:

> "Storm the fort, ye
>   Knights of Labor
> Battle for your cause:
> Equal rights for
>   Every neighbor
> Down with tyrant laws."

# PREAMBLE

## AND

## DECLARATION OF PRINCIPLES

### OF THE

# KNIGHTS OF LABOR

## OF AMERICA.

TO THE PUBLIC:

The alarming development and aggressiveness of great capitalists and corporations, unless checked, will inevitably lead to the pauperization and hopeless degradation of the toiling masses.

It is imperative, if we desire to enjoy the full blessings of life, that a check be placed upon unjust accumulation, and the power for evil of aggregated wealth.

This much-desired object can be accomplished only by the united efforts of those who obey the divine injunction, "In the sweat of thy face shalt thou eat bread."

Therefore we have formed the Order of Knights of Labor, for the purpose of organizing and directing the power of the industrial masses, not as a political party, for it is more—in it are crystallized sentiments and measures for the benefit of the whole people, but it should be borne in mind, when exercising the right of suffrage, that most of the objects herein set forth can only be obtained through legislation, and that it is the duty of all to assist in nominating and supporting with their votes only such candidates as will pledge their support to those measures, regardless of party. But no one shall, however, be compelled to vote with the majority, and calling upon all who believe in securing "the greatest good to the greatest number," to join and assist us, we declare to the world that our aims are:

I. To make industrial and moral worth, not wealth, the true standard of individual and National greatness.

II. To secure to the workers the full enjoyment of the wealth they create, sufficient leisure in which to develop their intellectual, moral and social faculties; all of the benefits, recreation and pleasures of association; in a word, to enable them to share in the gains and honors of advancing civilization.

In order to secure these results, we demand at the hands of the STATE:

III. The establishment of Bureaus of Labor Statistics, that we may arrive at a correct knowledge of the educational, moral and financial condition of the laboring masses.

IV. That the public lands, the heritage of the people, be reserved for actual settlers; not another acre for railroads or speculators, and that all lands now held for speculative purposes be taxed to their full value.

V. The abrogation of all laws that do not bear equally upon capital and labor, and the removal of unjust technicalities, delays and discriminations in the administration of justice.

VI. The adoption of measures providing for the health and safety of those engaged in mining and manufacturing, building industries, and for indemnification to those engaged therein for injuries received through lack of necessary safeguards.

VII. The recognition, by incorporation, of trades' unions, orders and such other associations as may be organized by the working masses to improve their condition and protect their rights.

VIII. The enactment of laws to compel corporations to pay their employees weekly, in lawful money, for the labor of the preceding week, and giving mechanics and laborers a first lien upon the product of their labor to the extent of their full wages.

IX. The abolition of the contract system on National, State and Municipal works.

X. The enactment of laws providing for arbitration between employers and employed, and to enforce the decision of the arbitrators.

XI. The prohibition by law of the employment of children under 15 years of age in workshops, mines and factories.

XII. To prohibit the hiring out of convict labor.

XIII. That a graduated income tax be levied.

And we demand at the hands of CONGRESS:

XIV. The establishment of a National monetary system, in which a circulating medium in necessary quantity shall issue direct to the people, without the intervention of banks; that all the National issue shall be full legal tender in payment of all debts, public and private; and that the Government shall not guarantee or recognize any private banks, or create any banking corporations.

XV. That interest-bearing bonds, bills of credit or notes shall never be issued by the Government, but that, when need arises, the emergency shall be met by issue of legal tender, non-interest-bearing money.

XVI. That the importation of foreign labor under contract be prohibited.

XVII. That, in connection with the post-office, the Government shall organize financial exchanges, safe deposits and facilities for deposit of the savings of the people in small sums.

XVIII. That the Government shall obtain possession, by purchase, under the right of eminent domain, of all telegraphs, telephones and railroads, and that hereafter no charter or license be issued to any corporation for construction or operation of any means of transporting intelligence, passengers or freight.

And while making the foregoing demands upon the State and National Government, we will endeavor to associate our own labors.

XIX. To establish co-operative institutions such as will tend to supersede the wage system, by the introduction of a co-operative industrial system.

XX. To secure for both sexes equal pay for equal work.

XXI. To shorten the hours of labor by a general refusal to work for more than eight hours.

XXII. To persuade employers to agree to arbitrate all differences which may arise between them and their employees, in order that the bonds of sympathy between them may be strengthened and that strikes may be rendered unnecessary.

**If you believe in organization, you are earnestly invited to join with us in securing these objects. All information on the subject of organization should be sent to the General Secretary-Treasurer of the Order, who will have an Organizer visit you and assist in furthering the good work.**

Frank J. Ferrell, a black member of the Knights of Labor, introducing Terence V. Powderly at the Richmond convention.

All human beings were equal in the sight of the order. Its attitude toward racial discrimination was illustrated in an incident that took place in 1886 at a national convention in Richmond, Virginia. New York had elected among its delegates Frank J. Ferrell, a black man. Ferrell was refused admittance to the hall because of his color. "Without hesitation," the report of the delegation stated, "the representatives of District Assembly #49 withdrew in a body, and secured quarters where there would be no objections to any one of their number."

Because of this, delegates proposed that Ferrell be given the privilege of introducing the grand master workman, Terence V. Powderly, to the convention. "One of the objects of our Order is the abolition of those distinctions which are maintained by creed or color," Ferrell told the delegates.

Of the thirty national unions in existence before

the Civil War, only the printers' and cigar makers' admitted women. While the role of women in the Knights of Labor was a controversial issue, the order was adamant. "The Knights of Labor is the only organization we know," said the western newspaper *The Los Angeles Union*, "which encourages the membership of ladies, demands for women exact equality and insists on equal pay for equal work."

"The working women and men of America, yes and of the world, have reason to hold in grateful appreciation the memory of . . . heroic women who struggle for freedom of opportunity for all," stated Terence V. Powderly, who was to become the order's most influential leader.

While the Knights spoke militantly of the needs of the people, its actions were often cautious, especially on the issue of work stoppages, calling for "the substitution of arbitration for strikes, whenever and wherever employers and employees are willing to meet on equitable grounds." As the years passed, the order was frequently compelled, by the nature of the times, either to call strikes or to support them. This was a constant cause of controversy and ultimately—

together with the loose nature of its organization— was to contribute to its disintegration.

Organization was also taking place among those small farmers who were oppressed for so long by large financial interests. Organization was needed to win the fight to regulate railroads, to win fair taxes, and in general to give expression to growing agrarian unrest. The National Grange of the Patrons of Husbandry was founded in New York in 1867, a social and fraternal organization concerned with the farmer's problems. By 1875, over twenty thousand local granges were organized with a membership, it was estimated, of three-quarters of a million.

Together with wage earners, the organized farmers fought in various state legislatures and in Washington for laws helpful to themselves and workers and against monopoly influence. The Greenback-Labor party later elected numerous candidates to office in local, state, and national elections, demanding better transportation and lower freight rates; an eight-hour workday; government control of railroads and telegraph; and that the nation's money be greenbacks, not based on coin.

Women delegates to the 1886 Knights of Labor convention. The smallest "delegate" was Lizzie Rodgers, daughter of Mrs. George Rodgers, mother of twelve. Housewives were eligible to join the Knights.

Mrs. Imogene C. Fales, president of the Sociologic Society of America in the 1880s, organized women to support unions and work for a new industrial system.

The Knights of Labor welcomed women. Susan B. Anthony, fighter for women's rights, and Frances Willard, temperance leader, were both members of the order; Mrs. Augusta Lewis Troup was a printing compositor and member of the Women's Typographical Union #1.

Mrs. Leonora O'Reilly was a child worker in New York's cellar factories. She joined the Knights of Labor at sixteen.

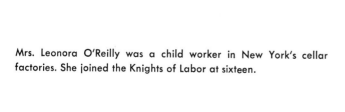

In the South, a summons to "fight" gained increasing support in rural areas of the nation. Leaders, such as Thomas E. Watson, later a Populist congressman, appealed, as C. Vann Woodward describes it, to the crisis laden. Watson said:

> To you who grounded your muskets twenty-five years ago I make my appeal. The fight is upon you—not bloody as then—but as bitter; not with men who came to free your slaves, but who come to make slaves of you. And to your sons also I call; and I would that the common spirit might thrill every breast throughout this sunny land, till from every cotton field, every hamlet, every village, every city, might come the shout of defiance to those Rob Roys of commerce and to the robber tariff, from whose foul womb they sprang."

In 1878, state and congressional elections were strongly influenced by the unity of farmers and workers. Fifteen candidates, representing the Greenback movement, were sent to Congress. The head of the Knights of Labor, Terence V. Powderly, himself was elected mayor of Scranton, Pennsylvania, on a Greenback-Labor ticket.

T. R. Allen, Master of Missouri.          Col John Cochrane, Master of Wisconsin.          S. H. Ellis, Master of Ohio.          F. H. Dumbauld, Master of Kansas.
John Weir, Master of Indiana.                              Mrs. J. C. Abbott, "Flora."                    Mrs. D. W. Adams, "Ceres."          C. D. Beeman, Gen'l Nat'l Deputy.
          Wm. Saunders, First Master, Nat'l Grange.          D. W. Adams, Master, Nat'l Grange.          O. H. Kelley, Secretary, Nat'l Grange.

SOME OF THE LEADING OFFICERS OF THE ORDER OF PATRONS OF HUSBANDRY.

The Knights of Labor cooperated closely with rural workers, such as the Patrons of Husbandry, who faced rising costs and falling prices. In 1869, wheat brought seventy-six cents a bushel; in 1894, the price was forty-nine cents a bushel. Each grange had certain offices called Flora and Ceres, to be filled only by women.

# SEVEN

# 1873-1886

# THE FOUNDING OF THE
# AMERICAN FEDERATION OF LABOR

*"Better to starve outright . . .*
*than to die by slow starvation."*

THE METROPOLITAN BANK SUSPENDS

Workingmen were realizing that labor unions were needed, and not merely locally based, but *national* unions—and even *federations* of unions.

But leaders were inexperienced, existing labor organizations were loosely built and, while dedicated to the cause of humanity, were not yet organized to serve the daily needs of working people. In addition, there were those recurring economic depressions that devastated the nation at irregular intervals, bankrupting small entrepreneurs and causing widespread unemployment and misery.

Few unions survived for long the ravages of such depressions. They simply fell apart and often had to

be rebuilt all over again when times were better. Those unions that survived were weakened as effective fighting instruments. On top of all this were the constant attacks leveled at labor unions—in newspapers, at legislative meetings, and through other means—by business interests.

By the 1870s powerful financial syndicates were in control of much of industry, especially the nation's all important coal fields. Coal corporations were just launching their policy of recruiting labor from overseas to work in the mines. Thousands of poverty-stricken working people from nations abroad, especially Slavs and Italians, were encouraged to come to

123

Italian immigrants were sometimes rushed into mine country when strikes were in progress and converted into strikebreakers.

America with promises of fortune-making as the lure.

These immigrants, usually uneducated, bewildered, and rapidly to be disillusioned, were herded into freight trains by the hundreds, bound for the coal fields. Such workers often replaced English-speaking miners, often members of labor organizations fighting to improve conditions. These miners, writes George Korson, "were compelled to give way in one coal field after another, either abandoning the industry altogether for other occupations or else retreating, like the vanishing American Indian, westward . . ."

The new arrivals in the mines were unable to read and often unable, because of language differences, to easily communicate with each other. They were, coal operators realized, unlikely to establish the fraternity among themselves that is the basis for unionism. At least for a while. This communication handicap, however, created serious immediate problems. Unable to read safety instructions, such workers faced constant hazards from violation of safety precautions, such as they were. Injuries and deaths in mine disasters, frequently reported in the newspapers, shocked the nation.

An example of the dangers surrounding work underground was vividly given by one miner who described how he was working with two others in a tunnel where they were going to sink a shaft.

I was up on a staging, and got down to ask one of the car men if I could ride his car out. With his assent, I started. A big rock on the front end of the car struck the first chute I came to, tipping it up so that my right hand got caught between the car and the bottom of the chute, getting badly mangled. My candle had been put out by the jolt, and I was left in total darkness. I groped my way back to where [a fellow miner] . . . was working in a crosscut. I called to him and he came out and walked with me to the doctor's office. . . . It was just a question of getting there somehow and keeping the bleeding hand from knocking against the wall as we went out . . .

Perhaps no area sustained greater deterioration of coal-mining conditions than Schuylkill County in

Life of a coal miner.

Pennsylvania in the 1870s, where twenty-two thousand coal miners labored underground. The daily routine of the miner was to crawl in the dim light of his lamp, in mud and trickling water, surrounded by coal dust and perhaps powder smoke.

There were early efforts to organize unions in the coal fields, providing a ray of hope for the men underground. Various early miners' songs expressed this:

> Step by step, the longest march
> Can be won, can be won;
> Single stones will form an arch,
> One by one, one by one.
> And, by union, what we will
> Can be all accomplished still.
> Drops of water turn a mill,
> Singly none, singly none.

But the struggle was a difficult one. When a miners' strike in the early 1870s under the leadership of the American Miners' Association was defeated, many of the workers, then largely Irish immigrants, turned—as a form of resistance—to their fraternal organization, the Ancient Order of Hibernians. The order eventually became associated, at least in reputation, with a group known as the Molly Maguires. Schuylkill County was rough country and when a series of violent murders occurred, blame was attached to the Molly Maguires.

Amid lurid newspaper sensationalism, leaders of the American Miners' Association and others, accused of being Mollys, were arrested and charged with the crimes. At the trial of the first group of accused unionists, Franklin B. Gowen, president of the leading coal company in the area, also acted as court prosecutor.

During the trial it was revealed that the Pinkerton Detective Agency was involved in the case, led by Allan Pinkerton, "originator of the business of labor spying," as Edward Levinson, a labor historian, put it. In summing up the case before the jury, the prosecutor stated that it is "almost inconceivable how this bad society has injured you and every property owner in the coal regions. . . . Capital . . . property . . . life, how everything has been imperiled . . ."

The accused men were found guilty, sentenced to death, and executed. During the years 1876 and 1877, trials of Molly Maguires were numerous throughout the region. It was usually enough to prove a man a member of the Ancient Order of Hibernians in order to find reasons for executing him.

"The facts show that there was much more terror waged against the Mollys than those illiterate Irishmen ever aroused," comments historian Aleine Austin.

Franklin B. Gowen himself was to state later: "The name of Molly Maguire being attached to a man's name is sufficient to hang him." The official record shows nineteen executions, although it is not possible to be accurate.

Allan Pinkerton, head of the private detective agency.

## LIST OF FUGITIVE MOLLIE MAGUIRES,
### 1879.

**WILLIAM LOVE.**—Murderer of Thos. Gwyther, at Girardville, Pa., August 14th, 1875. Is a miner and boatman; 26 years old; 5 ft. 9 in. high; medium build; weighs about 150 lbs.; light complexion; grey eyes; yellow hair; light mustache; has a scar from burn on left side of neck under chin, and coal marks on hands; thin and sharp features; generally dresses well. Lived at Girardville, Schuylkill Co., Pa.

**THOMAS HURLEY.**—Murderer of Gomer Jamas, August 14th, 1875. Is a miner; 25 years old; 5 ft. 8 in. high; well built; weighs about 160 lbs.; sandy complexion and hair; small piercing eyes; smooth face; sharp features; large hands and feet; wears black hat and dark clothes; lived at Shenandoah, Schuylkill Co., Pa.

**MICHAEL DOYLE.**—Murderer of Thomas Sanger and Wm. Uren, September 1st, 1875. Is a miner; 25 years old; 5 ft. 5 in. high; medium built; dark complexion; black hair and eyes; full round face and head; smooth face and boyish looking generally; wears a cap. Lived at Shenandoah.

**JAMES, ALIAS FRIDAY O'DONNELL.**—Murderer of Sanger and Uren, is 26 years old; 5 ft. 10½ in. high; slim built; fair complexion; smooth face; dark eyes; brown hair; generally wears a cap; dresses well; is a miner and lived at Wiggan's Patch, Pa.

**JAMES McALLISTER.**—Murderer of Sanger and Uren, is 27 years old; 5 ft. 8 in. high; stout built; florid complexion; full broad face, somewhat freckled; light hair and moustache; wears a cap and dark clothes, lived at Wiggan's Patch, Pa.

**JOHN, ALIAS HUMPTY FLYNN.**—Murderer of Thomas Devine, October 11th, 1875, and Geo. K. Smith, at Audenreid, November 5th, 1863. Is 53 years old; 5 ft. 7 or 8 in high; heavy built; sandy hair and complexion; smooth face; large nose; round shouldered and almost humpbacked. Is a miner and lived at New Philadelphia, Schuylkill Co., Pa.

**JERRY KANE.**—Charged with conspiracy to murder. Is 38 years old; 5 ft. 7 in. high; dark complexion; short brown hair; sharp features; sunken eyes; roman nose; coal marks on face and hands; wears black slouch hat; has coarse gruff voice. Is a miner and lived at Mount Laffee, Pa.

**FRANK KEENAN.**—Charged with conspiracy to murder. Is 31 years old; 5 ft. 7 in. high; dark complexion; black hair, inclined to curl and parted in the middle; sharp features; slender but compactly built; wears a cap and dark clothes. Is a miner and lived at Forrestville, Pa.

**WILLIAM GAVIN.**—Charged with conspiracy to murder. Is 42 year old; 5 ft. 8 in. high; sandy hair and complexion; stout built; red chin whiskers; face badly pock-marked; has but one eye; large nose; formerly lived at Big Mine Run, Pa. Is a miner. Wears a cap and dark clothes.

**JOHN REAGAN.**—Murderer of Patrick Burns at Tuscarora, April 15th, 1870. About 5 ft. 10 or 11 in. high; 40 years old; small goatee; stoop shouldered; dark hair, cut short; coal marks on hands and face; has a swinging walk; wears shirt collar open at the neck.

**THOMAS O'NEILL.**—Murderer of Patrick Burns, at Tuscarora, April 15th, 1870. About 5 ft. 9 in. high; 35 years old; light hair; very florid complexion; red moustache and think red goatee; stoop shouldered; walks with a kind of a jerk; think has some shot marks on back of neck and wounded in right thigh.

**PATRICK B. GALLAGHER, ALIAS PUG NOSE PAT.**—Murderer of George K. Smith, at Audenreid, November 5th, 1863. About 5 ft. 8 in. high; medium built; dark complexion and hair; latter inclined to curl; turned up nose; thick lips; wears a frown on his countenance; large coal cut across the temple; from 32 to 35 years old; has been shot in the thigh.

*Information may be sent to me at either of the above offices,*

**ALLAN PINKERTON.**

James (McKenna) McParlan was employed by the Pinkertons to spy on the Molly Maguires.

DUFFY'S FAREWELL TO HIS FAMILY AND FRIENDS.

FRIENDS OF THE CONDEMNED MEN AWAITING ADMITTANCE TO THE JAIL ON THE MORNING OF JUNE 21ST.

Interior of a cell; the gallows; the death march. Such tragic details of the Molly Maguires prosecutions were given lurid coverage in newspapers and magazines.

"What did they do?" asked the *Miners' Journal* of June 22, 1877, in reference to the Molly Maguires. "Whenever prices of labor did not suit them, they organized to proclaim a strike." Following the end of the last trial, an industrial spokesman declared: "Peace once more reigns in the anthracite coal regions. Mollie Maguireism is practically dead. The inhabitants of the anthracite coal regions are now enjoying the blessed peace which has recently come to them. God rules, justice must reign, and right must triumph."

some spokesmen for industry to assume that "labor is under control for the first time since the war," as the *Commerical and Financial Chronicle* put it in 1877. The words were scarcely written when one of the most explosive developments occurred in the entire history of American labor.

Those who worked on this country's railroads, by this time the largest industry in the nation, had suffered especially extreme deprivation. Wage cuts were frequent; the work week had been sharply curtailed; even the payment of the meager wages was often

Death on the rail. "When a workman was injured in shop, mine or on the railroad," a labor leader said, "the claim agent . . . would . . . present himself with an instrument of agreement for the injured man . . . to sign. By the terms of this instrument, the company would be released from all responsibility . . ."

"Impulsive strikes," they were called by one labor spokesman. This referred to the type of revolt by workers which was unorganized, spontaneous, and frequently lacking in discipline. As the fourth year of the depression of 1873 passed, the danger of such protests multiplied.

The fact that the organized labor movement was rendered helpless by economic conditions caused

delayed without explanation. There were, too, frequent rail catastrophies with attendant loss of life and limb.

Railroad workers, having to walk to work, usually lived near the railroad center itself, renting land owned by the railroads. Often the landlord exacted large rental. One report told how "track men of the Erie Road, who lived in shanties on land alongside

New Orleans unemployed wait for jobs.

the tracks where they raised little patches of potatoes and cabbages, were commanded suddenly by the company to pay ground rent of $20 to $25 a year or vacate the homes." Having no other place to go, most workers went deeply into debt.

Conductors were paid three dollars for a twelve-hour day. Locomotive engineers received the same remuneration, while railroad firemen were paid two dollars for twelve hours of work. Brakemen had the most dangerous jobs of all in the railroads. According to a railroad study by Peter Lyon,

They had to race along the narrow catwalk atop the swaying cars to spin the brake wheels on each car, a particularly zestful task in sleety weather. They had to stand between two cars being coupled so that they might steer link into socket and then let fall the pin that joined them, and this was tricky work, for in that instant when the two cars came together, a man could lose a finger, a hand or a life, and so the brake man with ten fingers was generally recognized as a new man on the job. The slaughter of brake men was fearful: hundreds killed and thousands maimed every year, during the 1870s, with no compensation for death or injuries and insurance rates priced out of sight.

"So long as brakes cost more than brake men," Dr. Lyman Abbott commented in 1874, "we may ex-

## RED WAR.

**Hostilities Fairly Begun in Chicago Yesterday Evening.**

**Desperate Contest Between Rioters and Police on Halsted Street.**

Details of the Protracted Combat---List of Dead and Wounded.

Morning Conflict Between Lieut. Vesey and a Lumber District Gang.

Broken Crowns on the North, South, and West Sides.

Obstructing the Street-Cars and Making Another Foray on the Factories.

Meeting of the Citizens---Addresses by Messrs. Swett, Colfyer, and Others.

The Council Meet and Pledge Themselves to Support the Authorities.

An Assembly of the Communists Sweetly Smashed by the Police.

Arrival of the Regulars---They are Greeted with Jubilant Cheers.

The Food Question---How the Railroads Are Situated---At the City-Hall.

**JULY 26, 1877**

A sensationalized newspaper clipping of the 1877 railroad strike.

pect the present sacrificial method of car coupling to be continued."

Nor were the unions among the railroad workers able to contend with these growing crises. Three railroad brotherhoods in existence, all of them newly formed, were without militant leadership. The Brotherhood of Railroad Conductors, as a matter of fact, forbade members to strike under penalty of expulsion.

Such was the situation in numerous railroad communities all over the country in the summer of 1877 when the president of the Baltimore and Ohio Railroad announced that all wages over one dollar a day would be cut 10 percent. This would bring weekly wages to something like five to six dollars a week. On the day when the new wage cut went into effect, there was a strange quiet in railroad centers.

The first sign of trouble was at Martinsburg, West Virginia, an important freight junction. Firemen abandoned their trains and large groups of sympathizers gathered together in their support. When city authorities arrested the leaders of the stoppage, their friends forced their release.

When the demonstration reached what was termed "alarming proportions," the governor of West Virginia, at the request of railroad officials, summoned the militia. However, the military, made up for the most part of relatives and friends of railroad workers, fraternized with the strikers. Two more companies of militia were dispatched. They, too, were ineffective.

"There is no disguising the fact," stated the *Baltimore Sun*, "that the strikers in all their lawful acts have the fullest sympathy of the community. . . . The singular part of the disturbance is in the very active part taken by the women, who are the wives and mothers of the firemen. They look famished and wild, and declare for starvation rather than have their people work for the reduced wages. Better to starve outright, say they, than to die by slow starvation."

The strike spread: Keyser, Grafton, Wheeling. Workers from the Chesapeake & Ohio Canal joined the strike. People demonstrated all along the railroad lines in protest. Strikes spread to Cumberland and Newark, Ohio. In Maryland, the governor called out the national guard. The first bloodshed took place at Camden Station where ten people in the crowd of sympathizers were shot. A three-day uprising took place in Baltimore with total casualties thirteen killed and fifty wounded. Even more violence was reported in the Pittsburgh area. "The inhabitants of Pittsburgh, including many businessmen, who felt that they were discriminated against in freight rates, were in accord with the strikers," writes the historian Samuel Yellen. Again the local militia fraternized with the strikers. A thousand troops were sent from Philadelphia. Some twenty persons were killed and twenty-nine seriously wounded. So great was the indignation of the people of the area that control of the city of Pittsburgh passed into the hands of the masses of the

An incident in the 1877 upheaval of railroad workers: the Sixth Regiment in Baltimore.

The city of Scranton, Pennsylvania, becomes a battleground between iron and coal company police and the strikers.

Robert Ammon, a youthful leader of the railroad strike, shown in a photograpic portrait and (opposite), in a contemporaneous magazine sketch, "directing the movements of the strikers" in Pittsburgh.

In Martinsburg, West Virginia, railroad strikers seek to remove strikebreakers.

Striking railroad workers.

Martin Irons, called the "leading spirit of the strike."

people, made up of the unemployed, the hungry, and strike sympathizers.

Still the strike spread! Altoona, Easton, Reading, Harrisburg, Johnstown, Bethlehem. Freight was tied up everywhere. In various communities, troops were instructed to fire into the crowd. Again there was resistance as troops were met with barrages of stones. Strike leaders were arrested and held without bail.

The strike spread to mining districts . . . to New York State . . . Rochester, Syracuse, Albany, Buffalo.

To demands for an increase in pay, or at least not a wage cut, William H. Vanderbilt, president of the New York Central, answered: "Although I may have my millions and they have the rewards of their daily toil, still we are about equal in the end."

Strikes spread far out from Michigan's lakefront, Fort Wayne, Chicago, Cincinnati, Saint Louis, Cleveland, on to the West Coast. On the Mississippi, steamers were stopped until captains granted seamen wage increases. Troops and warships were ordered to Washington for fear that public buildings might be taken over. President Rutherford B. Hayes issued

orders forbidding interference with the trains. He termed the demonstrations a rebellion against the government of the United States and threatened martial law.

Eventually the railway strike of 1877 was crushed. Leaders were blacklisted, pursued by railroad company agents, and hounded from their jobs for years.

There was a small minority voice that defended the strike: "It is certainly not my purpose," commented John Swinton, the journalist, "to lead any reader to suppose that the masses of men engaged in the various big strikes of recent times were all or always of quiet conduct. . . . Nor would I underestimate the amount of property destroyed in any case, probably by the strikers, but far more largely by the outside miscreants, who are sure to turn up in times of trouble, and to run amuck whenever an opportunity is offered. . . . There has been monstrous exaggeration by some of the press writers of the amount of violence and damage wrought by strikers in the strikes of recent times . . ."

Despite the horror and wastage of human life, a

Powderly addressing annual convention of the Knights of Labor.

consciousness of labor unity came about as a result of the conflict. Some labor unions that had been moribund came back to life. Among those that were helped by the new spirit was the Knights of Labor, even though it had not officially participated in the strike action. At the height of its influence, the order was made up of more than seven hundred thousand people. But the Knights were not destined to maintain influence for long. While the organization was involved in various sharply fought strikes, it was opposed to militancy. A developing movement for a shorter workday also failed to win the support of the order's conservative leadership. The strenuous times seemed to call for youthful, decisive action; leaders of the Knights were neither youthful nor decisive.

On the other hand, there were new and vigorous voices being raised within the ranks of labor. "The railroad strike of 1877 was the tocsin that sounded a ringing message of hope to us all," said Samuel Gompers, immigrant cigar maker, one of the young leaders of a new labor movement about to be born. This movement had its start at a conference in Pittsburgh in 1881, attended by some one hundred representatives of iron and steelworkers, coopers, cotton and wool spinners, cigar makers, and others. The result of the gathering was the creation of the Federation of Organized Trades and Labor Unions of the United States and Canada, made up for the most part of

John Swinton, liberal journalist.

Terence V. Powderly, a machinist, joined the Knights of Labor in 1874 in Scranton, Pennsylvania, succeeding Uriah Stevens as general master workman five years later. *Courtesy Chicago Historical Society*

J. W. Hayes, grand secretary-treasurer, Knights of Labor.

A BOY-COTT IS A RED HOT BED OF REBELLION AGAINST OUR AMERICAN INSTITUTIONS

James R. Sovereign of Iowa, successor to Powderly.

A.F. of L. early banner with insignia.

struggle is going on in all of the civilized world between oppressors and oppressed of all countries, between capitalist and laborer . . ." While the Knights of Labor and the federation were equally militant as far as their preambles were concerned, they were a world apart on most other issues. This rendered harmony between the two organizations difficult. "Talk of harmony with the Knights of Labor is bosh," Gompers wrote to a fellow union official. "They will not cooperate with a 'mere trades union,' as they call our organization . . ."

skilled workers. The basis for the new unionism was the need felt for separate organizations of workers employed in the same trade or calling.

Where the Knights of Labor was one mammoth organization, embracing almost anyone who cared to join, the new federation was oriented toward craft unions almost exclusively. Where the order was wedded to a broad idealism, the new federation was business-like and pragmatic. Where the Knights of Labor was loosely organized (admitting even physicians and employers) and nourished the hope of "changing the system," the closely knit federation developed a "philosophy of pure wage consciousness," as the historian Selig Perlman put it. Gompers insisted that the new federation "must be exclusively wage earners."

Five years after the federation was founded, it reorganized as the American Federation of Labor with Gompers as president and a preamble that began: "A

The formation of the A.F. of L. is announced.

## THE FEDERATION OF LABOR

### TRADES UNIONISTS FORM A NEW ORGANIZATION.

#### THE KNIGHTS OF LABOR IGNORED AND A CONSTITUTION FOR THE NEW BODY ADOPTED—OFFICERS ELECTED.

COLUMBUS, Ohio, Dec. 11.—It will doubtless prove a trifle galling to Terence Vincent Powderly and his old Executive Board to learn that the trades unionists, who have been in session here for the best part of a week, have elected as President of their new organization, the American Federation of Labor, Samuel Gompers, the man he so vilified in the "secret" circular that was printed in to-day's TIMES. The fact that Mr. Gompers was elected without opposition may give Mr. Powderly an idea of the estimation in which he is held by trades unionists.

The latter are now prepared to go their own way. They did not invite interference or opposition in the first place, and if Mr. Powderly's lieutenants with his knowledge had not abused their powers so grossly there would be peace to-day between organizations that are now rivals. The new organization has no fear of the Knights, for its membership was in existence long before they were thought of. It begins life with 25 trades unions as a nucleus. There is reason to suppose that as many more will join the fold before another convention is held. Its primary object is to secure as members every trade and labor union in the country, and some of the steps it has taken to attain this object show the shrewdness of the builders.

Heretofore the Knights have been enabled to enroll all the workers in small communities. A glance at the Federation's constitution will show that such a field will no longer be left exclusively to the "noble order." The Knights have been enabled to secure many members by a promise of general assistance in case of a strike or lockout. Such assistance has proved by experience but a broken reed. The Federation's

A Knights of Labor union card and Samuel Gompers's union card. Samuel Gompers was a member of the Cigar Makers' local union 144, and first president of the American Federation of Labor, 1886.

Gompers, a man of small stature but tremendous energy, believed that there was need for a new form of labor organization fundamentally built on attention to the *economic needs* of its members in various trades and crafts. He tried from the start to keep the federation close to principles of "pure and simple" trade unionism. The organization's goals were indeed simple. Instead of the slogan of the Knights of Labor, "An injury to one is the concern of all," the federation put forward the motto, "A fair day's wage for a fair day's work."

From the start, the new federation was aggressive in thought and action. It believed in strikes when necessary. It demanded control of wealth, which was "concentrating itself into fewer hands." It believed in

Adolph Strasser, president of the Cigar Makers' International Union, was a leader in the founding of the A.F. of L.

Samuel Gompers

"compulsory education laws . . . prohibition of labor of children under 14 years . . . sanitation and safety provisions for factories . . . repeal of all conspiracy laws . . . a National Bureau of Labor Statistics . . . protection of American industry against cheap foreign labor . . . Chinese exclusion . . ."

The new federation also believed in ties with labor of other nations. Frank K. Foster, secretary of the federation, reported to the 1884 convention that "the labor question is practically the same the world over . . . and the laborers of the world should clasp hands for their common weal." Later Gompers was to add: "The working people know no country. They are citizens of the world."

Dramatically important at the moment, the leaders of the federation, unlike those of its declining rival, the Knights of Labor, were staunchly in favor of the eight-hour day. And indeed, the eight-hour movement was the issue of the day.

Leaders of the Knights of Labor believed that the demand for a shorter workday was too impractical. The younger organization thus took over the leader-

Peter J. McGuire, first general secretary of the Brotherhood of Carpenters and first A.F. of L. secretary, is generally credited with being first to propose the idea of Labor Day. At first marching in a Labor Day parade was grounds for dismissal.

ship of the movement. At its convention in Chicago in 1884, the federation resolved that "eight hours shall constitute a legal day's labor from and after May 1, 1886, and that we recommend to labor organizations throughout this jurisdiction that they so direct their laws as to conform to this resolution by the time named." Gabriel Edmonston, president of the Brotherhood of Carpenters, also urged a series of national demonstrations toward this end. The federation invited the Knights to join them in the crusade, but without avail.

"It is evident that our members are not properly instructed, else we would not find them passing resolutions 'approving of the action of our executive officers in fixing the first of May as the day to strike for eight hours,'" Terence V. Powderly declared.

The executive officers of the Knights of Labor have never fixed upon the first of May for a strike of any kind, and they will not do so until the proper time arrives and the word goes forth from the General Assembly. No assembly of the Knights of Labor must strike for the eight-hour system on May first under the impression that they are obeying orders from headquarters for such an order was not, and will not, be given. Neither employer or employee are educated to the needs and necessities for the short-hour plan.

Matthew Maguire, secretary of the New York Central Labor Union in 1882, a machinist, is also credited with first proposing the idea of Labor Day.

Gabriel Edmonston, first general president of the Brotherhood of Carpenters and first A.F. of L. treasurer, sponsored the A.F. of L. proposal that "eight hours shall constitute a legal day's labor from and after May 1, 1886 . . . ," which resulted in the worldwide marking of May Day as a labor holiday.

The new A.F. of L. was primarily interested in organizing skilled workers into craft unions.

THE INTERNATIONAL UNION OF
JOURNEYMEN HORSESHOERS

JHU

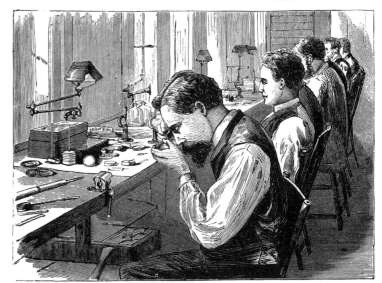

John Jarrett, president of the Amalgamated Association of Iron and Steel Workers; first president of Federation (1881).

Frank K. Foster, president of the Cambridge Typographical Union; Federation secretary (1881).

Thomas I. Kidd, general secretary of the Amalgamated Woodworkers International Union; A.F. of L. vice-president; a founder of the Labor-Populist Alliance of Illinois.

Robert Howard, secretary of the Cotton Spinners' Union; Massachusetts state senator (1885); Federation treasurer (1881).

Opposition to the eight-hour movement was further reflected in newspaper accounts, one New York daily stating: "Strikes to enforce the demand for eight hours work a day may do much to paralyze industry, depress business, and check the reviving prosperity of the country, but they cannot succeed."

Nevertheless, the federation was determined to summon a national demonstration in favor of the eight-hour day, both to be won legislatively as well as directly from local employers.

Frank K. Foster of the Typographical Union proposed a "universal strike for a working day of eight (or nine) hours to take effect not later than May 1, 1886."

The proposals were accepted by the federation.

Despite the fact that cooperation from the Knights of Labor was impossible, plans proceeded for the May 1 demonstration for a shorter workday. It was to develop implications far beyond anything its proposers could have imagined.

# EIGHT

# 1886-1892

# THE LABOR STRUGGLE
# AGAINST HUMAN EXPLOITATION

*"The Haymarket bomb in Chicago
destroyed our eight hour movement."*

While the call of the Federation of Organized Trades and Labor Unions for a strike in support of the eight-hour day was not endorsed by Knights of Labor leaders, the proposal met with a favorable response from working people, particularly in the large cities.

One call to action in Pittsburgh, Pennsylvania, declared:

The most pressing duty devolves upon all Working Men themselves . . . to unite with this motto of their programme:

*Eight Hours for Work
Eight Hours for Recreation, Rest
Eight Hours for Sleep . . .*

The introduction of the Eight Hour Standard Working Day would be only a small installment towards our full claims . . . for our eternal and inalienable rights of manhood.

The eight-hour movement spread not only through unions but through activities of eight-hour leagues that seemed to spring up everywhere.

On May 1, 1886, almost 350,000 workers took part in eight-hour-day demonstrations in Milwaukee, Saint Louis, Cincinnati, Washington, Baltimore, New York, Philadelphia, Boston, and other cities. In Chicago alone, 80,000 workers demonstrated. As an immediate result about 185,000 workers gained a shorter workday.

## WORKMEN'S HOLIDAY

### How May 1 Was Observed Throughout the Country.

### MANY BIG DEMONSTRATIONS.

### Everything Passes Off Peaceably and Without the Slightest Friction.

### DEMANDING AN EIGHT-HOUR DAY.

### Carpenters Inaugurate Strikes in Several of the Large Cities.

### AWAITING THE OUTCOME IN CHICAGO.

LOUISVILLE, Ky., May 1.—[Special.]—The greatest parade of organized labor ever seen in Louisville took place today. There were about 14,000 men in line representing every craft employed in this city. President Gompers of the National Federation of Labor rode with the local labor leaders in the line. The procession marched to National Park, where addresses were made by Judge Sterling, B. Tony, and President Gompers.

The carpenters today made a demand for eight hours. If the demand is refused the carpenters' strike will be inaugurated tomorrow.

cago area, was the violent rhetoric of a group of militant social revolutionaries within labor's ranks. Disillusioned with ballot-box irregularities and embittered against the system as a whole, these militant unionists had come under anarchistic influences, particularly that of Johann Most. This advocate of "propaganda of the deed" had come to America six years earlier after expulsion from the German Socialist party. At that time, the socialist movement in America was divided. There were those who believed in political action and trade unionism as a means of social progress, and those who, impatient with the slowness of these methods, were turning to violent tactics as a means of "arousing the masses."

While not much evidence was available of specific instances of actual violence, the radical grouping used much revolutionary rhetoric. These "heated phrases" supplied antilabor sources with "proof" of the violent nature of unionism, even though American labor, traditionally, did not look with favor on the use of organized force and violence.

Prior to the May 1 eight-hour demonstrations, particularly in Chicago, newspapers had given considerable attention to the militant speeches of certain social revolutionaries who, it was said, "represented a real threat of anarchy." This had caused tension in the city for fear that the eight-hour demonstrations might result in violent actions. Such was not the case. The eight-hour activity passed peacefully and without incident.

Nevertheless, despite the lack of violence, "The newspapers . . . ," states the biographer Charles A. Madison, "reported each strike or labor disturbance as if it were the first blow for the social revolution."

The fact was, as Professor Henry David reports in his study of the era, "The dreaded May 1 came, passed and left Chicago altogether unmarked. Despite the excitement which pervaded the city, the 'apprehension of serious trouble,' and the parades and demonstrations, the day passed in utter peace . . ."

The eight-hour movement was obviously gaining momentum, both in actions by state legislatures and direct gains from employers. Effects of the depression of 1884 were also easing, creating hope for the alleviation of other labor problems.

But there were those, some in positions of influence, who believed the security of the country was endangered by such labor gains. "Strikes may have been justifiable in other nations," wrote Henry Clews, a financial writer of the 1880s, "but are not justifiable in our country."

A conservative law journal observed: "Strikes as now managed are notoriously lawless, reckless and dangerous conspiracies against the public peace . . ."

Contributing to such alarm, especially in the Chi-

Johann Most

The first Labor Day parade in New York City, September 5, 1882.

However, two days after the demonstration, on May 3, violence did occur in Chicago at a strike that followed a lockout at the McCormick Harvesting Works.

The strike was bitter. Use of strikebreakers with police intervention had resulted in violence, the death of one striker, and serious injury to many more. Enraged by the incident, several militant Chicago labor leaders hastily summoned a protest "call to arms" meeting for the following evening, May 4, at Chicago's Haymarket Square.

The Haymarket meeting was not well attended,

# Secret Circular.

## Noble Order
#### OF THE
## KNIGHTS OF LABOR
### OF AMERICA.

PHILADELPHIA, PA., March 13, 1886.

The Recording Secretary will, on receipt of this circular, place it in the hands of the Master Workman, whose duty it shall be to issue a red-letter call for a full meeting, either regular or special, have a full attendance, and read it. Its extreme length must be excused, for I cannot go to each Assembly to speak on the present CRISIS, and take this method of reaching them.

An order was recently issued to suspend organization of new Assemblies for forty days. It did not go out until a careful review of the field had been taken. Had I not been convinced that it was absolutely necessary for the salvation of the Order, my vote would not be cast in favor of a cessation of the work.

One of the gravest emergencies that ever faced a human being stands squarely before the head of this Order to-day. It is not coming—*it is here*—and it must be firmly dealt with. Before taking another step in any direction I want to go before the great mass of our membership, through the medium of this circular—ask of them to speak to me as frankly as I now talk to them—and tell me what is best to be done. If the Order is to perform its mission as intended by its founders, and those who have worked with it from the beginning, a radical change must be effected, a stop must be called, and the ship brought back to her moorings. It has always been, and is at the present time, my policy to advocate conciliation and arbitration in the settlement of disputes between employer and employee. The law of knighthood demands at the hands of our members an adherence to that policy. Thousands of men, who had become disgusted with the ruinous policy of the strike as the only remedy for the ills we complain of, were drawn to us because we proclaimed to mankind that we had discarded the strike until all else had failed. The men and women who flock to our standard have a knowledge of their wrongs. They have endured these wrongs for years, and in reason are duty bound to learn how to right these wrongs by the least expensive and most satisfactory, as well as lasting, remedy. Six months will not teach men our principles and proper methods, yet men are impressed with the idea that they can learn them in six weeks or six days, and before the ground-work for a proper education is laid we find our Assemblies on strike or locked out, and in too many cases the provocation came from their own hasty and inconsiderate action. No matter what advantage we gain by the strike, it is only medicating the symptoms; it does not penetrate the system, and therefore fails in effecting a cure. The only natural sequence is a relapse, and a relapse alw... ...and a weaker patient than...

...is letter to th... ...I will ever write to you.

...he n... ...l cents. My policy

...nights of Labor

...s and

The "secret circular" of 1886 from Terence V. Powderly against strikes.

partly as the result of poor weather. Toward its conclusion, the rain increased, threatening to disperse even the few hundred spectators who had not yet left. At that point, a contingent of police arrived. The last speaker, Samuel Fielden, an organizer of the International Working People's Association, was concluding his remarks. The captain of the police ordered: "I command you, in the name of the People of the State of Illinois, to immediately and peaceably disperse." From the platform, which was a small wagon, Fielden replied: "We are peaceable."

At that moment, someone whose identity was never disclosed threw a bomb killing seven police officers, four workers, and injuring scores.

Hysteria and anger fused in the national convulsion that followed. The threat of "anarchy" had proved accurate. Sensational newspaper headlines made it clear that the guilty were obviously those revolutionaries who had been talking so loudly of force and violence. Among those arrested were eight social revolutionaries in the Chicago area. They included Albert R. Parsons, an American-born printer who evidently

**Attention Workingmen!**

**GREAT**

# MASS-MEETING

**TO-NIGHT, at 7.30 o'clock,**

**AT THE**

**HAYMARKET, Randolph St., Bet. Desplaines and Halsted.**

Good Speakers will be present to denounce the latest atrocious act of the police, the shooting of our fellow-workmen yesterday afternoon.

**Workingmen Arm Yourselves and Appear in Full Force!**

THE EXECUTIVE COMMITTEE

## Achtung, Arbeiter!

**Große**

## Massen-Versammlung

**Heute Abend, ½8 Uhr, auf dem**

**Neumarkt,** Randolph-Straße, zwischen Desplaines- u. Halsted-Str.

☞ Gute Redner werden den neuesten Schurkenstreich der Polizei, em sie gestern Nachmittag unsere Brüder erschoß, geißeln,

☞ Arbeiter, bewaffnet Euch und erscheint massenhaft!

Das Executiv-Comite.

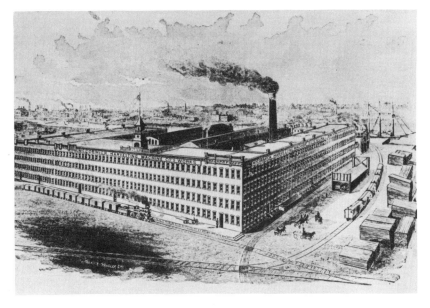

The McCormick Harvesting Works, Chicago, built in 1873, where the Haymarket affair had its beginning.

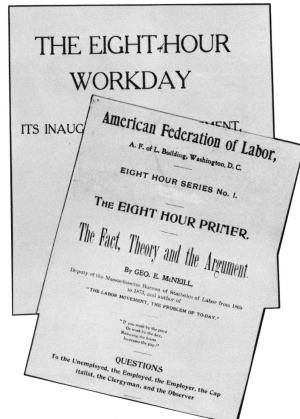

THE EIGHT-HOUR WORKDAY

ITS INAUG...

American Federation of Labor,

A. F. of L. Building, Washington, D. C.

EIGHT HOUR SERIES No. I.

THE EIGHT HOUR PRIMER.

The Fact, Theory and the Argument.

By GEO. E. McNEILL.

Deputy of the Massachusetts Bureau of Statistics of Labor from 1869 to 1873, and author of "THE LABOR MOVEMENT, THE PROBLEM OF TO-DAY."

"If you work by the piece Or work by the day, Reducing the hours Increases the pay."

QUESTIONS

To the Unemployed, the Employed, the Employer, the Capitalist, the Clergyman, and the Observer

One artist's conception of the Haymarket meeting.

1 Spot where Bomb Struck.  2. Point from which Bomb was Thrown.  3. Wagon In which Speaker Stood.  4. Desplaines Street.  5. Market Square.  6. Desplaines Street Police Station.

The Haymarket scene the day after.

believed so firmly in political action that he had recently been a candidate for Chicago alderman as a
socialist; August Spies, an editor of a radical newspaper; Samuel Fielden, George Engel, Adolph
Fischer, Michael Schwab, Oscar Neebe, and Lewis
Lingg, all involved, in one form or another, in radical
activities in the Chicago area.

At the trial, while it was proved that six of the
defendants had not even been present at the meeting
at the time of the explosion, their inflammatory rhetoric was used to prove that, if they did not throw
the bomb, they were capable of doing so, even of
offering encouragement for such deeds.

During the course of the trial, various labor organizations throughout the country called for mercy
for the accused. The youthful American Federation
of Labor adopted a resolution to this effect. "It was a
shocking story of official prejudice," said Gompers.
"Though the more even balanced rank and file does

not approve of the radical wing, yet they cannot
safely abandon the radicals to the vengeance of the
common enemies."

The Knights of Labor leaders, however, did not
join the defense movement. "Let it be understood by
all the world," Terence V. Powderly declared, "that
the Knights of Labor have no affiliation, association,
sympathy or respect for the band of cowardly mur-
derers, cut-throats and robbers known as anarchists . . ."

Numerous prominent citizens expressed concern
about the innocence of the accused. William Dean
Howells, the famous novelist, said: "I have never believed them guilty of murder, or of anything but their
opinions . . ." Henry Demarest Lloyd, the social critic,
wrote: "I have always had a doubt as to whether
the bomb was thrown by an anarchist at all . . ."

Professor Henry David observed: "Only . . . John
Swinton's paper retained some measure of sanity.

The trial of the accused men.

Four of the eight accused: Albert R. Parsons, Michael Schwab, Samuel Fielden, and August Spies. Parsons, Spies, George Engel, Louis Lingg, and Adolph Fischer were executed. Fielden, Schwab, and Oscar Neebe were imprisoned.

. . . This labor journal dared place much of the blame for the Haymarket bomb on the police." The bomb, said Swinton, was "a godsend to the enemies of the labor movement."

While a growing number of people sought justice for the accused men, the state's attorney urged the jury to "convict these men, make examples of them, hang them, and you save our institutions . . ."

In his final speech before the court, one defendant, August Spies, declared:

They thought eight hours hard toil a day for scarcely two hours' pay was enough. This "lawless rabble" had to be silenced! The only way to silence them was to frighten them, and murder those whom they looked up to as their leaders . . .

Now, these are my ideas. They constitute a part of myself. I cannot divest myself of them, nor would I, if I could. And if you think that you can crush out these ideas that are gaining ground more and more every day; if you think you can crush them out by sending us to the gallows; if you would once more have people suffer the penalty of death because they have dared to tell the truth . . . I say if death is the penalty for

# A. R. PARSONS' APPEAL
## TO THE PEOPLE OF AMERICA.

# APPEAL FOR AID.

## NOBLE ORDER
### OF THE
## KNIGHTS OF LABOR
### OF AMERICA

*Office of the General Secretary-Treasurer.*

PHILADELPHIA, September 10, 1886.

*To the Order Wherever Found, Greeting :*

The General Executive Board have received numerous requests recently for permission to appeal to the Order for assistance, caused by the large number of lock-outs and strikes which the members have been forced into since the special session of the General Assembly. Curtailing the power of Locals and Districts to strike seems to have had the opposite effect to what was intended with manufacturers and corporations, who have systematically locked our members out, and refused them employment unless they leave the Knights of Labor. When these firms and corporations have been approached by the members of the General Executive Board, with a view to arbitrate the difficulty, they were either insulted or arbitration positively refused.

We have at present on our hands the lock-out of the Augusta, Ga., cotton factories, where 3,000 of our members have been denied the right to work because 12 men, who were getting only 81 cents per day, asked for an advance of 15 per cent. in wages. The mill presidents of the Southern States combined, and said none of our employees shall work until these 12 men return to work at the price we have fixed, and leave the Order. They have now been out nine weeks. (L. A. 5030.)

The tanners and curriers of Salem and Peabody, Mass., requested a reduction of hours for a day's work, from 72 to 59 hours, when they were immediately locked out and refused work unless they leave the Knights of Labor. Nearly 3,000 have been involved in this struggle for the past eight weeks. (D. A. 77.)

The morocco-leather workers, of Wilmington, Del., asked for an advance of wages, or that the matter be submitted to arbitration, which was refused. These members have been out four months. (D. A. 94.)

The miners of Timberline, Mont., were locked out because they had organized an Assembly, and were refused employment until they renounced the organization by the Northern Pacific Coal Company. These members have been out seven weeks. (D. A. 98.)

The miners of Scott Haven, Pa., also were locked out for similar cause as above. (D. A. 80.)

The mill men of the McCullough Iron Company, Northeast, Md., (L. A. 5862,) asked for an advance of wages, which, after a five weeks' struggle, was acceded to as being just and proper. The manager of the company agreed to the advance and promised not to discriminate against the parties participating in the strike.

proclaiming the truth, then I will proudly and defiantly pay the costly price! Call your hangman!

Albert R. Parsons addressed the court at length along somewhat similar lines:

The great commercial stock centers were convulsed with apprehensions of a swift decline in values if the eight hour strike succeeded. . . . Something must be done to stop this movement, and it was felt that its strongest impulse was at the west, where 40,000 men were on a strike for eight hours in the City of Chicago . . .

I believe it was instigated by eastern monopolists to produce public sentiment against popular movements, especially the eight-hour movement then pending, and that some of the Pinkertons were their tools to execute the plan . . . I cannot accept a commutation to imprisonment. I appeal not for mercy but for justice.

While the effort to save the lives of the condemned Haymarket defendants continued up to the last, it was of no avail. Of the eight men brought to trial, seven were condemned to execution. One was sentenced to imprisonment. As a result of the wave of protest, three had their sentences commuted to life imprisonment. Four, including Albert R. Parsons, were executed on November 11, 1887. Six years later, two of the surviving Haymarket prisoners (one hav-

Illinois Governor John P. Altgeld issued a pardon years later to the surviving Haymarket prisoners on the grounds that they had not been given a fair trial. "It is an axiom of the law," said Altgeld, "that mere talk, no matter how abusive, does not constitute a crime."

Mrs. Lucy Parsons, wife of Albert R. Parsons, as a young woman when she began her efforts to free her husband; and many years later still active in an effort to prove his innocence.

A statue erected with funds from contributions by businessmen in honor of the police victims of the Haymarket tragedy. The statue was beset by misfortune. A streetcar knocked it down in 1920; in 1969, the statue was dynamited.

*On the statue base:* IN THE NAME OF THE PEOPLE OF ILLINOIS I COMMAND PEACE

ing committed suicide) were granted unconditional pardon by Governor John P. Altgeld of Illinois.

Although no branch of organized labor had been officially involved the night of the Haymarket tragedy, the development had a depressing effect on the movement for a shorter workday and general amelioration of labor's ills. "The Haymarket bomb in Chicago," said Gompers, "destroyed our eight hour movement."

Actually, it did not destroy the movement, but it did set it back for years to come. Not only did public sentiment turn against labor because of its seeming connection with violence, but many union members —having no taste for such tactics—tended to lose their enthusiasm for labor organizations. The Haymarket affair did not for long damage the forward movement of the young American Federation of Labor. But it did—together with failure to win important strike struggles—remove the Knights of Labor from the scene as an effective labor organization.

After Haymarket, repressive measures against la-

bor increased. Antiunion detectives, spies, ironclad antiunion oaths, use of courts, troops, injunctions—all multiplied. One especially effective antiunion technique was the fostering of bigotry and prejudice.

Black working people were sometimes imported from the South to replace striking Pennsylvania miners. Chinese were transported to America from their native communities to serve as cheap labor, frequently building the railroads. A brutal attack on Chinese workers took place in 1877 in San Francisco. Unemployed native Americans fanned the flames of anti-Chinese sentiment in a crusade to eliminate "cheap Chinese labor." The result was racially motivated disturbances with many casualties.

Prejudices against Irish and Hungarian immigrants, as well as others, often weakened possibilities of union organization, especially in the coal fields.

There were, indeed, instances where human sympathies outweighed bias. One miner's song illustrated this:

*On Chewsday last week as I laid on the sofa*
*Me backbone was sore, for that day I worked hard,*
*When in came the woman and sez to me, "Dinny,*
*There's a Hungarian man wants you in the yard."*
*Well, I pulled on me boots and went out in the garden,*
*There stood John Shalonsky; sez he as he smiled,*
*"I want yerself and the woman on next Sunday morning*
*To come to the Duck Pond and stand for me child."*

*Well, I tried to refuse but he'd take no excuse,*
*For Hungarians are divils whene'er they get riled;*
*The woman says no, but sez I, "Yes, we'll go*
*On next Sunday morning and stand for the child."*

*When Sunday came round, sure I dressed in my latest,*
*Shirt, necktie and collar and brand new black suit;*
*And me wife, Mary Ann, in her silk and her ribbons,*
*Faith, Old Jay Gould's daughter ne'er looked so cute,*
*Well, we christened the child and it cost five dollars,*
*When I handed it over, the clergyman smiled,*
*And sez he, "You're the first Far Down e'er come from*
*   Ireland*
*To stand for a Slavish Hungarian man's child."*

However, many English-speaking miners continued to resent their foreign-born co-workers, who spoke a strange language, and adhered to what appeared to be bizarre customs of dress and manner. This bias against immigrants, often encouraged by those who opposed the fraternity that breeds labor unionism, also showed itself in jeering, mockery, and other forms of intimidation.

Incited by attacks from newspapers and public speakers, English-speaking miners sometimes even stoned newly arrived immigrants when they dared leave their home surroundings. One newspaper contributed to this by stating that "foreigners feed upon the coarsest, cheapest and roughest fare . . . stalk about in rags and filth . . . and are neither fit associates for American laborers and mechanics nor reputable members of any society."

Anti-Chinese prejudice was largely based upon the fear that the Chinese might take the jobs of native workers.

Many Chinese laborers were imported to help in the construction of American railroads.

Jay Gould may have had this in mind when he declared he could "hire one-half of the working class to kill the other half."

Such attacks grew in vehemence and violence in periods of economic depression, which, at intervals, wrought havoc on the job market. Sometimes the influence of a depression lasted for a decade or more.

The result was savage competition for whatever jobs were available. Worker was pitted against worker for employment. Men were tempted to lose their self-respect as they, in desperation, often agreed to wage cuts and inhuman working hours to hold on to their jobs.

As agents of commercial interests continued to recruit foreign laborers, the number of immigrants to America increased. Emma Lazarus in 1883 wrote of the "huddled masses" arriving in the New World, "yearning to breathe free." As new workers arrived,

Racial and religious bigotry served the purpose of spreading suspicion and disunity.

ROMAN CATHOLICS DISGRACING THEMSELVES

A cartoon of the day represented a labor official
issuing orders.

REMINISCENCE OF ST. PATRICK'S DAY.
"Arrah, thin, it's a great pity yer not alive this day to see how yer descindents honor yer memory!"

Black workers were recruited in the South to enter mines, sometimes when strikes were in progress.

157

# HURRAH!

### FOR THE

## Working Men of New York!

In consequence of the success of the Working Men of New York in obtaining recognition of the necessity of shortening the hours of labor, we the Working Men of Pittsburgh, Pennsylvania, are induced to issue the following address to the whole body of Working Men of the United States, in accordance with the address of the New York Cabinet Makers to their fellow workmen:—

1. The accumulation of capital in ever fewer and fewer hands produces this result,—that the labor market is thereby overstocked.

2. Through the invention as well as the improvement of machinery, it comes to pass, that a large number of workmen with the present long hours of labor remain unemployed; of which fact many a struggling father of a family in the City of New York and other cities must be sufficiently convinced.

3. One class of men is not created, merely to procure the enjoyments of life for others; and the predominance of one class procured by the abasement of another class, is not in accordance with natural freedom.

4. The emancipation of the Working Class, however, must be won through the means of the working class itself.

5. The Congress of the United States some time since adopted the wise resolution that the working day for all employed in the government workshops should consist of eight hours.

In view of these facts, the most pressing duty devolves upon all Working Men themselves and upon those who come after them, to unite, with this for the motto of their programme:

## Eight Hours for Work,
## Eight Hours for Recreation, Rest,
## Eight Hours for Sleep.

An 1872 appeal for shorter hours.

resentment and fear increased. From such feelings grew political organization dedicated to hatred for the foreign born, especially the Irish and German Catholics.

The antiforeign movement prior to the Civil War called itself the Native American party, but became more popularly known as the Know-Nothing party, because of its members' refusal to publicly divulge its activities.

The roots of this native America movement remained long after the Know-Nothing movement disappeared. Incidents of hatred for national or racial groups were commonplace. So strong was the feeling for a time that the several hundred operatives in the weaving rooms of a Lowell, Massachusetts, mill struck and left the building because the company had put into their room an Irish washerwoman to scrub the floor. "They were native Americans and would not stand that," said one commentator.

Some unions realized the danger implicit in prejudice. "American mechanics," one labor publication warned, "recollect that you must unite as mechanics and as mechanics only. . . . The feeling of animosity which exists against foreign mechanics was originally started by employers to distract your attention from measures of importance . . . which would ultimately prove of real practical benefit to you."

Somewhat similar bias, and for somewhat similar reasons, developed toward the southern black worker. Numerous unions in the post-Civil War era barred

After Haymarket the weakening of unions left many working people without economic protection. Joblessness increased.

An Act to provide for the formation of Trade Union under the provisions of Article twenty-six of the Code of Public General Laws of this State, as the same was enacted by the act of eighteen hundred and sixty-eight. Chapter Four hundred and seventy-one and under the supplements thereto, and to define the powers of the Corporations so authorized to be formed.

Section 1 Be it enacted by the General Assembly of Maryland, That any five or more persons, Citizens of the United States, a majority of whom are Citizens of this State, who are engaged in the same occupation, or employment, or in similar occupations or employment, may organize and form as a corporation to be known as a "Trade Union" with such additions to the said name as they may adopt and set forth in their certificate, to promote the well being of their every day life, and for mutual assistance in securing the most favorable Conditions for the labor of its members, and as a Beneficial Society under the provisions of Article twenty-six of the Code of Public General Laws of this State, as the same was enacted by the Act of eighteen hundred and sixty-eight Chapter four hundred and seventy-one and its supplements in the manner in which other Corporations provided for in said Act are authorized to be formed; Each of said Trade Unions so organized and found as a corporation, shall possess all the powers and be subject to all the regulations, in said Act and in its supplements contained, affecting Beneficial Societies, or associations, authorized to be incorporated under the provisions of said Act and its supplements.

Approved this Eighth day of April 1884

Robert M. Lane
Governor

Henry Lloyd
President of the Senate

Speaker of the House of Delegates.

A reproduction of Maryland law, passed in 1884, officially recognizing the status of a trade union "to promote the well being of [citizens'] every day life . . ."

black workers from their ranks, but not without frequent discussion and differences of opinion. The birth of the National Labor Union in 1866 struck hard at anti-Negro prejudice.

The Knights of Labor continued to educate against discrimination, convinced that equal concern for all was necessary for effective unionism. One Negro member of the Knights of Labor wrote to his fellow white workers urging them to end habits of discrimination: "Take the colored man by the hand and convince him by actual fact that you will be true to him and not a traitor to your pledge . . . for there are not under heaven men in whose breasts beat truer hearts than in the breast of the Negro."

However, the demise of the NLU and the Knights of Labor marked also a loss of emphasis on certain aspects of unionism, available to all regardless of skill, sex, color, and other distinguishing traits. More specialized craft interests, perhaps an inevitable reaction to the impractical loose organization of its predecessors, was to be a feature of the American Federation of Labor structure.

The early A.F. of L. did not draw the color line, but expressed an "ideal of solidarity irrespective of race." Before long, however, the feeling changed. Whether a tendency to exclude black workers from craft unions was based more on fear of competition or racial prejudice carried over from slave days, it is difficult to decide. But the developing exclusion of the Negro worker from many unions brought with it serious problems—not just for the black worker seeking job security, but for the white worker seeking the same end.

Black workers of the South were continually encouraged by industry to leave the poverty-stricken, strife-torn Southland and to come north to work at lower wages than white workers. Sometimes blacks were imported to break strikes. "With the mines filled with colored men . . . the company will not be burdened with the expense of another strike for many years," wrote a director of a mining company in 1877.

The record shows that black workers—when ignorant, unaware, and uninterested in labor matters—have been used to break strikes. This availability has usually ended when the black worker has been shown that the union is open to black as well as white.

In their study, *The Black Worker*, Spero and Harris point out that "when all is said and done, the number of strikes broken by black labor have been few as compared with the number broken by white labor. . . . Employers in emergencies take whatever labor they can get and the Negro is only one of many groups involved."

At the beginning of the Civil War there were relatively few extremely wealthy people in America. By the 1890s there were more than four thousand millionaires. In a message to Congress, President Grover Cleveland took note of a widening gap between

...mittee appointed: ... and R. E. Weber.

Mr. GOMPERS, Chairman of the Committee on Plan of Organization, announced that the Committee was ready to report, and submitted the 1st article, as follows:

ARTICLE 1. This association shall be known as "The Federation of Organized Trades Unions of the United States of America and Canada," and shall consist of such Trades Unions as shall, after being duly admitted, conform to its rules and regulations, and pay all contributions required to carry out the objects of this Federation.

A motion was made to adopt the article as read, and discussion ensued.

Mr. WEBER hoped that the name of the Federation would read so as to include all laboring people.

Mr. KINNEAR—I want this organization to reach all men who labor, such as the 'longshoremen in our seaport towns. For that reason I desire the article so amended so as to read "Trades and Labor Unions."

Mr. GRANDISON (the colored delegate), of Pittsburgh—We have in the city of Pittsburgh many men in our organization who have no particular trade, but should not be excluded from the Federation. Our object is, as I understand it, to federate the whole laboring element of America. I speak more particularly with a knowledge of my own people, and declare to you that it would be dangerous to skilled mechanics to exclude from this organization the common laborers, who might, in an emergency, be employed in positions they could readily qualify themselves to fill.

Mr. POLLNER—We recognize neither creed, color, nor nationality, but want to take into the folds of this Federation the whole labor element of the country, no matter of what calling; for that reason, the name should read, "Trades and Labor Unions."

Mr. GOMPERS—The expression of the section, seems to me to be not thoroughly understood. We do not want to exclude any working man who believes in and belongs to organized labor.

Mr. JARRETT said he was in favor of accepting all men who worked for a living and belonged to an organized body of workers, but did not want to include those who would not work and maintain themselves.

Mr. COWAN—Do you want to exclude miners? We have many thousands of them, and we want them in this Federation. You will find them to be worthy your attention.

A VOICE—That is a trade.

From the text of the proceedings of the first convention of the early Federation, 1881, when Negro delegates urged admittance of all workers regardless of race.

J. P. Morgan

John D. Rockefeller

Henry George

Edward Bellamy

rich and poor when he stated: "As we view the achievements of aggregated capital, we discover the existence of trusts, combinations and monopolies, while the citizen is struggling far in the rear or is trampled to death beneath an iron heel. Corporations which should be . . . servants of the people, are fast becoming the people's masters."

If the wealthy had increased in number, so had the poor. The social ills of the country—and the refusal of the trusts to even recognize their existence much less seek to alleviate them—stimulated various reform movements. Many of those who gave voice or leadership to reform claimed to be socialists of one kind or another. Such a man was Edward Bellamy, a well-to-do New Englander, whose book *Looking Backward* became a best seller in 1888. Many Bellamy clubs sprang up throughout the country. Bellamy's vision for an America operated for use rather than for profit converted thousands of people to his social point of view.

Coxey's Army on the march.

Henry George, a self-educated sailor and printer, also wrote a book of broad and permanent influence. *Progress and Poverty* became a best seller in a short time. The book argued that land belonged to the people and that much of the land owned by railroads and speculators should be taken from them by taxation and placed in cultivation.

The "single tax" ideas of Henry George won him thousands of adherents. His popularity became so great that he was nominated in 1886 to run for New York's mayor.

Although the opposition termed him "an apostle of anarchy and destruction," all labor organizations in the city and a large number of individuals—including Terence V. Powderly and Samuel Gompers—endorsed George's candidacy.

While Henry George did not win, the support that he received and the high vote were instrumental in influencing the state legislature to approve of various new labor laws. Included were restrictions on child labor and the establishment of an agency to assist in mediation and arbitration of labor disputes.

Another reformer was Jacob S. Coxey, an Ohio businessman. Coxey was deeply stirred by the economic deprivations he saw around him. He sought to persuade the government to establish public works to help the unemployed, but without success. In 1893, he, himself, organized a march of unemployed men to the nation's capital to try to influence the administration to help solve the unemployment problem.

Coxey was convinced that the democratic system was no longer in operation and that peaceful, direct

A typical grange procession and mass meeting; the Reverend John Trimble, general secretary of the national grange; a farmer-labor cartoon of the day; and Mrs. Mary Elizabeth Lease.

action was the only way in which people would obtain the assistance they needed. While Coxey's movement was not successful, he reflected the needs of thousands of people—both on the farms and in the factories.

The march of "Coxey's Army" was an indication of the widespread unrest of the era. The march was largely organized by the youthful Populist movement that invaded almost every section of the United States where human exploitation was rife.

The Populist revolt was most expressive of the frustration of farmers that previously had been given voice in the national Grange movement. The rural population was bitter against business and industrial interests, most of all the railroads, who they felt particularly discriminated against agricultural areas.

In 1890, a meeting of militant rural representatives in Ocala, Florida, drew up a program of demands that were later adopted at a meeting in Omaha, Nebraska. This Populist platform demanded the nationalization of railroads, direct election of senators, who up to that point were elected through state legisla-

The first A.F. of L. legislative committee, elected at the 1881 Pittsburgh convention: Standing, Samuel Gompers and W. H. Foster; Seated, Charles F. Burgman, Richard Powers, and Alexander C. Rankin.

tures rather than popular vote, and other demands.

A symbol of the militancy of the movement was a Populist Kansas woman campaigner, Mrs. Mary Elizabeth Lease, who advised farmers to "raise less corn and more Hell." While the farmers cheered Mrs. Lease, opponents called her names.

"You may call me an anarchist, a socialist or a communist, I care not," said Mrs. Lease, "but I hold to the theory that if one man has not enough to eat three times a day and another man has $25,000,000, that last man has something that belongs to the first."

When the People's party, as it was sometimes called, organized in Georgia in 1891, Thomas E. Watson, later to be elected to Congress as a Populist, insisted that black people be included on committees.

"Now the People's Party says to these two men [a white and black farmer]," said Watson, "you are kept apart that you may be separately fleeced of your earnings. You are made to hate each other because upon that hatred is rested the keystone of the arch of financial despotism which enslaves you both. You are deceived and blinded that you may not see how this race antagonism perpetuates a monetary system which beggars both."

In 1892, the Populists nominated James B. Weaver, a Civil War general who had served in Congress, as candidate for the Presidency on the Populist party ticket. Weaver received over a million popular and twenty-two electoral votes. Ten Populist congressmen were elected, as well as a large number of state legislators and four governors.

The energy and militancy of the Populist movement, working together with many sections of labor and reflected in political action and in demonstrations, served to influence the American political scene through the two older parties for years to come.

Union women demonstrating in New York City.

# NINE

## 1892-1900

# THE CONFLICTS AT

# HOMESTEAD AND PULLMAN

*"United and acting together . . .*
*your power is invincible."*

The Haymarket affair and its widely publicized aftermath helped set back the onward progress of organized working people for many years. But Haymarket was just the latest of a series of violent conflicts for which responsibility was placed at the door of labor. The Molly Maguires, the railroad strike of 1877, Haymarket, and various other strikes and demonstrations—all accompanied by lurid newspaper and magazine publicity—had all helped create an unsympathetic view of organized labor.

"The Haymarket Affair," states the historian Joseph G. Rayback, "drove the terror deep into the nation's mentality and turned it into hysteria." The weakening of labor organization, following such events as the Molly Maguires' trials and Haymarket, helped depress working-class living conditions even further, if this was possible, than before.

Such was the case in the town of Homestead, Pennsylvania, in 1892, where the Carnegie Steel Company, a forerunner of the United States Steel Corporation, had its principal plant. The Carnegie Company was in control of almost the entire steel industry at this time, owning some twelve steel and coke works in the Pittsburgh area, and employing a total of thirteen thousand workers—some unionized and some not.

Three years before, a strike of Homestead workers

Wives of striking Ohio coal miners thumping pans at a "black leg" trying to take strikers' jobs.

against low wages had taken place and nonunion men had been brought in to work in the mill. By 1892, these "new" workers were finding wages, which they had helped to depress, intolerable themselves. Many joined the Amalgamated Association of Iron and Steel Workers, an A.F. of L. craft union. When this union sought renewal of its contract with the company, the Homestead manager, Henry C. Frick, responded with wage cuts. Shortly thereafter he announced that rather than renew the contract he would close the plant, which he did. Next day, the workers went on strike.

The Homestead plant, located on the Monongahela River a few miles east of Pittsburgh, employed some thirty-eight hundred workers. They performed the most difficult, hot, and dangerous kind of work, for the most part making structural iron and armor plate. Although the work was hard and the hours long, the wages were pitifully inadequate, starting at fourteen cents an hour and extending to $280 a month for the most highly skilled workers. Few employees, no matter how skilled, received more than fifty dollars a week.

"Mighty few men have stood what I have, I can tell you," a steelworker commented.

I've been 20 years at the furnaces and have been workin' a twelve hour day all that time, seven days a week. We go to work at seven in

Pouring cast iron in a foundry.

Newly arrived workers from overseas.

William Weihe, president of the Amalgamated Association of Iron and Steel Workers.

the mornin' and we get through at night at six. We work that way for two weeks and then we work the long turn and change to the night shift of thirteen hours.

The long turn is when we go on at seven Sunday mornin' and work through the whole twenty-four hours up to Monday mornin'. That puts us onto the night turn for the next two weeks, and the other crew onto the day. The next time they get the long turn and we get twenty-four hours off, but it don't do us much good. I get home at about half past seven Sunday mornin' and go to bed as 'soon as I've had breakfast.

I get up about noon so as to get a bit o' Sunday to enjoy, but I'm tired and sleepy all afternoon. Now, if we had eight hours it would be different. I'd start to work, say at six and I'd be done at two and I'd come home, and after dinner me and the missus could go to the park if we wanted to, or I could take the children to the country where there ain't any saloons.

One visitor to a steel mill described what he saw with horror: "One man jumps down, works desperately for a few minutes, and is then pulled up exhausted. Another immediately takes his place; there is no hesitation."

One steel official expressed the philosophy of the company:

Andrew Carnegie

We must be careful of what class of men we collect. We must steer clear of the west, where men are accustomed to infernal high wages. We must steer clear as far as we can of Englishmen, who are great sticklers for high wages, small production and strikes. My experience has shown that Germans and Irish, Swedes and what I denominate "buckwheats"—young American country boys, judiciously mixed, make the most effective and tractable force you can find.

The technique of cutting steel prices used by Frick's boss, Andrew Carnegie, greatest ironmaster of his age, led him inevitably into conflict with his employees. In his effort to reduce prices and destroy competitors, Carnegie insisted that his steel plants cut costs to the bone. This meant increasing production in Carnegie mills and decreasing the wage levels. "The mills have never been able to turn out the product they should," Frick wrote to Carnegie who was vacationing in his castle in Scotland, "owing to being held back by the Amalgamated men."

So in 1892 Frick closed the plant. As if by prearrangement, a small army of Pinkerton detectives, armed with guns, descended the Monongahela river in barges, apparently to replace locked-out workers. But when the men reached Homestead at four o'clock on the morning of July 6, they were met by armed workers. After a bloody battle the Pinkertons surrendered. Thirteen men lay dead: ten workers and three detectives.

Pinkerton detectives leaving barges after their surrender to steelworkers.

Carnegie's castle in Scotland.

## The Dual Carnegie.

*The Dual Carnegie, a critical cartoon of the era.*

WORKMEN CANNONADING THE BARGES.

WORKMEN ATTACKING THE BARGES.

COPYRIGHT 1892 BY EDWIN ROWE, HOMESTEAD, PA.
SURRENDER OF THE PINKERTON MEN

KUHZ & ALLISON·ART STUDIO, CHICAGO.
PINKERTON'S CAPTIVES ON THEIR WAY TO PRISON.

Writing later of the tactics of the detectives, to be used increasingly in future labor conflicts, John McBride, a United Mine Workers' officer, stated: "The Pinkertons have awakened the hatred and detestation of the working man of the United States. . . . They seem rather to invite trouble than to allay it . . ."

In the midst of the strike, an unexpected incident was to take place that helped turn popular sentiment against the strikers. An attempt was made to assassinate Frick by a youthful anarchist, Alexander Berkman. Evidently the man, enraged by the hanging of the Haymarket leaders, believed that assassinating the Carnegie official would help the Carnegie workers win their strike. The opposite proved the case. The event shocked the country and many placed the blame on organized labor. From that point on, public sympathy for the strikers began to shift.

As the strike continued, production was transferred to other Carnegie plants where no strike was in progress. More than eight thousand state troops were stationed at Homestead. The strikers, beset by hunger and seeing their jobs taken by strikebreakers, were finally forced to surrender. The strike was over and the union was eliminated at Homestead.

With some jubilation Frick wrote Carnegie in Scotland: "We had to teach our employees a lesson, and we have taught them one that they will never forget . . ." He added that it was "hard to estimate what blessings will flow from our recent complete victory." An equally happy Carnegie wired back from Skibo Castle in Scotland: "Life worth living again! Congratulate all around . . ."

The defeat of the Homestead workers convinced some labor unionists that the times required a different form of labor organization. The Amalgamated Association was a craft union, contending with a powerful corporation, with many plants, some organized and some not. Industrial corporations increasingly were manufacturing and distributing nationwide. "Why not organize unions on the same basis?" was a question being asked.

There had been various attempts at an industrial form of labor organization. The New England Association of Working Men in the 1830s was an early attempt at industrial organization. The Knights of Labor espoused a loose form of industrial unionism. However, the American Federation of Labor, convinced of the weakness of a too loosely knit labor movement, encouraged organization of workers on a *craft* basis.

One of the most determined advocates of the industrial form of unionism was a young railroad union officer, Eugene Victor Debs, an Indiana native and secretary-treasurer of the Brotherhood of Locomotive Firemen. "I was made to realize," Debs stated, "that the old trade union was utterly incompetent to deal successfully with the exploiting corporations. . . . A modern plant has a hundred trades and parts of trades represented in its working force. To have these

Membership certificate of Locomotive Firemen.

workers parceled out to a hundred unions is to divide and not to organize them. . . . The dominant craft should control . . . the union, and it should embrace the entire working force."

An effective speaker, Debs presented his views wherever railroad workingmen would listen. "Organize according to your industries," he insisted. "United and acting together . . . your power is invincible." Debs's views on industrial unionism were not restricted to speeches. He decided to resign his position with the locomotive firemen and try to organize railroad workers along industrial lines.

The year after the Homestead struggle ended, a new economic depression enveloped the land. Its

Eugene Victor Debs

A memorial to the Homestead workers killed in the strike, erected by the members of the Steel Workers Organizing Committee, September 1, 1941.

long, bony finger reached into every corner of the nation including the "model" city of Pullman, which was located near Chicago. This community was created and owned by George M. Pullman, head of the famous Pullman Palace Car Company. Some five thousand Pullman employees lived in this well-kept suburb. There were no saloons, there were no brothels. Public speakers were not permitted. No union activity was tolerated.

Actually the town gave George Pullman, a man who had started to work at the age of fourteen and overcome almost insurmountable obstacles, a subtle means of exploiting his employees. The method was simple. The cost to the Pullman Company of illuminating gas was only thirty-three cents a thousand cubic feet. Yet every worker living in Pullman had to pay at the rate of $2.25 a thousand. If the worker wanted

Locomotives—1893 and 1831. Railroading was one of the nation's most hazardous occupations.

George M. Pullman

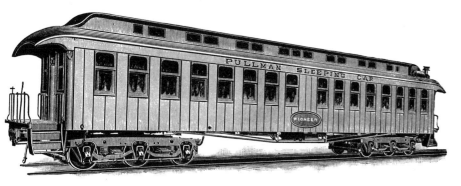

The luxurious Pullman palace cars.

to keep his job, he paid and kept quiet. The nearby city of Chicago supplied the Pullman Company with water at four cents a thousand gallons. For this same water, the company charged employees ten cents a thousand gallons, or about seventy-five cents a month.

When the panic of 1893 hit, the Pullman Company possessed assets worth $62 million, of which $26 million represented undivided profits. Despite this, however, it proceeded to cut wages 25 to 40 percent. When the workers demanded a return to the old scale of wages, the company refused.

Some aspects of the conditions facing the Pullman workers were described by John Swinton, a liberal journalist of the day:

Employees . . . were told that their interests and Pullman's were one and the same; that what would bring him greater prosperity would redound to their advantage. They were warned that to belong to a trade union would be inimical to their joint enterprise; and hence, any who formed a union among them was to be discharged—regarded as a common enemy, and driven out of town. His people were to depend upon his generosity and foresight in all things . . .

Illinois Governor John P. Altgeld spent a day inspecting conditions in the town of Pullman before he addressed a letter to Mr. George M. Pullman, which said in part:

> I examined the conditions at Pullman yesterday, visited even the kitchens and bedrooms of many of the people. Two representatives of your company were with me and we found the distress as great as it was represented. The men are hungry and the women and children are actually suffering. They have been living on charity for a number of months and it is exhausted. Men who had worked for your company for more than ten years had to apply to the relief society in two weeks after the work stopped . . .
>
> Something must be done and at once. The case differs from instances of destitution found elsewhere, for generally there is somebody in the neighborhood able to give relief; this is not the case at Pullman. Even those who have gone to work are so exhausted that they cannot help their neighbors if they would. I repeat now that it seems to me your company cannot afford to have me appeal to the charity and humanity of the State to save the lives of your employees. Four-fifths of those people are women and children. No matter what caused this distress, it must be met.

But nothing was done to remedy conditions facing the employees. Therefore, in the spring of 1894, Pullman workers went on strike.

It so happened that as the walkout was getting under way, the first national convention of the American Railway Union, a newly formed railroad union under the leadership of Debs, was meeting in Chicago. The ARU was dedicated to trying to organize all railway workers on an *industrial* basis. The new union had barely been launched and was in no condition to wage a major struggle when Pullman workers appealed to it for help. Reluctantly, it voted support.

As the stoppage spread, the union issued a call for a sympathy strike of railroad workers throughout the nation, including a boycott of Pullman trains. As a result, railroad transportation in the nation was largely paralyzed. The effectiveness of the industrial form of unionism was evident from the start.

"The American Railway Union immediately became the center of attention of railroad workers all over America," wrote Peter Lyon in his study of American railroads. "Section hands, switchmen, brakemen, roundhouse workers, firemen, engineers, even conductors signed membership cards to ARU lodges. They came in by the thousands."

At that point, United States Attorney General Richard B. Olney, a former railroad lawyer, went into action. When Governor Altgeld refused to call out troops to run the trains, Olney did so. Troops were summoned to Chicago—the nerve center of the strike.

Debs cautioned ARU unions throughout the coun-

Richard B. Olney held two posts in President Grover Cleveland's cabinet: attorney general, at which time he obtained the court injunction in the Pullman strike, and secretary of state, a year after the strike ended.

Peter M. Arthur, head of the Brotherhood of Locomotive Engineers.

Attempting to move a meat train from stockyards.

National guardsmen in action in the Pullman strike.

try to "commit no violence. Have every man stand pat. Troops cannot move trains." But Olney dispatched thirty-six hundred deputy marshals to Chicago to "preserve order and protect property." The opposite effect resulted. Up to that point, the strike had been orderly. Now the violence broke out. Railroad cars were overturned and burned.

Debs commented later: "Peace and order were

*The Longshoremen's Noon* by John George Brown, showing workingmen on the docks.

fatal to the railroad corporations. Violence was as necessary to them as peace was to the employees . . . I have never advocated violence in any form . . . I have always made my appeal to the conscience of the people."

The violence provided reason for the issuance of a court injunction forbidding Debs and his associates "from in any way or manner interfering with . . ." any business activity of twenty-two railroads. It charged the ARU leaders with conspiracy—hindering the delivery of United States mail.

From that point on the strike deteriorated. Armed men began to move the trains. Debs, trying to turn back the attack, ignored the injunction and issued an appeal to the workers of Chicago for a general strike.

A.F. of L. officials, dubious of the new form of unionism, were loath to act. Gradually the strike was broken and its leaders either jailed or blacklisted. From this time on the use of the injunction in union struggles was to increase.

The Pullman strike was over. The American Railway Union suffered a defeat from which it never recovered. Nevertheless, Debs told his membership: "No strike has ever been lost, and there can be no defeat for the labor movement."

Debs's experience in the strike and his exposure to new political views were to make a lasting impression on him. From that time on, he was to devote himself almost exclusively to promoting the socialist point of view.

# TEN

# 1900-1920

# AMERICA ENTERS
# THE TWENTIETH CENTURY

*"The laboring man will be protected . . .
not by labor agitators,
but by . . . men of . . . property."*

Although Eugene V. Debs began to look toward socialist solutions to problems facing workingmen and women, there were large numbers who still retained hope in the existing system. And, indeed, despite the tragic depths to which many were reduced by economic inequities, the prevailing system showed extraordinary resilience and flexibility.

If industrial America had created hideous injustices, coexisting with them was a youthful verve and exciting potential for good. The America of which Walt Whitman sang, with its confidence in the new democracy and its people, was only slightly tarnished by events. If a dreaded depression sucked the last

penny from a worker's family, sent children into sweatshops and young girls into the streets, it was usually followed by a respite sufficient to keep alive hope for better times to come.

The railroads had spanned the nation and labor had participated importantly in the feat. The railroad worker, long the victim of carnage on wheels, now saw the coming of an improved locomotive, the automatic coupler, the air brake, a new interlocking switching system. This railroad, the canals he helped build, the bridges, roads—all gave the worker a new mobility. Even if people found that their economic problems dogged their footsteps wherever they went,

177

nevertheless, many welcomed the fact that they needed no longer be tied to one industrial plant or region.

There were other frontiers opening up, too. The world of learning was becoming available, if not to all workers, at least, they hoped, to their children. Following the Civil War, a slow but continued advancement took place in public education. The one-room country schoolhouse began to be supplemented by consolidated schools. After 1880, public schools proliferated. By 1909, there were ten thousand public high schools in the expanding nation. By 1926, the number had increased to 21,000, serving more than 3,500,000 students.

Important progress was also being made in education for health. Relatively fewer babies were dying; people were living longer because of spreading knowledge of physiology, hygiene, public sanitation, preventive medicine, and need for physical training.

The onward march of science and invention not only affected the lives of almost everyone, but aroused hopes that, if economic pressures were difficult today, they might well be alleviated tomorrow. Had not the horse and wagon begun to be supplanted by the horseless carriage? Inventions of all kinds tumbled forth, one after the other: the sewing machine, the telegraph, refrigerated cars, barbed wire, typewriters, electric lights, machine tools. If many of these devices tended to further harry and hurry those who operated them, they did create jobs and pay.

The forward movement of the nation now numbering some seventy-six million people was scarcely interrupted in 1898 by what was described by an American ambassador as a "splendid little war" with Spain, nominally for the independence of Cuba.

The war may have seemed "splendid" to those far from battle. But, as one writer put it, "for . . . sailors,

Sweatshop workers.

John Mitchell

certainly for sweltering stokers, and for . . . soldiers . . . it was as grim, dirty, and bloody as any war in history."

It was a disillusioning war, too. The sympathies of the American people had been aroused by sensational journalism to support intervention. When President McKinley issued a call for volunteers, there was a rush to sign up, as young men sought to help "right great wrongs." On the production front working people turned out the guns, caissons, balloon material, projectiles. Exhausted stevedores, at loading ports in Florida, slept on piers after their shift, ready to return to work the next morning.

Speaking on the floor of Congress, Senator Albert J. Beveridge of Indiana reflected the spirit of the times when he declared:

God . . . has made us the master organizers of the world. . . . He has marked the American people as His chosen Nation . . . to finally lead in the regeneration of the world. This is the divine mission of America, and it holds for us all the profit, all the glory, all the happiness possible to man . . .

When a union leader—like John Mitchell, mine workers' leader—came to Shenandoah, Pennsylvania, in 1902, it was a big event.

## S. J. Atwood's Employment Agency

### 12 STATE STREET, NEW YORK

### STATEMENT of LABOR CONTRACT

in accordance with Chapter 700 of the Laws of 1910.

| | |
|---|---|
| Name of Employer<br>Name des Stellungsgebenden<br>Imie pracydającego<br>Alkalmazást ado neve<br>Pracu dajuceho meno<br>Namn af arbetsgifvaren<br>Nome del padrone | Cohoes Company |
| Address of Employer<br>Adresse des Stellungsgebenden<br>Adres pracydającego<br>Alkalmazást ado czime<br>Pracu dajuceho adress<br>Adress af arbetsgifvaren<br>Direzione del padrone | Cohoes N.Y. |
| Name of Employee<br>Name des Angestellten<br>Imie robotnika<br>Alkalmazott neve<br>Robotnikow meno<br>Namn af arbetstagaren<br>Nome del Lavorante | Uno Palmer |
| Address of Employee<br>Adresse des Angestellten<br>Adres robotnika<br>Alkalmazott czime<br>Robotnikow adressa<br>Adress af arbetstagaren<br>Direzione del Lavorante | 4219 - 7th Ave Bklyn |
| Nature of work to be performed<br>Art der auszuführenden Arbeit<br>Jaka praca<br>A munka minősége<br>Jaka robota<br>Det arbete som skall utföras<br>Specie di Lavoro | Carpenter on Concrete forms.. |
| Hours of Labor<br>Anzahl der Arbeitsstunden<br>Ilosc godzin robocsych<br>Munka orák száma<br>Kelo hodini robit<br>Arbets-timmarne<br>Ore di Lavoro | 9 hours per day |
| Wages offered<br>Angebotener Lohn<br>Jaka placa<br>Felajánlott munkabér<br>Kelo placu<br>Den lön som erbjudes<br>Paga offerta | 35 to 40 cent per hour |
| Destination of the persons employed<br>Bestimmungsort der Angestellten<br>Miejsce przeznaczona do roboty<br>Az alkalmazottak küldetési helye<br>Dze je poselanim<br>Destinationen af de anställda personerna<br>Destinazione delle persone impiegate | Cohoes N.Y. |
| Terms of Transportation<br>Transport-Bedingungen<br>Warunki jazdy<br>Szállitási feltételek<br>Jak budu poslane<br>Villkoren för deras transportering<br>Condizione di viaggio | Paid own fare........ |
| Remarks<br>Anmerkungen<br>Uwaga<br>Megjegyzések<br>Poznamka<br>Anmärkning<br>Osservazioni | |

If more than one person is engaged, list of names and addresses will be found attached.

New York,.........June 29th............... 1914

A 1914 labor contract printed in English, German, Polish, Hungarian, Slovak, Swedish, and Italian. Wages were thirty-five to forty cents an hour for a nine-hour day.

"The tone of Beveridge's speech," commented one historian, "was in the spirit of the times."

Cities were growing at a phenomenal rate and, while agriculture still ruled the nation, impatient farm boys and newly arrived immigrants continued to bolster the industrial work force. Cities would double their size in a few short years.

Carl Sandburg wrote of the Chicago of the era:

Hog Butcher for the World,
Tool Maker, Stacker of Wheat,
Player with Railroads and
     the Nation's Freight Handler;
Stormy, husky, brawling,
City of the Big Shoulders.

In 1900, the nation produced at least half the world's cotton, corn, oil, and copper; about a third of its silver, pig iron, and steel; and much of its coal. There were two hundred thousand miles of railroads completed and two hundred thousand miles of telegraph wire strung. Soon there would be a million miles of telephone wire stretching across the nation.

The country was burgeoning, but it was also becoming fertile territory for developing trusts that President Cleveland had already described, years before, as "fast becoming the people's masters." In 1901, the world's largest corporation, United States Steel, was put together like a jigsaw puzzle. It soon would outdistance any other company in accumulated resources. The steel combination was organized under the personal direction of J. P. Morgan, the man with the greatest "command of money . . . in America." U.S. Steel's attitude toward labor was made clear from the start when it refused "bluntly to deal with

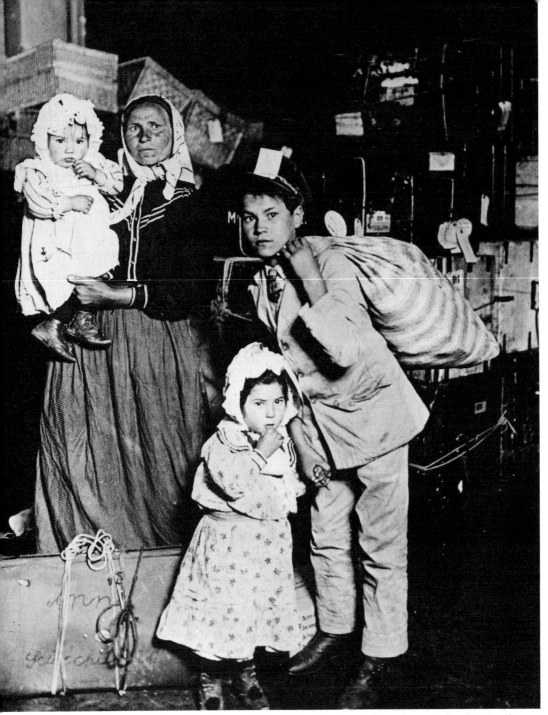

Men often arrived from abroad to seek jobs. When they found them, they sent for their families.

union labor under any circumstances." According to historian Selig Perlman, "The Board of Directors . . . took what amounted to an oath to extirpate unionism."

J. P. Morgan seemed to feel, as one of his biographers stated, that the "business machinery of America should be honestly and decently managed by a few of the best people, people like his friends and associates."

Samuel Gompers and the A.F. of L. executive council, of course, thought differently. In 1897, the council elected a committee to present a memorial to Congress urging enforcement of the eight-hour law in public-work projects. In addition, labor urged larger appropriations for public works, rivers and harbors, and currency reform—in an effort to ensure the country against economic depressions. The A.F. of L. at this time repeatedly spoke out against the use of injunctions against labor and, as the new century arrived, set to work to present to Congress a "bill of grievances," setting forth the ills it claimed were being suffered by American working people.

This bill of grievances, drawn up by fifty-one A.F. of L. international, state, and city labor bodies, charged, among other things, that the Sherman Antitrust Act was not being used to limit the growth of

$ACRED $MOTHERHOOD

"Chee! Annie, look at de stars, thick as bed-bugs."

monopolies. These sentiments of labor were presented to the President of the United States and Congress in the early spring of 1906.

All of this did not bother men like J. P. Morgan or his associates. They felt comfortable that their affairs, both economic and political, were in the control of the few rather than the many. That was why the election campaigns of 1896 and 1900 were a source of anxiety to them. Despite the passage of the much publicized Sherman Antitrust Act of 1890, the trend toward the creation of trusts never halted, or even slowed down. The era, which culminated at the turn of the century, was the most rambunctious period of industrial combination up to that time. By 1904, some 40 percent of the nation's manufacturing capital was in the hands of trusts.

Discussing this situation, Senator Orville Platt of Connecticut contended that the conduct of the Senate in approving the Sherman law "has not been in the line of honest preparation of a bill to prohibit and punish trusts. It has been in the line of getting some bill with that title that we might go to the country with . . ."

A few years later a congressional investigation by a committee headed by Senator Arsène P. Pujo held hearings and concluded that "an integration had taken place of big finance and big industry which unitedly controlled banks, railroads, public utilities, insurance companies and major industries." Industrial capitalism, it was found, had given way to finance capitalism.

Hand in hand with the growth of monopoly power was industry's rejection of labor unions, particularly militant ones. It had cause. Labor organizations not

Almost every community had its "hello girls."

Bakery worker

Sweatshop worker

only could demand a share of the fortunes being made, but could serve to hinder the freewheeling operations of the fortune makers. "The greatest danger lies in the recognition of the union," stated David M. Parry, president of the newly created National Association of Manufacturers in 1903. "Organized labor . . . does not place its reliance upon reason and justice, but on strikes, boycotts and coercion. It is, in all essential features, a mob knowing no master except its own will."

High government officials of the era were also frequently hostile to labor unions. President Theodore Roosevelt wavered in his attitude toward both industry and labor. Although he was known as a "trust-buster," there were those who believed he might equally have been dubbed a "union buster." "The worst foe of the poor," he stated, "is the union leader . . . who tries to teach him he is a victim of . . . injustice."

Roosevelt's successor, William Howard Taft, revealed what his biographer described as "a shocking hostility" toward the railway strikers of 1894. Taft wrote to a friend: "It will be necessary for the military to kill some of the mob before the trouble is stayed." And in another letter: "Word comes tonight that 30 men have been killed by the Federal troops. Though it is bloody business, everybody hopes that it is true . . ."

The defeats at Homestead and Pullman were not the only losses suffered by labor around the turn of the century. Workers in gold and silver mines of the Coeur d'Alene section of Idaho faced an array of antilabor forces—strikebreakers, injunctions, and the state militia—in their efforts to reject a dollar-a-day wage reduction. As a result of the conflict, troops thrust several hundred union men into hastily erected bullpens and kept them there until the strike was broken. From the struggle, however, was to develop a new union, the Western Federation of Miners, which supplied a new militant labor leadership to those in the metal mine country.

The Western Federation of Miners was actually conceived in the Idaho bullpens in 1892. William D. Haywood, secretary-treasurer of the Western Federation of Miners, said, "We are not ashamed of having been born in jail." It was not the only union to come into existence in the period immediately before and after the start of a new century. The United Mine Workers, the International Ladies' Garment Workers, the National Seamen's Union—these and others were born then.

As the metal miners in the western country organized on an industrial union basis, so did the coal miners of the anthracite region.

Even the children of Pennsylvania coal miners had unions. "Almost as soon as the breaker boy's certificate is accepted and placed on file in the colliery office,"

"Breaker boys."

one turn-of-the-century report stated, he makes application to become a member of the "junior local," the members of which are all boys under sixteen. Their weekly meetings take place at night, and are conducted with the utmost secrecy, the members being admitted only by password. The monthly dues range from ten to twenty-five cents, in accordance with the wages received by the members.

These junior locals evidently had officers, from president to corresponding secretary, as well as weekly meetings.

At Harwood, a village about four miles from Hazelton, I attended a meeting of a Junior Local. Promptly at eight o'clock the boys, about fifty in number, gathered in the schoolhouse. Their oily caps and grimy overalls gave evidence of their having only recently left their day's toil in the mines and breakers. After the blinds had been drawn, and the door locked, the president mounted the teacher's platform and called the meeting to order by pounding on the desk with his fist. Comparatively few of the members who filled the benches in the room would have been pronounced by any observer of ordinary perspicacity outside the perjured world of Anthracite as being more than ten years of age.

"How old are you?" I asked the assembled meeting, and the answer came back in a grand chorus, "Thirteen." An accord of ideas, as well as ages, worthy of a union.

Both in the East under the leadership of the United Mine Workers and in the West under the leadership of the W.F. of M., miners engaged in continuing bitter conflicts. Even so, wages continued at low levels. This was particularly unbearable in view of the frequency of mining accidents, of chronic diseases from working underground, and of the high ensuing death rate. "Coal mining is more hazardous," said the Anthracite Coal Commission, "than any other class of underground work."

The ten-hour day for miners was particularly injurious to life and health.

A not unusual sight was that of families and friends waiting at the pithead to find out what miners, if any, had survived an underground explosion or cave-in.

The exploitation of human beings for profit in this era was nowhere more flagrantly demonstrated than in the prisons of the nation. Since the time of the earliest labor organizations, mechanics and artisans

Miners testing for fumes underground.

Families waiting at the mouth of a mine at Monongahela, Pennsylvania, after a disaster.

had protested against the use of convict labor, which they claimed was used to drive down wages and price levels. This practice, while occasionally controlled, reached its most objectionable status in the coal mines of the South, starting in the post-Civil War era and extending well into the 1900s. Most southern states exploited prison labor. This was done in two ways: the first was the contract system through which a convict's labor was for hire within the prison itself. The second method was a system by which prisoners were farmed out to private corporations, especially coal mine operators. By paying a moderate fee, the company was thus able to extract a high rate of profit from rented prisoners.

The convict-rental system was highly successful—for some corporations. Not only were they able to buy ample labor for a small fee, but there was an additional increment for them. The system was a useful weapon against labor union organization. The use of convict miners was an influential factor in breaking strikes of nonconvict miners and helped weaken the mine workers' union where convict hiring was practiced.

Aside from the evils of convict labor, general conditions in coal mines—before the United Mine Workers began to demand improvements—were bad, often beyond description. This was dramatized in the summer of 1895 by a group of miners in Spring Valley, Illinois, who "offered to go into voluntary slavery in return for reasonably comfortable homes, some fuel, clothing and enough food to keep themselves from starving."

While the *Hartford Courant* was of the opinion that "there are too many millionaires and too many paupers," the employers of mine workers were not equally sensitive to conditions. George F. Baer, president of the Philadelphia and Reading Railway, pointed out that "anthracite mining is a business, and not a religious, sentimental, or academic proposition."

If conditions in the mining countries were deplorable for mine workers and their families, in the big cities sweatshops were also presenting constant threats to the life and health of many urban workers. In the garment industry, in cities such as Boston, New York, and Chicago, men, women, and children toiled seemingly endless hours for a pittance. "As to hours," said one labor organizer, "there is practically no limit, except the endurance of the employee."

Conditions in garment sweatshops, tanneries, and cotton mills were dirty, dark, and damp. Some earned eight or ten dollars a week and seldom saw the daylight. "I am a stranger to my own children," one New York worker said.

Workers usually were at their machines at seven o'clock in the morning. And they stayed there, except for a brief lunch period, until eight o'clock at night, or later. Sometimes they worked by hand. Other times they worked with machines, which went like mad all day. "Sometimes in my haste," one operator reported, "I get my finger caught. The needle goes right through it. It goes so quick, though, that it doesn't hurt much. I bind the finger up with a piece of cotton and go on working. We all have accidents like that."

One garment worker, Pauline Newman, described how

during the winter months, we were extremely uncomfortable—if not actually freezing. The only heating facility in these places was a stove, put

The convict system in operation.

in the middle of the floor. The warmth was insufficient for all—but especially for those of us who were placed near the windows. I recall several places in which when a window happened to be broken, a cardboard would, as a rule, be substituted for the glass. Thus adding to the cold and depriving us of what bit of daylight that window afforded. How we suffered from the cold! In the summer we suffered from the heat, for these places were suffocating. The gas jets only added to the general humidity and discomfort.

In these disease-breeding holes, we, the youngsters together with the men and women, toiled from seventy and eighty hours a week! Saturdays and Sunday included! . . . A sign would go up on Saturday afternoon: "If you don't come in on Sunday, you need not come in on Monday." Children's hopes trampled upon—children's dreams of a day-off shattered. We wept, for after all, we were only children.

Another eyewitness, a visitor, Jacob A. Riis, wrote of a trip to a tenement that often served as a workshop,

A woman carrying work home for the family to sew.

# Philadelphia & Reading Railway Company.
## President's Office.

### Reading Terminal. Philadelphia.    17th July 1902.

My dear Mr. Clark:-

I have your letter of the 16th instant.

I do not know who you are.   I see that you are a religious man;  but you are evidently biased in favor of the right  of the working man to control a business in which he has no other interest than to secure fair wages for the work he does.

I beg of you not to be discouraged.  The rights and interests of the laboring man will be protected and cared for  - not by the labor agitators, but by the Christian men to whom God in His infinite wisdom has given the control of the property interests of the country, and upon the successful Management of which so much depends.

Do not be discouraged    Pray earnestly that right may triumph, always remembering that the Lord God Omnipotent still reigns, and that His reign is one of law and order, and not of violence and crime.

Yours truly,

Geo. F. Baer

President.


Mr. W. F. Clark,

Wilkes-Barre,

Pennsylvania.

Famous letter from industrialist George F. Baer.

# Fellow Workers!

Join in rendering a last sad tribute of sympathy and affection for the victims of the Triangle Fire. THE FUNERAL PROCESSION will take place Wednesday, April 5th, at 1 P. M. Watch the newspapers for the line of march.

צו דער לויה שוועסטער און ברידער !

די לויה פון די היילינע קרבנות פון דעם טרייענגעל פייער וועם זיין סיטוואָר, דעם פֿטען אפריל, 1 אחר נאכמיטטאָג.

קיינער פון אייך מער נים פערבלייבען אין די שעפער ! שליסם זיך צו אין די רייהען פון די מארשירענדע ! דרוקם אוים אייער סימפאטיע און מיטפֿון בעדוירערגען אייף דעם נרויסען אנלומס וואָם די ברכיישערוואעלם האָם געהאַם.

געבראָנגען די קעפ – סים ציעטעתע העראצער וועלען מיר פֿיהראן אונזערע סחײיערע שמעסרם צו וויער לעצמער רוה.

וואָמם די ציהזונגען דורך וועלכע מיר וועלען לאטען וויסמן וואו איהר קענס זיך צוויסנאַנקומען.

צו דער לויה פון די היילינע קרבנות,

סטם שוועסטער און ברידער !

# Operai Italiani!

Unitevi compatti a rendere l'ultimo tributo d'affetto alle vittime dell'imane sciagura della Triangle Waist Co. IL CORTEO FUNEBRE avra luogo mercoledi, 5 Aprile, alle ore 1 P M. Traverete nei giornali l'ordine della marcia.

up two flights of dark stairs, three, four, with new smells of cabbage, of onions, of frying fish, on every landing, whirring sewing machines behind closed doors betraying what goes on within, to the door that opens to admit the bundle and the man. A "sweater," this, in a small way.

Five men and a woman, two young girls, not fifteen, and a boy who says unasked that he is fifteen, and lies in saying it, are at the machines sewing knickerbockers, "knee pants" in the Ludlow Street dialect. The floor is littered ankle-deep with half-sewn garments. In the alcove, on a couch of many dozens of "pants" ready for the finisher, a bare-legged baby with pinched face is asleep. A fence of piled-up clothing keeps him from rolling off on the floor.

The faces, hands, and arms to the elbows of everyone in the room are black with the color of the cloth on which they are working. The boy and the woman alone look up at our entrance. The girls shoot sidelong glances, but at a warning look from the man with the bundle they tread their machines more energetically than ever. The men do not appear to be aware even of the presence of a stranger.

The "sweating system," as it was called, was in full effect at the turn of the century and after, and helped bring into existence the International Ladies' Garment Workers' Union. After a bitter strike, the ILGWU achieved an agreement with manufacturers outlawing subcontracting within their shops, prohibiting employers from sending out homework, and declaring a preference for the employment of union members.

One of the most frightening hazards affecting workers in the dilapidated factories or tenement homes in which they toiled was fire. Employers frequently kept factory doors locked to keep workers from leaving early or to maintain an optimum temperature for handling fabrics or other products.

One Saturday afternoon in the spring of 1911 a fire broke out on the eighth floor of the Triangle Shirtwaist Company building in downtown New York City. When the thousand employees tried to escape, they found the doors locked. Firefighting equipment was inadequate. As a result, 146 workers lost their lives. Hundreds more were injured.

The nation was aghast at the tragedy. "The Triangle fire," said the future secretary of labor, Frances Perkins, one of those investigating the tragedy, "was a torch that lighted up the whole industrial scene." Among the results was the introduction of legislation in many states strengthening safety requirements in factories.

In the food industry, for another, especially meat-packing, conditions were deplorable as far as employees were concerned. In his novel, *The Jungle,* Upton Sinclair described some of the daily conditions facing a packinghouse worker of that period.

> Here a man put shackles about one leg [of a steer] and pressed another lever, and the body was jerked up into the air. There were fifteen or twenty such pens, and it was a matter of only a couple of minutes to knock fifteen or twenty cattle and roll them out. Then once more the gates were opened, and another lot rushed in; and so out of each pen there rolled a steady stream of carcasses, which the men upon the killing beds had to get out of the way.

The Triangle fire in New York claimed scores of victims.

## IF YOU DON'T COME IN SUNDAY DON'T COME IN MONDAY.

THE MANAGEMENT

"If you don't come in Sunday . . ." signs were common in New York sweatshop garment factories.

The manner in which they did this was something to be seen and never forgotten. They worked with furious intensity, literally upon the run—at a pace with which there is nothing to be compared except a football game. It was all highly specialized labor, each man having his task to do; generally this would consist of only two or three specific cuts, and he would pass down the line of fifteen or twenty carcasses, making these cuts upon each. First there came the "Butcher," to bleed them; this meant one swift strike, so swift that you could not see it— only the flash of the knife; and before you could realize it, the man had darted on to the next line, and a stream of bright red was pouring out upon the floor. This floor was half an inch deep with blood, in spite of the best efforts of men who kept shovelling it through holes; it must have made the floor slippery, but no one could have guessed this by watching the men at work.

The carcass hung for a few minutes to bleed; there was no time lost, however, for there were several hanging in each line, and one was always ready. It was let down to the ground, and there came the "headsman," whose task it was to sever the head, with two or three swift strokes. Then came the "floorsman," to make the first cut in the skin; and then another to finish ripping the skin down the center; and then a half dozen more in swift succession, to finish the skinning. After they were through, the carcass was again swung up; and while a man with a stick examined the skin, to make sure that it had not been cut, another rolled it up and tumbled it through one of the inevitable holes in the floor.

There was scarcely a craft or occupation, including clerks, servants, waiters, that was not victimized by insecurity and exploitation. And usually, with jobs scarce, there was no means of protection or effective protest. Household servants were sometimes cruelly exploited as described by the writer Rheta Childe Dorr in 1910:

I remember a young girl who waited on table at a women's hotel where I made my home. One morning I sent this girl for more cream for my coffee. She was gone some time and I spoke to her a little impatiently when she returned. She was silent for a moment, then she said: "Do you know that every time you send me to the pantry it means a walk of three and a half blocks? This diningroom and the kitchens and pantries are a block apart, and are separated by three flights of stairs. I have counted the distance there and back, and it is more than three blocks."

"But Kittie," I said to her, "why do you work in a hotel, if it's like that? Why don't you take a place in a private family?"

"I've tried that," said the girl. "I had a place with the ——— family," mentioning an historic name ". . . My room was up in the attic, with only a skylight for ventilation. During the day, except for the time I spent sitting on the area steps after nine o'clock, I was waiting on the

Packinghouse worker

cook in a hot kitchen. They let me out of the house once every two weeks. Here I have some freedom, at least."

Clerks were another group of hard-worked employees, according to an expert on the old-time country store.

The boy who obtained a post as store clerk came up against reality—long hours, a considerable amount of physical labor, the cussedness of customers, and the sedentary monotony of working on the ledger. . . . All through the 19th century, and well into the present one, store goods came in large packages that weighed up to two hundred pounds. It took a great deal of pushing, heaving, and grunting to handle the barrels of vinegar, flour, and whale oil. Molasses came in a hogshead, nails in kegs, each large package identified only by its geographical origin. All stock had to be placed or stored somewhere—in a back room, in the store itself, in the cellar, or raised above the first floor with a windlass.

Later all merchandise had to be rolled out again to the farm wagons of the customers', or else scooped, poured, cut, weighed, and wrapped up by hand at the counters. The clerk cleaned out the fireplace or stove, mended the fire, swept out the store, took down and put up the heavy shutters, ground the coffee by hand, and not infrequently found himself with a lame back or a pulled ligament . . .

Upton Sinclair's novel, *The Jungle*, helped expose conditions in the nation's slaughterhouses.

Turn-of-the-century women factory workers.

Finally, Marie Van Vorst in 1908 wrote of the mill-worker:

Over there is a woman of sixty, spooling, behind the next side is a child, not younger than eight, possibly, but so small that she has to stand on a box to reach her side. Only the very young girls show any trace of buoyancy; the older ones have accepted with more or less complaint the limitation of their horizons.

They are drawn from the hill district with traditions no better than the loneliness, desertion and inexperience of the fever-stricken mountains back of them. They are illiterate, degraded; the mill has been their widest experience; and all their tutelage is the intercourse of girl to girl during the day and in the evenings the few moments before they go to bed in the millhouses where they either live at home with parents and brothers all working like themselves, or else they are fugitive lodgers in a boarding-house or a hotel, where their morals are in jeopardy constantly.

As soon as a girl passes the age, let us say of seventeen or eighteen, there is no hesitation in her reply when you ask her: "Do you like the mills?" Without exception the answer is, "I hate them . . ."

Child labor in twentieth-century America was not a new practice. From the start of industrialization, children had entered the textile mills and glassblowing factories. But as years passed, the demand grew in volume—usually led by organized labor—for free pub-

The golf links are so near the mill
That almost every day
The laboring children can look out
And see the men at play.
Sara N. Cleghorn

lic schools and an end to the labor of children. Several states passed laws, if not abolishing child labor, at least restricting it. Some states, such as Massachusetts, introduced state regulations for compulsory schooling for children.

Actually no demand of labor unions, from the earliest days, was so determinedly put forward as "the education of mechanics' children." The Knights of Labor as well as the American Federation of Labor both placed high on their list of demands the abolition of child labor and the free education of the children of working people.

However, economic crises made abolition of child labor difficult. Haunted by poverty and starvation, working families often found it necessary for even young children to work. Family income was so meager, every penny earned was needed. Then, too, employers in certain industries found the nimble fingers of young children useful for certain occupations and processes. It was also possible to pay children less than adults, often for the same work.

In the coal fields, boys were sent to the mines when they were eight, nine, and ten years of age, usually starting in the breaker room, where coal is picked over to separate it from slate. "It is a painful sight," a

Toiling in the field.

Young miner and mule.

Boy worker in a glass factory.

Cotton field hand.

Child miner bent from years of premature toil.

correspondent of *The Labor Standard* wrote, "to see the men going so silently and gloomily about their work, but it is a thousand times worse to see these boys . . . these little fellows go to work in this cold, dreary room at seven o'clock in the morning and work 'til it is too dark to see any longer. For this they get from $1 to $3 a week."

Where there were miners there were often mills that employed cheap girl labor. "It was estimated that nearly ninety percent of the females were girls who had not yet reached womanhood," according to a report in *McClure's* magazine in 1903.

They worked ten hours a day. Most of them worked standing all of the time except at the noon hour. . . . The pay was poor for the long hours, but the money was needed in a miner's family. Indeed, some of the girls were working because their fathers had been injured in the mines or even killed. Wages ranged from $1.25 to $3.00 per week . . .

Just as the boys in the mines had junior locals, so did their sisters in the mills have a union. The weekly meeting, it was reported, was the great event in the life of every child in the coal fields. When attending meetings members of the girls' unions wore "the same clothes that they would wear to church." The debates were about wages and hours and working conditions. Often the discussions led to serious action, strikes.

The girls asserted themselves almost as often and with almost as much strength as the dirty, grimy miners. Sometimes an injustice done to one girl would arouse the feelings of her sisters.

One strike was called when a very little girl began to grow crippled from operating a treadle. She became so lame and ill that she had to stay home for a week and go to bed. During that time a large boy was hired to do her work. He was, of course, paid more money. When the girl returned, the boy was fired and the girl put back on the treadle. The boss refused to find other work for her.

In the words of a young leader of the union, "Shall we stand for it, girls, for seeing her grow up a cripple and the union not doing nothing, not reaching out no hand for to help? We that believes in the rights of man?"

Some had fathers who were striking, but the vote was unanimous.

"We had the resolution [to strike] written out nice on a typewriter," the leader said. After two days the boss gave in. The boy worked at the treadle and the girl was placed at work at a bench.

John Mitchell, president of the United Mine Workers, himself once a child worker in the mines, said that it is

hard to reconcile the humanity and flaunted intelligence of this era with the wholesale employment of children in industry. Childhood should be a period of growth and education. It should be the stage in which the man is trained for future efforts and future work. . . . It is difficult to conceive of anything more fatuous, anything more utterly absurd and immoral, than the wholesale employment of children in industry. . . . The policy of extracting work from children and exploiting their slow-growing strength is utterly vicious and entirely self-destructive . . .

But there were those who thought child labor was not an evil but, in some ways, a benefit.

"Are you in sympathy with child labor?" a clergyman from Lawrence, Massachusetts, was asked in 1912 at a senatorial hearing looking into the matter of child labor. "Do you think these mills should employ children to do the work that older and stronger and grown people should do or could do?"

"The work that the children do in the mill, most of it, is perfectly proper for children to do," was the reply.

"I presume that is true; but that does not in any manner enlighten the committee or answer the question," said a senator.

"Why, it expresses my conviction that the work is such as children might properly do."

"And ought properly to do; and ought to do?"

"Well, children have got to be occupied, whether they are laboring in the mill or toiling on the farm, or going fishing; they have got to be occupied."

Said the *Textile World*, on the same subject, "They have to be constantly watched or they will go from bad to worse in order to make more time for play."

The nation was obviously ready for a tidal wave of reform.

Popular discontent was about to usher in a period of change. The activity of reformers was to merge with growing demands from the labor movement as well as the militant protests of the Populists.

This combination produced eloquent spokesmen for the people's cause. One of these was William Jennings Bryan, "the great commoner," several times the Democratic party candidate for the Presidency of the United States. His powerful voice thundered calls to action: "The humblest citizen in all the land, when clad in a righteous cause, is stronger than all the hosts of error. I come to speak to you in defense of a cause as holy as the cause of liberty—the cause of humanity."

Many saw in the Bryan platform—which included the championing of working people and farmers, the free coinage of silver, the opposition to big business—a way out for the poverty stricken and oppressed.

"I supported Mr. William Jennings Bryan," said Eugene V. Debs, " . . . not because I regarded the

*From the Depths,* a popular illustration of the day.

Campaign poster for William Jennings Bryan, "the great commoner."

free coinage of silver as a panacea for our national ills, but because I believe that the triumph of Mr. Bryan and free silver would blunt the fangs of the money power . . ."

Although there was a surge of support for the candidacy of Bryan, it was not sufficient for victory. After the election of William McKinley, a conservative Republican, was announced, Philip D. Armour, the meat-packer, wrote to a friend: "We are all feeling better here this morning. We have the consolation of knowing the country is safe for four years . . ."

The defeat of Bryan did not end the popular demand for reform. The common man was demanding—in this "Progressive era"—the right to a better life. Upton Sinclair's book exposing conditions in the meat-packing industry, which sold hundreds of thousands of copies, contributed to a federal investigation of the industry. "I aimed at the public's heart," said Sinclair, "and by accident hit it in the stomach."

In 1906, as a result of the popular clamor, the federal Pure Food and Drug Act was passed, which required labels to indicate contents, banned manufacture for sale of adulterated or misbranded foods or drugs, and outlawed harmful additives to foods.

Although President Theodore Roosevelt called exposing the indifference to human values "muckraking," it was urgently needed. The spirit of the Populist was in the air, reaffirming, as the Populist platform stated, "allegiance to the principles declared by the founders of the Republic and also to the fundamental principles of just government . . . the country has reached a crisis in its national life . . . and . . . prompt and patriotic action is the supreme duty of the hour . . ."

Reformers—not usually directly connected with labor—tried in a variety of ways to improve a society that they felt was unjust in countenancing human exploitation. Many wealthy men and women, aghast at the human devastation they saw about them, tried to hasten change.

"There were two things I wanted to do," said Lewis W. Hine, the socially conscious photographer whose pictures of children at work did much to expose the evils of child labor. "I wanted to show the things that had to be corrected. I wanted to show the things that had to be appreciated."

Jane Addams, the Chicago social worker who pioneered among the poor, reminded the privileged: "It is well, sometimes, to remind ourselves that, after all, the mass of mankind works with their hands."

Jack London, the famed novelist, wrote a definition of a strike breaker or "scab"—"a two-legged animal with a cork-screw soul"—that was widely quoted.

Women like Miss Mary E. Dreier and Mrs. Raymond Robins gave leadership to the Women's Trade Union League, which permitted nonworking-class women to work with labor on causes it considered most important, especially those involving women's rights.

Lillian Wald, whose Henry Street Settlement in New York welcomed the poor and homeless, told how she learned of trade unionism from a neighbor's visit:

Our pleasure was mingled with consternation to learn that she wished aid in organizing a trades union. Even the term was unknown to me. She spoke without bitterness of the troubles of her shop-mates, and tried to make me see why they thought a union would bring them relief. It was evident that she came to me because of her faith that one who spoke English so easily would know how to organize in the "American way," and perhaps with a hope that the union might gain respectability from the alliance.

Florence Kelley, the first inspector of factories in Illinois, was a leading fighter against child labor, working largely through the National Child Labor Committee. Her chance visit to a glassmaking factory influenced her views the rest of her life. "The picture of these little figures moving about in the shadows, carrying trays of glass, cutting themselves occasionally upon broken glass in the dark, or being burned by the hot bottles" never left her.

There were many more reformers, and their work and influence had a lasting effect on the developing social consciousness of the nation.

Another influence for social change was the philosophy of socialism. Numerous founding A.F. of L. leaders—such as Adolph Strasser and Peter J. Maguire—were socialists and, as a young man, Samuel Gompers was influenced by socialist thought.

"In those days, New York was a haven for over-zealous soldiers in the European struggle for freedom," said Gompers, ". . . they were men of imagination, courage, ideals. They sought their ends through revolution . . . their talks stirred me deeply . . ."

Gompers studied socialist ideas, and even learned German so he could read the original writings of Karl Marx. Later he drifted away from the socialists. But their influence on the labor movement continued. In A.F. of L. convention after convention, socialist delegates—sometimes in substantial number—tried to influence labor to adopt its program or part of it. This program was based on the conclusion that "capitalism has fulfilled its mission . . . it can no longer control the productive forces of society." The socialists called for public ownership of means of production, for independent political action by labor, for industrial unionism, generally for a greater consciousness on the part of labor of its class differences from employers.

By energetic work, socialists built a considerable following. At the turn of the century numerous socialist candidates for mayor and alderman were elected to office as well as to the state legislatures. In 1910, one

Jacob A. Riis

Helen Keller

Jane Addams

Jack London

Miss Mary E. Dreier and Mrs. Raymond Robins

Lewis W. Hine

Florence Kelley

Lillian Wald

Reformers urged help for the underprivileged.

The well-to-do were often oblivious to the problems of the poor.

socialist—Victor L. Berger from Milwaukee—was elected to the United States House of Representatives. In 1917, Max Hayes, a socialist and a member of the International Typographical Union from Cleveland, ran as a candidate against Samuel Gompers for the A.F. of L. presidency and received one-third of the votes.

By 1912, the party had more than one thousand of its members in public office. They included one congressman, fifty-six mayors, and three hundred aldermen. The socialists were also influential in the passage of national and state reform legislation, urgently needed at the time, such as state laws setting limits on how many hours women may work, the minimum age children may be employed, and factory health and safety regulations.

What some called "the Continental Congress of the working class" was held in Chicago in the winter of 1905. There were several hundred delegates present from thirty-four local, state, district, and national labor organizations. Membership represented about 150,000 working people and included the Western Federation of Miners, the United Metal Workers, and the Socialist Trade and Labor Alliance.

Victor L. Berger from Milwaukee, Socialist United States congressman.

Cartoon satirizing a factory overseer.

Slaughtering hogs

Garment worker in a sweatshop.

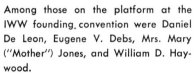

Among those on the platform at the IWW founding convention were Daniel De Leon, Eugene V. Debs, Mrs. Mary ("Mother") Jones, and William D. Haywood.

ch veteran labor leaders
d of the Western Federa-
r of the Socialist Labor
f the Haymarket victim;
organizer; and Eugene
ocialist leader in the na-

ial Workers of the World
organization took a posi-
ith the American Federa-
ught "one big union" whose
orm society but to "abolish

d the IWW a "dual union,"
duplicated the efforts of
e IWW called the A.F. of
."

n Federation of Miners,
affiliate, was William D.
who contrasted physically
way with Samuel Gompers.
"we are going down in the
workers and bring them up
."

e the IWW recruited many of
le, the turpentine and lumber

# Craft Unionism—
# Why It Fails

Printed in U. S. A.

IWW meeting of Denver miners.

*Craft Unionism is foundering on the rocks of Capitalism. Only Industrial Unionism as exemplified by the I.W.W. can save the day...*

Published by the
Industrial Workers of the World
1001 W. Madison St. Chicago, Ill., U. S. A.

**Price Ten Cents**

I WILL WIN

companies treated many of their workers as if they were slaves. As one worker reported:

> They have deliberately cultivated the narcotic drug habit among the workers. At every company store, cocaine, morphine and heroin are sold. The workers, once addicted, cannot think of going away from their source of supply, even if they could scrape together enough money to pay for the journey. These workers move about from camp to camp, but never get away from a district.

The aggressive spirit of the times even caused the long exploited cowboys of western ranches to strike for higher pay. Receiving only twenty-five to fifty dollars a month, Wyoming cowhands of "panhandle" ranches demanded higher pay and better food. The strike involving half a dozen ranches was lost. But the militant spirit was spreading.

The IWW sought in its announcements to unite all workers on an industrial basis behind a common philosophy: "The working class and the employing class have nothing in common. There can be no peace so long as hunger and want are found among millions of

WE ARE IN HERE FOR YOU; YOU ARE OUT THERE FOR US

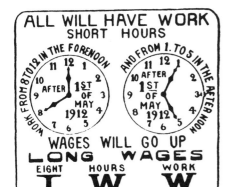

## Preamble of the Industrial Workers of the World

The working class and the employing class have nothing in common. There can be no peace so long as hunger and want are found among millions of working people and the few, who make up the employing class, have all the good things of life.

Between these two classes a struggle must go on until the workers of the world organize as a class, take possession of the earth and the machinery of production, and abolish the wage system.

We find that the centering of the management of industries into fewer and fewer hands makes the trade unions unable to cope with the ever growing power of the employing class. The trade unions foster a state of affairs which allows one set of workers to be pitted against another set of workers in the same industry, thereby helping defeat one another in wage wars. Moreover, the trade unions aid the employing class to mislead the workers into the belief that the working class have interests in common with their employers.

These conditions can be changed and the interest of the working class upheld only by an organization formed in such a way that all its members in any one industry, or in all industries if necessary, cease work whenever a strike or lockout is on in any department thereof, thus making an injury to one an injury to all.

Instead of the conservative motto, "A fair day's wage for a fair day's work," we must inscribe on our banner the revolutionary watchword, "Abolition of the wage system."

It is the historic mission of the working class to do away with capitalism. The army of production must be organized, not only for the every-day struggle with capitalists, but also to carry on production when capitalism shall have been overthrown. By organizing industrially we are forming the structure of the new society within the shell of the old.

# COLLECTIVE BARGAINING

LABOR'S PROPOSAL TO
INSURE GREATER

## INDUSTRIAL PEACE

WITH QUESTIONS AND
ANSWERS EXPLAINING
THE PRINCIPLE

By SAMUEL GOMPERS

PRICE, TEN CENTS PER COPY

PUBLISHED BY AMERICAN FEDERATION OF LABOR
WASHINGTON, D. C.

FRANK MORRISON          SAMUEL GOMPERS
SECRETARY                PRESIDENT

---

## CHAPTER 48.

### CONSTITUTIONAL AMENDMENT.

(S. B. No. 89, by Senator Moore.)

## AN ACT

TO SUBMIT TO THE QUALIFIED ELECTORS OF THE STATE OF COLORADO AN AMENDMENT TO ARTICLE FIVE (V) OF THE CONSTITUTION OF THE STATE OF COLORADO BY ADDING THERETO A NEW SECTION, TO BE KNOWN AS SECTION TWENTY-FIVEa (25a), DIRECTING THE GENERAL ASSEMBLY TO PROVIDE BY LAW AND PRESCRIBE SUITABLE PENALTIES FOR THE VIOLATION THEREOF, FOR A PERIOD OF EMPLOYMENT NOT TO EXCEED EIGHT (8) HOURS WITHIN ANY TWENTY-FOUR (24) HOURS (EXCEPTING IN CASES OF EMERGENCY WHERE LIFE OR PROPERTY IS IN IMMINENT DANGER), FOR PERSONS EMPLOYED IN UNDERGROUND MINES OR OTHER UNDERGROUND WORKINGS, BLAST FURNACES, SMELTERS; AND ANY ORE REDUCTION WORKS OR OTHER BRANCH OF INDUSTRY OR LABOR THAT THE GENERAL ASSEMBLY MAY CONSIDER INJURIOUS OR DANGEROUS TO HEALTH, LIFE OR LIMB.

*Be it Enacted by the General Assembly of the State of Colorado:*

Section 1. That there shall be submitted to the qualified electors of the State of Colorado, at the next general election for members of the General Assembly,

*Approved March 14, 1901*

working people and the few . . . have all the good things of life." The IWW conviction was that there was need for "one great industrial union . . . founded on the class struggle."

The IWW membership was largely recruited from the unskilled and semiskilled workers, the least privileged and the most exploited, lumberjacks, migratory workers, farmhands, western miners.

The Wobblies, as the IWW members were sometimes called, developed the practice of using "flaming language"—as one writer put it—rhetoric that made free use of such terms as "sabotage" and "direct action." Such references were duly used to discredit the organization among working people.

However, historians Philip Taft and Philip Ross have pointed out in their comments on violence in labor history that "IWW activity was virtually free of violence. . . . It is of some interest to note that a speaker who advocated violence at a meeting at the IWW hall in Everett [Washington] was later exposed as a private detective."

The IWW was involved in numerous strike situations and, in almost all, made a peaceful and constructive contribution. However, the inability to consolidate gains and to build lasting organization—as well as the anti-IWW persecutions that developed—ultimately caused the weakening of the organization as an effective labor group.

As might be expected, the voices of dissent, arising from socialists and IWW sources, spread considerable alarm in conservative circles. While there were those who believed in repression as a method of silencing such raucous noises, a growing number of leading industrial spokesmen were coming to the conclusion that there was another way. This "other way" took form in an organization, known as the National Civic Federation, "dedicated to the fostering of harmony and collaboration between capital and organized labor."

The federation, founded around the turn of the century, included some of the most prominent industrial and labor figures as active members: Marcus A. Hanna, head of the Republican party; Andrew Carnegie, retired steelmaster; August Belmont, the banker; John D. Rockefeller, Jr., heir to the oil fortune. Labor was prominently represented by Samuel Gompers, A.F. of L. head; John Mitchell, president of the United Mine Workers; and numerous leaders of A.F. of L. craft unions such as Warren Stone of the Brotherhood of Locomotive Engineers; J. J. Hannahan, grand master of the Locomotive Firemen; James O'Connell and James Duncan, A.F. of L. organizers.

Participation by union leaders in the National

Colorado amends its constitution to approve the eight-hour workday in 1901.

The A.F. of L.'s powerful executive council (left to right seated): Joseph F. Valentine, Iron Molders' Union; Frank Morrison, International Typographical Union; Samuel Gompers, president; James Duncan, Granite Cutters; Daniel J. Tobin, International Brotherhood of Teamsters. (Left to right standing): T. A. Rickert, United Garment Workers; William Green, United Mine Workers; Jacob Fischer, Barbers' International Union; W. D. Mahon, Amalgamated Association of Street, Electric Railway & Motor Coach Employees; Frank Duffy, Brotherhood of Carpenters; Matthew Woll, AFL Union Label & Service Trades Department.

Civic Federation's activities was to become a point of sharp controversy in labor's ranks. The historian Norman Ware states that through its participation, the A.F. of L. thus "became a 'Morgan partner' in attacking radicalism wherever it appeared."

While certain unions, from time to time, disengaged from the federation, it was not until 1935 that the A.F. of L. ruled that its officers withdraw from the Civic Federation, then chiefly involved in an anticommunist crusade.

To many, there was nothing actually contradictory in Samuel Gomper's support of the Civic Federation.

Under the energetic and shrewd leadership of Gompers, the A.F. of L. became, for approximately forty years, the dominant labor organization in the country. By 1900, it had grown to over one million members; fourteen years later, it had doubled that number. Gompers was proud of being a "practical" man. He believed in applying sound business practices to the union movement. He was not a theorist, but was convinced of the importance to labor of fighting for immediate aims. Once asked the objectives

## Should a Political Labor Party Be Formed?

AN ADDRESS BY

### SAMUEL GOMPERS
President of the American Federation of Labor

### TO A LABOR CONFERENCE
Held at New York City, December 9, 1918

Endorsed and Directed to be Published by the Executive Council of the American Federation of Labor Headquarters, A. F. of L. Building Washington, D. C.

PRICE, TEN CENTS PER COPY

FRANK MORRISON
Secretary

SAMUEL GOMPERS
President

A.F. of L. brochure of early 1900s.

of the A.F. of L., he reportedly answered with one word: "More."

Early in the history of the A.F. of L., a revealing insight into its philosophy was given when Adolph Strasser appeared before a United States Senate hearing in 1883:

Question: You are seeking to improve human matters first?

Answer: Yes, sir, I look first to the trade I represent; I look first to the cigarmakers, ·the interests of men who employ me to represent their interests.

Question: I was only asking you in regard to your ultimate ends.

Answer: We have no ultimate ends. We are going on from day to day. We are fighting only for immediate objects—objects that can be realized in a few years . . . we say in our constitution that we are opposed to theorists . . . we are all practical men . . .

Decades later, in 1914, Gompers himself appeared before another body, this time the United States Commission on Industrial Relations, to discuss A.F. of L. objectives. He was questioned by Morris Hillquit, a leader of the Socialist party:

Hillquit: Then, the object of the labor union is to obtain complete social justice for themselves and for their wives and for their children.

Gompers: It is the effort to obtain a better life every day.

Hillquit: Every day and always . . .

Gompers: Every day. That does not limit it.

Hillquit: Until such time . . .

Gompers: Not until any time.

Hillquit: In other words . . .

Gompers: In other words, we go further than you. You have an end; we have not.

Samuel Gompers did much to develop the idea of "business unionism."

President Woodrow Wilson, Samuel Gompers, and William B. Wilson, a former United Mine Workers' official, who was appointed the nation's first secretary of labor in 1913.

DEVOTED TO THE INTERESTS AND VOICING THE DEMANDS OF THE TRADE UNION MOVEMENT

Vol. XV.                    APRIL, 1908.                    No. 4

# LABOR'S PROTEST TO CONGRESS

WASHINGTON, D. C., *March 19, 1908.*

WE, THE official representatives of the national and international trade and labor unions and organization of farmers, in national conference assembled, in the District of Columbia, for the purpose of considering and taking action deemed necessary to meet the situation in which the working people of our country are placed by recent decisions of the courts, now appear before Congress to voice the earnest and emphatic protest of the workers of the country against the indifference, if not actual hostility, which Congress has shown toward the reasonable and righteous measures proposed by the workers for the safeguarding of their rights and interests.

In the name of Labor we now urge upon Congress the necessity for immediate action for relief from the most grave and momentous situation which has ever confronted the working people of this country. This crisis has been brought about by the application by the Supreme Court of the United States of the Sherman anti-trust law to the workers both organized and in their individual capacity.

Labor and the people generally look askance at the invasion of the court upon the prerogatives of the law-making and executive departments of our government.

The workers feel that Congress itself must share our chagrin and sense of injustice when the courts exhibit an utter disregard for the real intent and purpose of laws enacted to safeguard and protect the workers in the exercise of their normal activities. There is something ominous in the ironic manner in which the courts guarantee to workers:

The "right" to be maimed and killed without liability to the employer.

The "right" to be discharged for belonging to a union.

(261)

Early A.F. of L. political action—March 1908.

The A.F. of L. under Gompers avoided politics in the usual sense. "No party politics, be they democratic, republican, populist, socialist or any other, shall have a place in the Federation," said Gompers. But the A.F. of L. did play an important role, under pressure from its members, in helping win social and labor legislation, nationally and in the states. Gompers was skeptical of some legislative proposals supported by liberal leaders, even opposing as a socialist trend government health, unemployment insurance, and old-age pensions. Gompers believed labor's gains should be won largely by collective bargaining. But he did lend the A.F. of L. influence, which was considerable, for or against numerous other legislative efforts.

In March 1906, the A.F. of L.-approved labor's bill of grievances was sent to President Theodore Roosevelt. The list of grievances that confronted the

Mrs. Mary Kenney O'Sullivan, a Boston bindery worker, was the A.F. of L.'s first woman organizer.

Change of shift in a Nevada silver mine

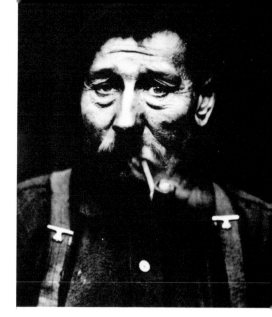

Worker from Ireland

A. Philip Randolph, head of the Brotherhood of Sleeping Car Porters.

working people of the era included the demand for passage of an anti-injunction bill, restrictions on immigration, a bill to free seamen from involuntary servitude and, as mentioned earlier, stronger antitrust laws.

Many of these demands were realized in the years ahead, particularly under the administration of President Woodrow Wilson.

An idea for a United States department of labor had been put forward by labor as early as 1865. It was not until March 1913, however, that such an agency was created. The department's purpose, briefly, was to "foster, promote, and develop the welfare of the wage earners of the United States . . ." The one time coal miner, William B. Wilson, was named the first secretary of labor.

In 1915, the La Follette Seamen's Act was passed, which guaranteed the rights of seamen to seek a limit to working hours, to obtain part of their pay on demand when reaching any loading or discharging port, and other benefits. Much of the long years of work that resulted in passage of the act was done by Andrew Furuseth, general secretary and president of the International Seamen's Union of America. During his years of working in behalf of seamen, Furuseth was once asked what he would do if served with an injunction restraining him from certain of his union activities.

"I would put the injunction in my pocket," said Furuseth, "and go to jail and in jail my bunk would be no narrower, my food no worse, nor I more lonely than in the forecastle."

Other social reforms of the era included the Hep-

Sidney Hillman, youthful organizer of the Amalgamated Clothing Workers of America, said: "We need a new type of labor leader . . . men and women more dedicated to social service."

Andrew Furuseth, who fought for the International Seamen's Union of America.

burn Act of 1906, which strengthened the powers of the Interstate Commerce Commission to fix fair and reasonable railroad rates. A constitutional amendment, providing for the direct election of United States senators, was passed by Congress and ratified by the American voters in 1913. The direct primary was approved at the turn of the century, which gave people greater control over the selection and nomination of candidates; this was accompanied in some states by the initiative, referendum and recall. State laws for workmen's compensation were either passed or strengthened in many states, as were those for improved factory inspection.

The Adamson Act of 1916 was approved, which established an eight-hour day for workers in all interstate railroads. The Clayton Antitrust Act of 1914, which Gompers hailed as "Labor's Magna Carta," was passed, declaring "the labor of a human being is not a commodity." Although the act purported to exclude labor unions from the provisions of antitrust laws, the bill promised more than it delivered. It was found to include loopholes that did not prevent courts from using injunctions against labor after all.

In 1920, after more than seventy years of effort,

Labor proclaims its grievances.

Susan B. Anthony and Elizabeth Cady Stanton, pioneer fighters for the woman's vote, both had been members of the Knights of Labor.

## Federal Child Labor Law Is Held Invalid

Supreme Court Declares It Is Invasion of Local Powers of States

Four Justices Join in Dissenting Opinion

InterstateCommerceActNot Intended to Regulate Production, Majority Says

## Highest Court Nullifies Child Labor Statute

Taft Delivers the Decision Holding Law Unconstitutional in Encroaching on Powers of the States

Penalty of Excise Tax Is Attacked

Rules Congress Exceeded Its Authority; No Dissenting Opinion Filed

WASHINGTON, May 15. The child labor law was declared unconstitutional

Reports of rulings of the United States Supreme Court in 1918 and 1922, which declared unconstitutional laws to outlaw child labor.

## SUFFRAGE FORCES VICTORIOUS

### RATIFICATION COMES AFTER BITTER FIGHT

RATE DECISION IS POST...

STUMPING TOUR...

House Votes 50 to 46 to Ratify Amendment After Two Roll Calls on Motion to Table Show Ti...

largely by women suffragists, and with occasional labor support, a constitutional amendment extending the vote to women was ratified. The movement to abolish child labor made progress, with labor among its most staunch advocates, but twice it was blocked. When the Congress of the United States approved laws abolishing child labor, twice the United States Supreme Court, once in 1918 and once in 1922, ruled the laws unconstitutional.

The first part of the twentieth century was a period of social progress. But a large number of working people, at the bottom of the economic heap, were unaware of changes for the better. These included, particularly, thousands of immigrants from abroad, many unskilled. Also included were workers, black and white, in the southern part of the country, the chief victims of the permanent economic crisis that had followed the Civil War. The factories of the land, expanding tremendously, were filled with men and women whose daily grievances were seldom expressed in any organized fashion—and even less often satisfied.

# ELEVEN

# 1900-1920

# LABOR IN THE
# WORLD WAR I ERA

*". . . the scaffold has never yet*
*and never will destroy*
*an idea or a movement . . ."*

Some leaders of industry and labor may have had class harmony in mind. For was not America now able to claim, and with growing accuracy, to be the wealthiest nation in the world? Were there not enough natural resources on the North American continent for all to share? There were, by the early 1900s, thousands of automobiles in operation; telephones were now a commonplace; airplanes no longer sent most horses into panic. Motion pictures were able to transfer even the most impecunious into new worlds of grandeur and adventure. The magic of radio was about to enter almost every home that had electricity. These, and many other exciting innovations, recognized no class lines.

But for workers in many of the mines, offices, and factories of the nation, life was not that much better. Although leaders might discuss collaboration for the common good, within these workshops conditions were anything but satisfactory or harmonious.

Such was the situation in the textile mills of Lawrence, Massachusetts, in the winter of 1912.

By this time the "rosy cheeked maidens," who had entered the textile mills of Lawrence, Lowell, and other New England towns, had long since departed. The warm glow of paternalism—which had inspired lectures, poetry readings, church activities, and social gatherings—had been extinguished years before. The mill operators were now in the undisguised business

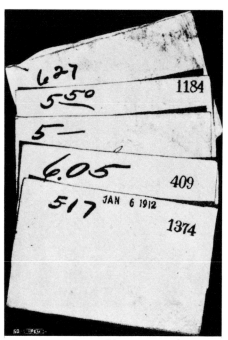

Pay envelopes of Lawrence workers.

Conditions of work in Lawrence mills were often deplorable.

of making money, in the fastest and most direct manner they could. Competition, absentee owners, premium pay for production quotas—all had long since drained any feelings of benevolence from factory management that may have existed hitherto.

Most of the thirty thousand working men, women, and children employed in Lawrence in 1912 were unskilled, low paid, and overworked. Most had recently arrived in America from a variety of nations overseas, lured here by the promise of a land of plenty. Instead, they found conditions in the textile mills that endangered their health; exhausted them physically and mentally; and community-living facilities that were scarcely adequate for animals; and no way to register their grievances.

A subsequent federal investigation of the situation was to reveal additional information as to conditions in the mill such as:

Employee: In regard to the wages, I stated that I made as much money in one week as I used to make in a week and a half. Of course, I wish I would have that money. But I must tell you that the speed was speeded up not by that engineer, but it was speeded up from the boss down to the weaver, for instance—

Congressman: You mean instructions to work faster?

Employee: Yes; for instance, there are belts that run the wheels of the machinery in every room. That belt since the 1st of January was speeded up by putting some kind of soap on it, or whatever it is called, and it was running with a much faster speed than it used to be; in fact

Strikers of Lawrence marching. The children are workers, not young people on a holiday.

that we could not attend to the work. But it is also speeded up by the loom fixer—the one that fixes the weaving machines, because he gets the premium when more cloth comes off from that machine, and the second hand in that room gets the premium when more cloth comes on in that room. It is a premium just on the working man, that one push the other, one is trying on the other, tell him to go ahead and make the machine faster and faster, and so they do. Many people work a week or two and have to stay out a week and spend half a week's wages for doctors and medicine, and in spite of that, they have a premium system that kills the people there by inches, not at once—we haven't got that lucky chance like a miner, he is killed at once—we are killed by inches every day; for instance, the speed usually used to run fast enough all the time, but the premium was a thing to compel the man or woman or child to speed up themselves, and the weaver, if he does not make the premium a month, he is called up to the office and told, or to the second hand, and told, "Now, you know that you did not make as much premium this month, and look out for the next month if you want to keep that job." No matter if the man is sick, or the woman is sick, she is compelled to stay at the machine in order not to lose the job . . .

Accidents became commonplace as a result of the speedup, general fatigue, and faulty nourishment. In some departments there was scarcely an employee who had not lost a finger in the whirling machinery.

A movement for shorter working hours had resulted the year previous in the passage of a state law that cut the work week for women and minors from fifty-six to fifty-four hours. When the law officially went into effect on January 1, the companies had cut the working hours of men, women, and children; but they also had cut the wages, too, and, at the same time, speeded up production.

Lawrence was dominated by the American Woolen

AT LAWRENCE

These children must remain at home in want because it would be a case of "neglect" to send them away to strike sympathizers.
—New York Tribune, Feb. 28.

Company, which *The New York Times* referred to as "the $65,000,000 wool trust." The company's "Wood Mill," named after President William Wood, stretched into the distance almost as far as the eye could see.

"Husky, able bodied men would steal by the watchmen and get into the mill," said an article in *American Magazine,* describing conditions in Lawrence at the time, "and then beg . . . for a job where they could make any wages at all . . . There are many able bodied men in the Lawrence mills doing children's jobs, taking children's places, and receiving the pitiful children's wages . . ."

Discrimination in the mills was widespread. One nationality, pitted against another, kept workers disunited. In one department of the American Woolen Company, the Polish workers had been threatened with replacement by Italians unless they worked faster. Hours of work averaged sixty a week. Women were encouraged to enter the mills, as one worker testified later, "not that their wages be levelled up to men, but that the men be forced to compete with women."

The result of years of deprivation had its dramatic climax in the middle of January when more than twenty-five thousand millworkers—including men, women, and children—marched from their jobs.

Thousands of textile workers milled through the streets, leaderless. When representatives of strikers decided to call on the IWW for help, two organizers were dispatched to Lawrence: Joseph J. Ettor and Arturo Giovannitti.

"Solidarity is necessary," the youthful Ettor told the strikers, "division is the surest means to lose the strike. . . . Among workers there is only one nationality, one race, one creed. . . . By all means make this strike as peaceful as possible." Ettor told the textile workers, "In the last analysis, all the blood spilled will be your blood."

Early in the strike the militia was called to the scene to maintain order. From that point on violence was more frequent. In one incident, a striking woman was shot and killed. Both Ettor and Giovannitti were arrested and charged with involvement in the murder, and held in prison without bail. But still the strike maintained its solidarity.

A city judge stated: "The only way to teach them is to deal out the severest sentences." And a stockholder remarked: "The way to settle this strike is to shoot down 40 or 50 of 'em."

An attempt was made to plant dynamite and blame it on the strikers. "When the strikers used or prepared to use dynamite," said one daily newspaper, "they display a fiendish lack of humanity." Some weeks later, a local merchant was arrested, charged with planting the dynamite in an effort to discredit the strikers. Even later, the president of the American Woolen Company, William Wood, was himself indicted, charged with involvement in the dynamite plot.

On March 12—sixty-three days after the strike began—the mills of Lawrence surrendered. The demands of the workers were met including overtime pay, a wage increase, and no discrimination. Two days later, twenty-five thousand men, women, and children gathered on the Lawrence Common and solemnly voted on the settlement as they had done on most other issues of the strike.

Following the settlement began the trial of Ettor and Giovannitti charged with being accessories to murder. It was a strange case since even the prosecution admitted that neither man had been within miles of the place where the crime was committed.

"Does the District Attorney believe," asked Ettor in his address to the court, "that . . . the gallows . . . ever settled an idea? If an idea can live, it lives because history adjudged it right . . . the scaffold has never yet and never will destroy an idea or a movement . . ."

Influential in the outcome was the sensational news, made known during the trial, that President Wood had been indicted, charged with complicity in the dynamite plot during the strike. After this revelation, the jury was not convinced of the guilt of the two men. On November 23, they were found not guilty.

Less than a year later another dramatic struggle erupted, this time in the distant state of Colorado.

Confrontation at Lawrence.

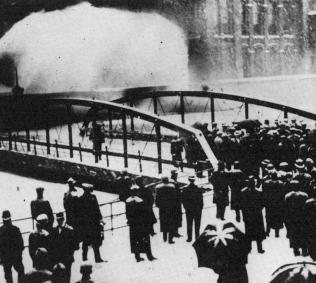

Strikers were sprayed with water.

IWW organizers Elizabeth Gurley Flynn and William D. Haywood with textile strikers' children in Paterson, New Jersey.

Miners in Trinidad, Colorado, in protest march at attack on fellow unionists.

Joseph J. Ettor and Arturo Giovannitti

Miners of the Ludlow area lived under conditions that, by 1913, were becoming increasingly intolerable. The United States Commission on Industrial Relations reported:

Many camp marshals, whose appointment and salaries are controlled by local companies, have exercised a system of espionage and have resorted to arbitrary powers of police control, acting in the capacity of judge and jury in passing the sentence: "Down the canyon for you," meaning thereby that the miner so addressed was discharged. . . . Miners generally fear to complain of real grievances because of the danger of their discharge or their being placed in unfavorable position in the mines.

Conflict finally flared up between workers affiliated with the United Mine Workers and the Rockefeller-owned Colorado Fuel & Iron Company. Rather than grant union recognition the company preferred to fight.

More than nine thousand miners in the fall of 1913, with their families, quit company property and set up tents in adjacent land. They were prepared to stay out of the pits until their employers agreed to improve conditions. They were protesting against being forced to live in a company town, being paid with company scrip, and working more than the eight-hour day that was on the statute books. In addition, hundreds of men were killed annually in accidents in the mines. "They value a mule more . . . highly than a human being," one union leader commented.

The strike continued through the winter of 1913 and 1914. The miners were evidently prepared to live in the tents until they won their fight. At length the state militia was summoned, arriving with machine guns and rifles. One night, after a series of unsuccessful efforts to dislodge the strikers, the troopers riddled their tents with bullets. When women and children crawled into holes they had dug inside the tents to escape the onslaught, the troops poured oil on the tents and set them on fire. Eleven children and two women, who had taken refuge in one of the holes, were burned to death or suffocated.

The widely publicized event shocked the nation. Many of the strikers managed to escape to the hills where other workers joined them in a running battle with the troopers. Finally President Wilson sent federal troops to disarm both sides. But not before thirty-three men, women, and children had been shot or burned to death.

"The mine operators won the strike," reported the *United Mine Workers' Journal*, ". . . but old John D. [Rockefeller] lost some of his public affection and had to begin the practice of giving away dimes to placate opinion."

The strike was a defeat of national significance for labor. From it developed the "Rockefeller Plan" for handling industrial personnel problems. Under this plan, unions that lacked militancy were encouraged.

A congressional hearing on labor conditions was attended by Mrs. William Howard Taft, wife of the President.

Some Ludlow survivors.

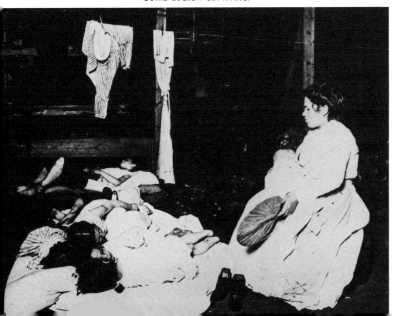

A monument to those who died at Ludlow, Colorado.

"The early rise of company unionism in nearly all other large-scale capitalistic industries," wrote Professor Malcolm Keir, "was traceable to the publicity which was given to the 'Rockefeller Plan.' "

But, side by side with "company unionism," a new approach to containing the militancy of labor was being born.

Fundamental to nearly all antiunion efforts of this era was an employer crusade known as the "American plan," or "open shop." This symbolized an organized effort by management to prevent the coming of unions or to weaken and eliminate them where they existed.

"There never has been any doubt in the minds of the trade union workers," wrote Samuel Gompers, "as to what is back of the 'open shop' movement. They know that it is a movement backed by the powerful enemies of labor."

Industrial spokesmen disagreed with Gompers. "I think it is the proper thing to protect the open shop principle," said Eugene C. Grace, president of Bethlehem Steel Corporation.

The popular columnist of the day, Finley Peter Dunne, wrote of the open shop through his creation, Mr. Dooley:

"Wat's all this that's in the papers about the open shop?" asked Mr. Hennessey.

"Why, don't ye know?" said Mr. Dooley. "Really, I'm surprised at yer ignorance, Hinnissey. What is the open shop? Sure, 'tis where they kape the doors open to accommodate the constant stream of men comin' in to take jobs cheaper than the men that has the jobs . . ."

"But," said Mr. Hennessey, "these open shop men ye mention say they are for unions if properly conducted."

"Sure," said Mr. Dooley, "if properly conducted. And there we are: and how would they have them conducted? No strikes, no rules, no contracts, no scales, hardly any wages and damn few members."

An effort was made, as part of the open-shop campaign, to glamorize the role of the strikebreaker. In a magazine article appearing in 1903, Charles W. Eliot, president of Harvard, described the strikebreaker as "a very good type of modern hero." In the crusade for the open shop, the role of detectives and undercover men in labor situations increased, involving such organizations as the William J. Burns International Detective Agency and the Pinkerton Detective Agency, which was involved in the Molly Maguire trials, the Homestead strike, and others.

The courts appeared to respond to the prevailing atmosphere. One famous case in 1902 involved hat

Fur workers

workers in Danbury, Connecticut, who had declared a national boycott against the D. E. Loewe Company in support of a local strike for recognition. The company sued, charging the union was conspiring in restraint of trade. Triple damages were asked, not against the union but against individual union members on strike. In 1916, the United States Supreme Court, with Justice K. M. Landis issuing the decision, ruled in favor of the company. Some $252,000 was assessed against union members, many of whom were threatened with loss of their homes and savings.

Differences between labor and management, during this period, frequently resulted in violent actions.

"I have an abhorrence of violence," Samuel Gompers once said, ". . . It is invariably the labor movement that suffers most from connection with violence . . ."

"No major labor organization in American history," states Philip Taft and Philip Ross, "ever advocated violence as a policy. . . . Trade unions from the beginning . . . stressed their desire for peaceful relations . . ."

In agreement, Professor Michael Wallace, in his study of violence in America, points out that "most moderate labor demands have called forth ferocious resistance; our 'labor violence,' in fact, might be more aptly renamed 'capitalist violence.' "

However, violent conduct has often been charged against labor. For example, in 1905 the former governor of Idaho was killed by a bomb. Shortly after, the Pinkerton Detective Agency was called in. The crime was traced—so it was claimed—to officials of the Western Federation of Miners: William D. Haywood, treasurer; Charles H. Moyer, president; and George A. Pettibone, a former member.

There was much sensational publicity. President Theodore Roosevelt joined in condemning the accused labor leaders, referring to them as "undesirable citizens."

As the case developed it was found that James McPharlan—who had supplied evidence against the Molly Maguires a quarter of a century earlier—was now manager of the Pinkerton western division and was involved in the accusation against the three union leaders.

A defense organization was established, and Clarence Darrow, the noted labor lawyer, was hired as defense counsel. Darrow told the jury: "Don't be so blind . . . as to believe that when you make three fresh new graves, you will kill the labor movement . . ." As the case dragged on, the prosecution failed to establish the guilt of the three union leaders and they were freed.

When news of the acquittal reached mining camps of the West, there was much celebration. "In Goldfield when I went there later," reported Haywood years afterward, "they showed me the dents that had been made in the mahogany bars in the saloons by the hobnails of the boys who had danced to celebrate their joy at my release. There is no way of estimating how much whiskey was drunk for the occasion . . ."

Developments on the home front were soon overshadowed by war clouds that developed in the spring

Check and receipt in the Danbury Hatters case.

World War I poster.

William D. Haywood, Charles H. Moyer, and George A. Pettibone. Because of a childhood accident, Haywood lost the sight of one eye. He usually turned his face away from the camera for this reason.

of 1914 with the assassination of Archduke Francis Ferdinand, heir to the throne of Austria. The First World War was launched.

There were those who believed that the United States should enter at once. Gompers was among these. The historian Philip Taft wrote, "As war approached, Gompers was convinced that labor had to cooperate or lose the possibility of influencing decisions."

However, there were some A.F. of L. leaders who opposed America's entrance. John P. White, president of the United Mine Workers, viewed the conflict as "a commercial war." Daniel J. Tobin, president of the Brotherhood of Teamsters, was another opponent of American involvement.

At a meeting of the IWW General Executive Board held in Chicago in July 1917, a statement was approved on where the IWW stood on the question of war. "Since its inception our organization has op-

posed all national and imperialistic wars," the IWW statement said in part.

Our songs, our literature, the sentiment of the entire membership—the very spirit of our union, give evidence of our unalterable opposition to both capitalism and its wars. All members of the IWW who have been drafted should mark their claims for exemption, "IWW opposed to war."

However, in the spring of 1917 the United States entered the conflict. At the start of the war many union members still worked a twelve-hour day and a seven-day work week. The average wage was about fifteen dollars a week. This was to change.

The somewhat benign attitude of government toward labor, and the scarcity of available working people during the war, placed unions in an advan-

Military recruits

War workers

Wood was recognized as a serviceable cheap material for a wide variety of uses—including submarine chasers, ships, airplanes, and for the fuel that the armed forces needed.

The relatively new automobile industry was also called upon to assume an important role. The making of passenger cars shifted to production of shells, guns, tractors, and aircraft engines. And the workers—men and women—learned new skills to keep the production lines moving.

During World War I, large numbers of women were taken out of the house and entered factories for the first time to help produce the goods the armed forces needed. Thousands of women worked fabricating bronze, brass, and copper. Many others were employed making hardware parts, such as those for typewriters and sewing machines. "It was during this war," says Elizabeth Faulkner Baker, "that women for the first time began to work directly with machines, a function which men had denied her capability for so many years. . . . With the end of World War I, it was found that women were in industry permanently. There was no getting her back to the home and kitchen."

One employer was quoted as saying: "We can't get women back at the old wages . . . [they] are sticking to their war jobs." Said the *Textile World Journal:* "Women may be regarded as fixtures in the machine shops and foundries . . ."

Prior to America's entrance into the war there was much talk of preparedness. Demonstrations and pa-

tageous position. The government was interested in winning support for the war from all sections of the population. To help achieve this in the ranks of organized labor, the War Labor Board endorsed the principle of collective bargaining and the employment of union workers in projects executed under government contract. These, and other such measures, inevitably helped the A.F. of L. membership grow. By 1919, there were over three million A.F. of L. members, not including independent unions such as those in the railroad industry. As a consequence, wages also rose sharply.

"No important measure vitally affecting labor is now taken," said the *New Republic,* "without consultation with the leaders of the American Federation of Labor, and on the most important government boards the wage earners are represented."

The demands of war affected new industries and old. Emphasis was placed upon the traditional role of wood. "Wood will win the war," became a slogan.

British labor delegates confer with American A.F. of L. leaders. Gompers is at extreme left. Fifth from left is Secretary of Labor William B. Wilson.

Thomas J. Mooney, saying good-bye to his mother.

rades, seeking to stimulate support for America's entrance into the war, took place in various cities. On July 22, 1916, such a parade was marching down San Francisco's Market Street to the tunes of martial music when, shortly after two o'clock in the afternoon, a bomb exploded. Nine people were killed and forty more wounded.

Newspaper headlines blamed the crime on "anarchistic elements." Four days later a number of arrests were made, including Thomas J. Mooney, a thirty-four-year-old organizer for the International Molders' Union A.F. of L. and a onetime IWW member. Also arrested was twenty-two-year-old Warren K. Billings, a shoe worker and friend of Mooney.

Thus began the Mooney-Billings case, which was to last for more than two decades and cause repercussions not only in America but literally throughout the world. Although Mooney and Billings were attacked as anarchists, the labor movement defended them as victims of the antiunion, open-shop drive. At Mooney's trial the jury was urged by the prosecution to "place this fiend where never again he can repeat this act. . . . Mooney . . . [was] determined to

Warren K. Billings

earned him a commutation to life imprisonment. But Mooney demanded his freedom. "I demand that you revoke your commutation," he said, "I prefer a glorious death sentence to a living death . . . I am innocent."

The secretary of labor spoke out for freeing Mooney. Both houses of Congress held hearings on the Mooney-Billings affair. At a special legislative session in the California State House in 1938, Mooney, now grown from a young to an old man, stated: "Billings and I stood in the way of an open shop town."

"He will be kept in San Quentin," said the defense lawyer, Arthur Garfield Hays, "until public opinion so changes that it will be to the political advantage of a governor to let him out of jail, or until he dies."

It was not until twenty-one years after his imprisonment that a young California governor, elected largely by the vote of organized labor and pledged to free Mooney, acted. In 1939, Mooney was officially pardoned. Shortly thereafter Billings also gained his freedom.

bring about a reign of terror in San Francisco." In such an atmosphere Mooney was found guilty and condemned to death. In a separate trial Billings was convicted and—because of an earlier conviction—sentenced to life imprisonment according to California law.

A few days after Mooney's trial, the Molders' Union, Local 164, voted Mooney an expression of confidence, even electing him a delegate to the union's next convention.

In the days and years that followed, Mooney and his defenders produced an array of facts to support their claim that he could not have been guilty of the crime. One sensational piece of evidence was a photograph that identified him as watching the parade miles away at the time of the crime. A clock in the picture appeared to prove the point. Additional information was procured bearing upon the unreliability of witnesses that had testified against Mooney.

By 1923, all the living jurors were on record in favor of a full pardon for Mooney. As increased evidence was made available, the trial judge, Franklin A. Griffin, stated: "The Mooney case was one of the dirtiest jobs ever put over, and I resent the fact that my court was used for such a contemptible piece of work . . ."

The ground swell in defense of Mooney, including requests from President Woodrow Wilson, finally

Mooney behind bars.

The parade in San Francisco honoring Mooney when he was released after twenty-one years in prison.

There were other celebrated cases of the era. Civil rights have always been important to working people. Without them, they lose their democratic right to seek redress of their grievances, and they become doomed to a descending standard of working and living.

This is why, when civil rights appear to be violated, labor has frequently participated for the defense.

In 1914, a young IWW organizer and songwriter, Joe Hill, was arrested in Salt Lake City, Utah, charged with robbery and murder. He denied guilt. The Joe Hill case became a national and even international cause. Thousands had sung his songs, "Casey Jones," "Pie in the Sky," "Preacher and the Slave," "The Rebel Girl," on picket lines wherever there had been labor struggles. Many believed him a victim of an antilabor frame-up.

However, on November 19, 1915, he was executed by firing squad according to the law of the state. His last words were reputed to have been: "Don't waste time in mourning; Organize!"

"The adherents of Joe Hill," stated Barrie Stavis in the preface to his play about Hill, "say that he was framed; that he was shot by the state of Utah not for the murder of a grocer and his son, but because he was *Joe Hill,* labor's poet, the man who wrote songs expressing the deepest needs of the working class. . . . They say that he was framed because he was a member of the Industrial Workers of the World; the most militant section of the labor movement at that time."

The coming of the war increased agitation for similar repressive action.

Claiming the IWW was "hampering the war effort," government and vigilante groups raided dozens of IWW offices in various communities around the country. Hundreds of workers, some IWW members and some not, were arrested, their patriotism under question. Sometimes mobs took the law into their own hands.

Frank Little, a militant IWW organizer in a strike of metal miners in Butte, Montana, in 1913, was seized by an armed mob, beaten, and then hung to a railroad trestle. In 1919, Wesley Everest, another

The funeral of Joe Hill

Joe Hill

## JOE HILL'S LAST WILL

(Written in his cell, November 18, 1915, on the eve of his execution)

My will is easy to decide,
For there is nothing to divide.
My kin don't need to fuss and moan—
"Moss does not cling to rolling stone."

My body?  Ah, if I could choose,
I would to ashes it reduce,
And let the merry breezes blow
My dust to where some flowers grow.

Perhaps some fading flower then
Would come to life and bloom again.
This is my last and final will,
Good luck to all of you,

—JOE HILL.

Frank Little

A report of the 1919 Seattle general strike.

Wesley Everest

Boston police on strike in 1919.

IWW leader still in his "doughboy" military uniform, was attacked while helping the unionization of lumber workers in Centralia, Washington. The IWW headquarters was broken into and Everest taken captive. "You haven't got the guts to lynch a man in the daytime," he accused his captors. That night Everest was mutilated, shot, and hung to a bridge.

Hundreds of other IWW members and suspected members were arrested for impeding the war effort, including William D. Haywood, members of the IWW

executive board, and IWW editors. Almost one hundred leaders were brought to trial in Chicago. In the prevailing atmosphere, almost all were found guilty. Many served long terms in prison.

A general strike in Seattle in 1919, in support of shipyard workers' demands for higher wages, involved sixty thousand people. The strike was brief and peaceful. But Mayor Ole Olson branded it a Bolshevik plot, an accusation—widely publicized—contributing to the national unease.

At about the same time nineteen Boston policemen, non-IWWers, but leading a movement to orga-

Eugene V. Debs, prisoner number 9653.

Debs released from prison.

nize an A.F. of L. union, were discharged. A strike of policemen followed, bringing from Massachusetts' Governor Calvin Coolidge the dictum: "There is no right to strike against the public safety by anybody, anywhere, anytime." The strike was lost.

On the afternoon of June 16, 1918, Eugene V. Debs, now a frail, sixty-eight-year-old man, rose to his feet to deliver an address at a socialist picnic in Canton, Ohio. People came miles to listen to one of his speeches. On this day Debs had resolved to speak out on the war, in defiance of recently passed legislation that placed heavy penalties on persons interfering with mobilization of military forces. When he rose to speak, he knew there were agents in the audience who were there to take down his address and report it to authorities. But he was not the kind of man who would employ caution on such occasions.

"I may not be able to say all that I think," he told the audience, "but I am not going to say anything that I do not think. . . . If it had not been for the men and women who, in the past, have had the moral courage to go to jail, we would still be in the jungles." He then went on to speak critically of the war and, in effect, give encouragement to those who opposed it.

Four days later, Debs was indicted for violation of the Espionage Act. At the trial, which attracted wide attention, Debs said:

Years ago I recognized my kinship with all living things, and I made up my mind that I was not one bit better than the meanest on earth. I said

then, and I say now, that while there is a lower class I am in it, while there is a criminal element, I am of it, and while there is a soul in prison, I am not free.

Rather than follow the advice of his lawyers and use legalities to avoid conviction, Debs refused to withdraw anything he had said in the Canton speech. Found guilty, he was sentenced to serve ten years in prison.

Debs served three years in the Atlanta Federal Penitentiary. During that time, he received thousands of letters of support from a wide variety of people including Carl Sandburg; Sarah N. Cleghorn, the poet; Laurence Housman, the playwright; Hellen Keller; Max Eastman; Upton Sinclair; James Whitcomb Riley; Louis Untermeyer; George Bernard Shaw; and Romain Rolland.

While in prison, the Socialist party nominated Debs to run for the Presidency of the United States. It was the first time in American history that an imprisoned man had been nominated for the highest office in the land. Debs received 920,000 votes.

In March 1921, Warren G. Harding, succeeding Woodrow Wilson to the White House, issued an order releasing Debs from prison. One of his first acts upon leaving confinement was to donate his prison money, the few dollars that are given to a prisoner when discharged, to the defense fund of two men who were also in jail, facing execution.

In the spring of 1920, police officers boarded a streetcar in Brockton, Massachusetts, and arrested two men—one a factory worker and the other a fish peddler. At first the men believed they were being held because of their radical philosophy. A recently

Sacco and Vanzetti

A Sacco-Vanzetti protest.

passed law called for the deportation of aliens who were anarchists; but the men—Nicola Sacco and Bartolomeo Vanzetti—were being charged with a much more serious offense. A murder and robbery had been committed and they were placed under arrest as suspects.

Both men had strong sympathies for exploited working people, both had helped raise funds for various strikers including the textile workers of Lawrence. Vanzetti himself had led a strike of Plymouth shoe workers and, as a result, had been blacklisted from regular employment and took up fish peddling for a living. Both men dreamed of the day when, as Vanzetti stated, "a society free of hate and exploitation" would come into existence.

## Sacco's Goodbye to His Son

My son, do not cry. Be strong to comfort your mother. Take her for walks in the quiet country, gathering wild flowers, resting beneath shady trees, and visiting the streams and the gentle tranquillity of the Mother Nature.

Do not seek happiness just for yourself. Step down to help the weak ones who cry for help. Help the persecuted because they are your better friends. They are your comrades who fight and fall, as your father and Barto fought and fell, to conquer joy and freedom for all the poor workers.

A widely used postcard of the era.

# The New York Times.

VOL. LXXVI....No. 25,413.    NEW YORK, TUESDAY, AUGUST 23, 1927.

## SACCO AND VANZETTI PUT TO DEATH EARLY THIS MORNING; GOVERNOR FULLER REJECTS LAST-MINUTE PLEAS FOR DELAY AFTER A DAY OF LEGAL MOVES AND DEMONSTRATIONS

*This is the five dollar bill received by me from the U.S. Government on leaving the Atlanta prison and contributed by me to the Sacco Vanzetti Defense Fund Dec. 25th 1921. Eugene V. Debs*

Debs contributed his prison money to Sacco and Vanzetti.

During the course of the seven-week trial, a number of defense witnesses swore that both Sacco and Vanzetti were engaged elsewhere at the exact time of the murder. "By a systematic exploitation of the defendant's alien blood, their imperfect knowledge of English, their unpopular social views, and their opposition to the war," stated Felix Frankfurther, a young attorney destined later to be a Supreme Court Justice, "the District Attorney invoked against them a riot of political passion and patriotic sentiment . . ."

As a result, in the spring of 1921 the pair were found guilty and sentenced to death in the electric chair.

For six years the two men fought for their lives, encouraged by a growing defense movement, supported by numerous labor unions. The 1922 A.F. of L. convention petitioned for a new trial. Two years later it adopted a resolution describing the two men as "victims of race and national prejudice and class hatred." As the years passed, organized labor continued to call for a new trial: the International Ladies' Garment Workers' Union; the United Mine Workers; labor groups from the furriers in New York to the Dallas Central Labor Council in Texas. More than six thousand Colorado miners demonstrated for their freedom.

"I was prompted by my nature to an ideal of freedom and justice to all," said Vanzetti, "and this is the worst of the crime to my enemies. . . . Had I negated my principles after my arrest, I would not find myself now, on the threshold of a death house. I neither boast nor exalt, nor pity myself. I follow my call. I have my conscience serene . . ."

Sacco wrote a friend: "It is true, indeed, that they can execute the body, but they cannot execute the idea which is bound to live."

Although a large defense movement demanded commutation of the sentences, it was the words of the two men that did most toward rallying support to the last. When every recourse had been blocked, and final sentence had been passed, Vanzetti spoke his final words:

If it had not been for these thing, I might have live out my life talking at street corners to scorning men. I might have die, unmarked, unknown, a failure. Now we are not a failure. This is our career and our triumph. Never in our full life could we hope to do such work for tolerance, for justice, for man's understanding of man, as now we do by accident.

Our words—our lives—our pains—nothing! The taking of our lives—lives of a good shoemaker and a poor fish peddler—all! That last moment belongs to us—that agony is our triumph.

As black soldiers returned from fighting in France, they encountered racial problems. W. E. B. Du Bois, the historian, wrote: "Make way for democracy! We saved it in France, and . . . we will save it in the United States of America, or know the reason why!"

While black and white troops had been fighting presumably to "make the world safe for democracy," on the home front racial bias had not abated. "The greatest outbreaks of racial violence in our history," according to Michael Wallace, "have come in war time." The years 1917 to 1919 were marked by bloody anti-Negro mob actions, in East Saint Louis, Chicago, and elsewhere. It was a familiar story. Black workers

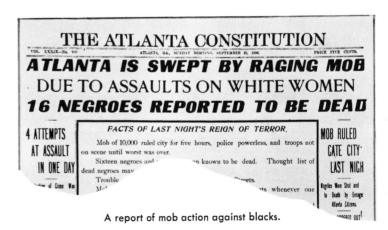

A report of mob action against blacks.

A "silent parade" of black people led by the NAACP in 1917. The sign condemned the disenfranchisement of the southern black by giving white voters undue voting power.

were leaving the South. White workers in the North feared for their jobs. The movement of black migrants north was reflected in a sampling of family letters written in 1917:

Bryan, Tex., Sept. 13, 1917.
Dear Sir: I am writing you as I would like to no if you no of any R. R. Co and Mfg. that are in need for colored labors. I want to bring a bunch of race men out of the south we want to work some whear north will come if we can git passe any whear across the Mason & Dickson. please let me hear from you at once if you can git passes for 10 or 12 men. send at once.

Anniston, Ala., April 23, 1917.
Dear Sir: Please give me some infamation about coming north i can do any kind of work from a truck gardin to farming i would like to leave here and i cant make no money to leave i ust make enought to live one please let me here from you at once i want to get where i can put my children in schol.

Dear Sir: I saw your add in the Chicago *Defender* for laborers. I am a young man and want to finish school. I want you to look out for me a job on the place working morning and evening.

Postwar arrests of "radicals."

I would like to get a job in some private family so I could continue taking my piano lesson I can do anything around the house but drive and can even learn that. Send me the name of the best High School in Chicago. How is the Wendell Phillips College. I have finish the grammar school.

Blacks left the South for good cause. Lynchings took place at a rate of three a week. Between 1882 and 1927, about five thousand persons were lynched in the nation, mostly black. However, the blacks had never adapted themselves to the campaign to keep them in a position of subordination. In 1887, Wallace reports,

9,000 blacks working the Louisiana sugar plantations, together with a thousand whites, struck for $1.00 a day. The planters persuaded the Governor to send in the militia, which shot into a crowd of strikers at Pattersonville, killing several. Strike leaders were lynched. Finally, at Thibodaux, the "most prominent citizen" organized a private vigilante force, massacred 35 strikers, and broke the strike. In 1919, when black Arkansas sharecroppers formed a union, their meetings were shot up; when the blacks fired back and

killed some attackers, whites went on a week-long rampage . . .

It was against such habitual terrorization that the blacks protested and formed unions; and when these tactics failed, they went north.

When admitted to northern labor unions, black workers often made the most loyal and dedicated members. But they were often barred from membership not only because of their color but because most blacks were deprived of a chance to learn a craft or skill; and most A.F. of L. unions did not admit unskilled mass-production workers.

The war abroad was over in 1919; but the home front had its special brand of terror partly, one historian wrote, as "an exaggeration of war time passions."

The "Red scare," as Professor Stanley Coben pointed out, was brought on by a combination of conditions, . . . runaway prices, a brief but sharp stock market crash and business depression, revolutions throughout Europe . . . fear of domestic revolt."

During this period there were more than thirty-five hundred strikes in the nation involving some four million working people. Evidently those in authority believed that the security of America demanded strong action.

It seemed that bloody revolution was hovering everywhere; and the most innocuous liberal was—with a phrase or two—in the position of overthrowing the most powerful government on earth. "The worst of it is," said one congressman, "that every movement, every new idea, every new suggestion, every new thought that is advanced is immediately denounced as Bolshevism. It is not necessary to argue any more with a man who advances a new idea; it is enough to say, 'That is Bolshevism.'"

Voices seeking to calm the national agitation were largely ignored. Governor Alfred E. Smith of New York was given scant heed when he stated, in connection with the expulsion of five newly elected socialist lawmakers from the state legislature:

Although I am unalterably opposed to the fundamental principles of the Socialist Party, it is inconceivable that a minority party, duly constituted and legally organized, should be deprived of its rights to expression as long as it has honestly, by lawful methods of education and propaganda, succeeded in securing representation . . .

When the legislators were reelected by their constituents, three of them were expelled. In Washington, Victor L. Berger, the lone Socialist congressman, was barred from office although reelected by his constituents.

The New York *World* pointed out editorially that there was "no Bolshevik menace in the United States and no IWW menace that an ordinary, capable police force is not competent to deal with." However, there were those in authority who acted as if every militant unionist was about to overturn the government. On the night of January 2, 1920, the first of a series of nationwide raids under the auspices of the Department of Justice took place. In approximately seventy cities around the country some three thousand "dangerous aliens" were rounded up for deportation. Schools, offices, meeting halls, union headquarters, even private homes were entered on the vaguest suspicion of violating an act calling for the deportation of dangerous aliens.

Men and women were hustled from their homes without warrant or explanation, frequently kept in jails, or "pens," for long periods of time; many were deported without the possibility of even a good-bye to their families or friends. It did not seem to matter whether there was evidence of any kind available. Even those who visited the victims were often themselves seized or thrust into jail.

The "Red scare," of course, influenced the labor movement, causing disunity in union ranks where militant leaders were suspected of subversion. It was to be years before the nation would recover.

By 1909, the last of the mills of the United States Steel Company had been declared free of unionism. Lacking any organized voice in the conditions of their work, steelworkers found themselves faced with increasingly serious grievances.

Hours in the industry, in steel centers throughout the country, despite the hot and heavy nature of the work, were long. One-quarter of the men usually worked seven days a week with a twenty-four-hour shift every two weeks in addition. "Their lives are one constant round of toil," a union organizer said, "they have no family life, no opportunity for education or even for recreation. . . . At 40 the average steel worker is played out."

It was a common practice in the steel mills, as in the textile mills of New England, for employers to reward plant superintendents for a constantly accelerating standard of production. Thus, superintendents and foremen would urge on the men at the furnaces, by threat of layoff, to meet the ever-rising production ratio.

"What's he been doin'?"
"Overthrowin' the guvment."

A humorous cartoon during the period of the "Red scare."

Hot work in the steel mill.

Anti-eight-hour-day notice.

# WHAT THE 8 HOUR DAY MEANS

¶ The Employers' Association of Pittsburgh will show in a series of advertisements:

¶ That the **8**-hour day is not practical.

¶ That it is not economical.

¶ That it is not for the best interests of the employe or the employer.

¶ That it cannot be put into successful operation in our plants.

¶ That the men themselves want to work more than **8** hours a day.

¶ That it will drive industries away from Pittsburgh and destroy its prestige as a manufacturing center.

¶ That, if enacted here, it would place Pittsburgh at a disadvantage in its competition with other American manufacturers.

¶ That, if in effect throughout the United States, it would prevent successful competition with carefully fostered industries abroad.

¶ That it would place an additional burden of millions of dollars annually on the public.

### The Employers' Association of Pittsburgh

A Yale undergraduate decided to see for himself how it was to work in a steel mill. His alarm clock woke him for a day's work.

I fought myself out of bed and shut it off; stood up and tried to think. Pretty soon a thought came over me like an ache; it was "Fourteen hours!" That was beginning in fifty-five minutes —fourteen hours of backwalls, and hot ladles, and —Oh, hell!—I sat down again on the bed, and prepared to lift my feet back in.

Then I got up, and washed fiercely, threw on my clothes, and went downstairs, and out into the afternoon sun.

Down by the restaurant, I met the third-helper on Eight.

"Long turn wouldn't be so bad, if there weren't no next day," he said, with a sort of smile.

In the mill was a gang of malignant men; things all went wrong; everybody was angry and tired; their nerves made mistakes for them.

William Z. Foster, A.F. of L. leader in Chicago's steel strike, with Mrs. Mary ("Mother") Jones.

"I only wish it were next Sunday!" I said to someone.

"There aren't any goddam Sundays in this place," he returned. "Twenty-four hours off between two working days ain't Sunday."

The young worker wrote further of his experiences:

When I came back from the spout, Fred was in front of the furnace, blue glasses on his nose, inspecting the brew. He put his glasses back on his cap, glanced at me, and pointed to a pile of dolomite and slag which had been growing in front of Number 3 door.

"All right," I said, and picked up a shovel from the dolomite pile. For a couple of minutes, I shovelled the stuff down the slag hole, and re-membered vividly the bygone pit-days. Then I would have been cleaning up around the buggy. For a minute I felt vastly superior to pit people. I earned two cents more an hour, and threw down a hole the dolomite and dirt they cleared away.

I began to feel a little tired in back and legs, and repeated Fred's formula on how to get away with a long turn: "Take it like any other day to five o'clock. Then work for midnight. Anyone can stand it from midnight to morning."

Steelworkers who talked unionization lived in ter-ror of discharge and the blacklist. They worked the long exhausting hours at furnaces, hearths, and ovens silently, as if waiting somehow for deliverance.

There were various concessions made by the steel companies such as sanitary facilities, profit sharing,

A steelworker

A street scene in a steel town

John Fitzpatrick, A.F. of L. Chicago leader and chairman of the committee to organize iron and steelworkers.

and pensions. And there was considerable discussion of "industrial democracy" and "employee representation plans." But none of this was organization.

No effective organization had been carried on in steel for more than a decade. But in the summer of 1918 labor leaders met in Chicago at which time the National Committee for Organizing Iron and Steel Workers was established with John Fitzpatrick, president of the Chicago Federation of Labor, as president and William Z. Foster, who had successfully led the A.F. of L. drive to organize Chicago packinghouse workers, as secretary-treasurer. Foster's idea was to introduce industrial unionism without conflicting with existing craft unions.

The war had created conditions unusually favorable for union organization. There was actually a shortage of workers. However, it was well known that the steel industry was "unalterably opposed to any extension of union labor." As the organization campaign began, union members began to lose their jobs. "We don't discharge a man for belonging to a union," one steel corporation spokesman stated, "but of course we discharge men for agitating in the mills." Then came the barring of halls and even entire communities to union meetings. "Does the United States

The strike ballot

*Black Smith*

# BALLOT

## IRON & STEEL WORKERS

The Union Committees are now seeking to get **higher wages, shorter hours and better working conditions** from the steel companies. Are you willing to back them up to the extent of **stopping work** should the companies refuse to concede these demands?

### TAJNO GLASANJE

Odbor junije sada traži da se dobije bolja plaća, kraći radni satovi i bolji uvjeti za rad od kompanija čelika. Dali ste voljni isti do skrajnosti podupreti da se prestane sa radom ako bi kompanija odbila da udovolji zahtevima?

### SZAVAZZON!

Az Union Bizottsága, az Acél Társaságoktól való—magasabb fizetés, rövidebb munka idő és jobb munka feltételek—elnyerése után törekszik. Akar ezek után törekedni? s a végsőkig kitarta—ni? és ha a társaságok ezen kivánalmaknak nem tesznek eleget a munkát beszüntetni?

### VOTAZIONE.

I comitati dell'Unione stanno cercando di ottenere paghe piu' alte, ore di lavoro piu' brevi, e migliori condizioni di lavoro. Desiderate voi assecondarli, anche quando dovesse essere necessario di fermare il lavoro se le Compagnie rifiutassero di accettare le domande?

### HLÁSOVACÍ LÍSTOK

Výbor uniový chce dosiahnuť podvyšenie mzdy, menej hodín robiť a lepšie robotnícke položenie od oceliarskych spoločnosti. Ste vy ochotní ich podporovať do krajnosti; až do zástavenia práce, v páde by spoločnosť odoprela žiadosťučiniť tým požiadavkám.

### BALOT

Komitet Unii stara się obecnie o uzyskanie od Stalowych Kompanij większej płacy, krótszych godzin i lepszych warunków pracy. Czy jesteś gotów poprzeć nas aż do możliwości wstrzymania pracy na wypadek, gdyby Kompanie odmówiły naszym żądaniom?

**VOTE YES OR NO.**      Mark X in square indicating how you vote

 Yes  [ X ]      No  [   ]

**National Committee for Organizing Iron and Steel Workers**
WM. Z. FOSTER, Secy-Treas.      303 Magee Bldg., Pittsburgh, Pa.

Constitution apply to Pennsylvania?" asked a union organizer. "Is the right of assembly fundamental or is it a thing to be granted or withheld . . ."

Barred from speaking at an organizational meeting, Mrs. Mary ("Mother") Jones, eighty-nine-year-old organizer of railroad workers and miners, declared: "We are to see whether Pennsylvania belongs to Kaiser Gary [Elbert H. Gary, chairman, U.S. Steel Corporation] or Uncle Sam." Despite her age, she was taken off to jail.

Hostility toward the union campaign increased. Workers loath to lose even one needed paycheck reluctantly were convinced that a strike would be necessary. Demands were drawn up which, summarized, amounted to "eight hours and the union." But requests for conferences were ignored. As the threat of strike increased, Fitzpatrick suggested to Gompers that President Wilson intervene. But the President was deeply involved with his efforts to create a League of Nations and was unavailable.

Still the companies refused to confer. "Whatever may have been the condition of employment in the long past," stated Gary, ". . . there is at present no necessity for labor unions. . . . As you know, we do not confer, negotiate, or combat labor unions as such."

Finally on September 22, 275,000 steelworkers walked out on strike in the chief steel plants of America: Chicago, Pittsburgh, Cleveland, Gary, Homestead, Weirton, and many others.

"It is industrial war," commented *The New York Times* of that day, "the leaders are radicals, social and industrial revolutionaries." Said the New York *Tribune:* "Another experiment in . . . Bolshevizing American industry."

"The future industrial destiny of this country," stated Gary, "is dependent to the greatest degree on . . . the maintenance of [the] open shop." To this, J. P. Morgan, Jr., cabled from London: "Heartiest congratulations on your stand for the open shop. . . . I believe American principles of liberty deeply involved and must win if we all stand firm."

The strike lasted until the end of the year. The unity of the steelworkers was maintained in the face of a wide variety of efforts to convince them to return to work without union recognition—use of mounted police, attacks on the foreign born, strikebreakers, a back-to-work campaign, attacks on the union leadership.

Finally in January of the following year the strike was ended. The workers were forced back to their jobs without winning improved conditions.

In its long report on the strike, the Commission of Inquiry of the Interchurch World Movement stated: "The steel strike . . . in one sense is not over. The main issues were not settled. The causes still remain . . ."

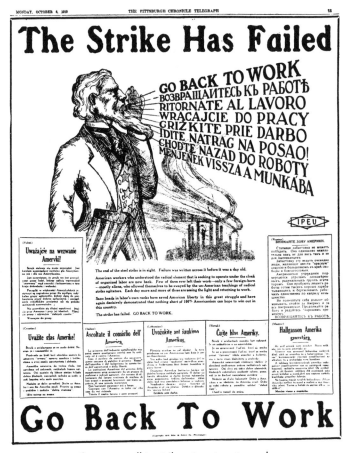

Company call to strikers to return to work.

# TWELVE

# 1920-1932

# THE POSTWAR
# "PROSPERITY"

*"Everybody ought to get rich."*

With the union upsurge weakened and the Bolshevik "menace" somewhat under control, the nation entered the 1920s eager to return to what President Warren Harding called "normalcy." Indeed, almost everybody was tired of strife. The war abroad had cost tens of thousands of American lives; while postwar economic conflict at home had bred its own violent disorder. Perhaps after all, opinion molders commented, the way to tranquillity was to let business do it. "Never before," said *Nation's Business,* "here or anywhere else has the government been so completely fused with business."

What was wrong with that? Had not Calvin Coolidge, who succeeded to the Presidency after Harding's death, announced that "the business of America is business?" And later added: "The man who builds a factory, builds a temple . . . the man who works there, worships there."

Armed with such a philosophy, the nation looked to its businessmen for leadership, such as Andrew W. Mellon, head of a financial group of banks and corporations with assets of approximately $13 billion. After becoming secretary of the treasury, Mellon revealed his primary public interest was to reduce government spending and the rate of taxes on large income earners.

John J. Raskob, an official of E. I. du Pont de Nemours & Company, wrote a magazine article entitled "Everybody ought to get rich." But United States Steel doubled its take-home profit from 1924 to 1929 without granting a single general wage increase.

The era brought forward various new theories of scientific management, particularly those of Frederick W. Taylor, who helped establish a methodology for making factory men and machines produce more while costing management less. Henry Ford, whose "horseless carriage" now could be assembled at the rate of one every ninety-three minutes, proclaimed: "Machinery is the new Messiah."

The scientifically computed piecework system increasingly made the worker a victim of the machinery he tended. "I think that piece work is a very unjust method of paying workers," one woman worker said.

If we realized how piece work harms us mentally and physically, we might take it a little bit more seriously. Piece work is paid on a plan that is more like guess work than anything else. The employer cannot resist the temptation to cut prices when he sees that we are making more than he thinks we ought to make.

Often the employer picks the fastest girl in the place and gives her a certain amount of work to turn out, with a time-study method of ascertaining the time required. When she turns out more than the average worker, and so earns

The production lines moved fast . . .

. . . to provide the cars people wanted.

Victory for men's clothing workers
in New York in 1919.

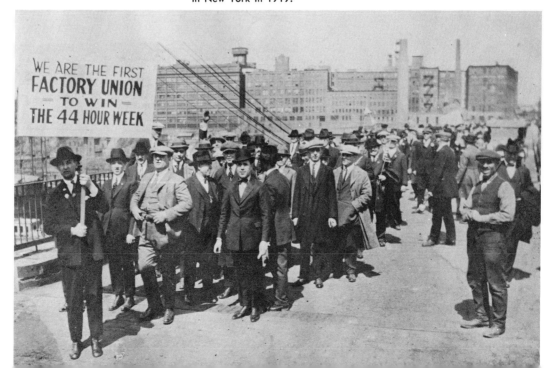

A pioneering production line.

more, the employer usually cuts the prices accordingly. He may cut the rate again and again. And we have to work faster and faster in order to get a living wage.

One physician commented on the system:

Medically, the piece work system is perhaps the most pernicious thing that could be devised to weaken what, for a better term, might be described as the dynamic efficiency of the nervous system. I am referring, of course, to the unregulated piece work system in which there is no maximum or average amount of work set down to keep the worker from speeding beyond his capacity. The pay that the piece worker obtains for his labor is ingeniously devised, and subject to change in amount, so that he must work at top speed to make it worth while. With the increased efficiency of the pieceworker, the price per piece of work turned out is commonly decreased, so that a greater and increasingly more intense effort is necessary to reach the individual's maximum reward for his labor. It needs no argument to convince even a sturdy advocate of that new idol, called efficiency, that such methods

are bound, in the long run, to use up the worker . . .

But there was considerable evidence publicized that the nation was in a state of all-encompassing prosperity. There were 4,800,000 automobiles being produced each year; construction of buildings and roads was up; the invention of new machines and methods was stimulating business; profits had never been so high.

Working people participated in their communities in much of the gaudy activities of the era. Violation of Prohibition became a way of life; jazz became the national anthem; everybody laughed with Will Rogers or Ed Wynn on the radio, when they could afford a radio. It was the era of the flapper and shocking one-piece bathing suit. The Charleston dance craze knew no class barriers. Clara Bow, the "It" girl, and Rudolph Valentino filled the theatres with people from all occupations and interests. Lindbergh became the popular hero, and scarcely was there a red-blooded man who would not have traded most anything, if he had anything, for going out to the park to see Babe Ruth hit one over the fence.

But it was an unhealthy and unrealistic prosperity. Newspapers did not feature the fact, but by the end

The birth of the "Jazz Age."

of the 1920s, only four corporations were producing 64 percent of all iron and steel; half of all bank resources were in the hands of 1 percent of the existing banks; about two hundred corporations controlled half the corporate wealth.

"On the surface it appeared that we had found a formula which would insure permanent prosperity," writes Professor William H. Miernyk, "but underneath, the foundations of laissez-faire capitalism were rotting away."

Despite the much publicized affluence, the working people were not enjoying many of the fruits of prosperity. Over 70 percent of the American people had incomes of less than twenty-five hundred dollars a year. The average worker's annual income was about fifteen hundred dollars for a work week that often extended to sixty hours or longer. The income of farmers was falling, too.

The ineffectiveness of organized labor to cope with the situation was yielding inevitable results. "A prevalent attitude among the business class," stated Robert S. and Helen Merrell Lynd in their sociological study, *Middletown*, "appears in the statement of one of the . . . leaders, 'Working men don't need unions nowadays. . . . We are much more in danger of coddling the working men than abusing them . . .'"

According to William E. Leuchtenburg: "With no counteraction from labor unions, which were weak, or from government . . . business increased profits at twice the rate of the growth of productivity . . ."

In the boom 1920s in Gastonia, North Carolina, workers received ten dollars a week for a twelve-hour day. One southern paper observed: "Labor is . . . contented. . . . It has the will to work. Strikes are unknown."

Conditions of the era were reflected in testimony

given by working people before the United States Senate Committee on Manufactures in 1929.

SENATOR TYSON. How long did you work at the plant at Nashville?
MISS BOWEN. At one time I worked 9 months, and I fell down the steps and torn my back all to pieces and was at home 13 months, and then went back to . . . and worked two months.
SENATOR TYSON. What did you get when you started in?

For many there was little prosperity and often no work.

Separate entrances.

MISS BOWEN. When I started work at . . . I was taken on as a stenographer. I got $15 a week and I had a nervous breakdown and then I went into the mill to work and that accounts for my being in Elizabethton today . . .

SENATOR METCALF. Did you say you worked 10 hours a day?

MISS BOWEN. Yes, sir, the girls work 10 hours a day, and then on Saturday you can not eat a bite of lunch from the time you get in the plant until you get out Saturday, and when you think about working until 11:30 through the week and getting a lunch at 11:30 and then have to work until 1 o'clock on Saturday before you get anything to eat, you are exhausted.

SENATOR METCALF. That is on Saturdays you have to go right through to 1 o'clock?

MISS BOWEN. Yes, sir. If they catch you eating anything you are discharged, for the simple reason that they claim you are liable to drop a crumb on the silk and that damages it, of course; and they also stopped the girls from using cosmetics in the plant for the simple reason of ruining silk.

Across the country, conditions facing West Coast longshoremen were also growing increasingly intolerable. There were more workers in the ports than were needed, leaving hundreds without employment fruitlessly strolling the docks, hoping for the possibility of a job. Graft in the procuring of jobs became commonplace. A representative of the United States Bureau of Labor Statistics declared:

In normal times, only a small part of this supply [of longshore labor] is earning what may be considered decent wages. Probably a larger proportion is earning a subsistence wage, i.e., just about enough to make ends meet on a comparatively low standard of living. The balance is always on the brink of starvation and depends largely on outside support, chiefly charity. At the present time, a very conservative estimate would probably place more than 50% of all the longshoremen on the relief roles.

Union membership in general was dropping. From five million members in 1920 the figure declined during the decade to three and a half million or less.

Striking Broadway chorus girls, members of the Actors Equity Association.

The "shape-up" method of hiring waterfront workers encouraged kickbacks and favoritism.

Children toiled in the fields.

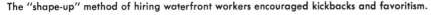

N.º 1241

*To Committee of Employee Representatives:*

*I do hereby promise to return to my regular place of employment at the* ~~Corporation~~ *Corporation plant and do further promise to work in harmony and peace with my fellow employees and my employer. In violation of this promise I hereby agree to relinquish my position and leave the Corporation's property at once.*

*Signed* _____ *Clock No.* _____

*Interviewed by* _____

A "yellow dog" contract.

THE COUPONS IN THIS BOOK ARE PAYABLE ONLY IN MERCHANDISE

**BRANDON CORPORATION STORES**  $2.00

**BRANDON STORE**

ISSUED TO _____

ISSUED BY _____ DATE _____

N.º ____ NOT TRANSFERABLE - VOID IF DETACHED

Script for a "company store."

There was reason. Workers' efforts to partake of some of the prosperity were repeatedly defeated. In the summer of 1922 some four hundred thousand railroad shopmen struck against wage cuts. An injunction was obtained through the efforts of United States Attorney General Harry M. Daugherty, who within a few years would be on trial in a national scandal.

The injunction, one of the strictest ever issued against a labor organization, forbade union activities of all sorts, including meetings. With other railroad unions failing to participate in the effort, the strike was lost. In the same year, when operators refused to renew their union contract, 500,000 soft-coal miners went on strike and were soon joined by 150,000 miners from the anthracite field. It was the first time that both groups had fought for better conditions together. However, strikebreakers were used; violence developed; troops were called. Gradually, the strike collapsed.

At about the same time, the International Seaman's Union struck against wage cuts and abolition of the three-watch system. Shipping was at a standstill from New England to Texas. However, this strike also failed as did that shortly thereafter of meat-packers in Chicago in an effort to resist a wage cut.

The defeats were caused not only by lack of labor unity, but by open-shop advocates perfecting their arsenal of antilabor techniques. These included, as later governmental investigations revealed, labor spies to report to management of union activity and, on occasion, to provoke violence; their introduction of "yellow dog" contracts—once known as "iron clad oaths"—which required a worker to pledge, as a condition of employment, not to join a union.

Perhaps the best known of the professional strikebreakers of the 1930s was Pearl Bergoff, a small, redheaded man, evidently proud of his trade. Bergoff admitted:

The A.F. of L. Executive Council. When Samuel Gompers died in 1924, after forty-two years of A.F. of L. leadership, he was succeeded by William Green (center front), United Mine Workers secretary-treasurer.

I've been thirty years in harness to American industry. I've shipped armies of men to Cuba and Canada. Railroad strikes, dock strikes, transit strikes and textile strikes, I've broken them all in my time. And there's still plenty of demand for my service . . .

I've broken strikes for the City of New York and the City of Chicago. I've worked for the United States government and have letters of thanks for it. There's not a city I haven't broken a strike in. There's not a railroad running out of New York I haven't worked for.

Then there was a constant stream of injunctions—court orders requiring a person or people to refrain from doing certain acts—which were frequently obtained against unions, particularly when on strike. There was a rise in the number of company stores that working people were compelled to patronize. There was an increased use of gunmen and a revival of the Ku Klux Klan, particularly in the Midwest, which utilized terroristic actions particularly against the foreign born, nonwhites, Catholics, Jews, and union workers.

In addition to the issuance of injunctions against labor, court orders played an increasing role in movements for social progress in general. The United States Supreme Court during this period upheld the use of injunctions and opposed establishing minimum wage regulations. In this latter case the court ruled that "there can be no difference in the case of selling labor and the case of selling goods."

Confronted by such oppressive developments, the A.F. of L., for the first time, supported an independent political candidate for the Presidency—a friend of labor, Senator Robert La Follette.

The senator from Wisconsin was an eminent progressive, dedicated to championing socially beneficial causes. Elected governor in 1900, he introduced liberal reforms in areas of education, industry, labor, and public utilities. But, when he ran for the Presidency on a third ticket, in 1924, "most voters preferred," as Charles A. Madison put it, "Coolidge prosperity" to "La Follette liberalism." Although La Follette received five million votes, Calvin Coolidge was elected.

As the nation drifted further into control by conservative forces, A.F. of L. leaders seemed impotent to do much about it. They were not aware that their

Field hand

Laundry workers were among the most underpaid.

Black workers were warned not to join unions.

the recognized trade-union movement. The worker was unskilled or semiskilled for the most part; the work was fragmented so that lines distinguishing trades, or crafts, were veritably obliterated. Most jobs could be learned in a few days, if not a few hours. Then, too, the new industrial worker was usually poorly paid, frequently foreign born and subjected to language handicaps and nonconforming customs.

John S——— was typical of many Detroit auto workers in the early days of the industry. A new arrival from farm country, he was unskilled in factory work.

Even low-paid jobs were hard to find.

industrial society was long ready for a new form of unionism. In 1924, Samuel Gompers died at the age of seventy-four. He was replaced by William Green, former secretary-treasurer of the United Mine Workers, a follower in the Gompers's nonmilitant tradition. When Green was elected, according to the historian Foster Rhea Dulles, "The business community . . . breathed a sigh of relief."

Among the industries that now employed millions of workers, the burgeoning automobile industry had not been unionized. Mass-production methods created a type of worker and work function that was alien to

Miners on their way below ground.

Telephone linesman

In the early 1920s, it was estimated that some seventy-five thousand young, unmarried men were, like John S———, taken into the auto industry as part of a so-called "suitcase brigade." They were given work during the rush season, and discharged when slack time came. Like so many others, John S——— learned to operate a machine, but not to develop a skill.

Life on the assembly line was described in an article in *The New York Times* from the time when

the car begins to come to life. It begins as part of a chassis placed on a moving platform, or belt. It is scarcely more than a frame, just a few pieces of iron held together by the necessary bolts. The belt moves and the frame with it. Workmen stand on each side of the line.

As the frame comes by, a man slips a wheel on the axle nearest him. The next man tightens the bolts that hold it. Some one puts in the steering post, some one else attaches the fenders, and so on down the line, each man doing the same thing to each car as it passes. Near the end of the line, the body is lowered from above. It is fitted and bolted in place and the car, now looking like an automobile, moves on.

A man with a hose puts a gallon of gas in the tank, another jumps into the driver's seat, and the car runs off the line under its own power, ready to take the road. In less than an hour from the time a chassis frame starts at one end of the line it comes off a complete car at the other.

A few half-hearted attempts at unionization of the automobile industry were made before the first World War, and again in the 1920s. There were dissidents of various shades of radicalism who, from time to time, sought more militant action. After the IWW, the Trade Union Education League was one. Others included its successor, the Trade Union Unity League. But even though there were organizational results, particularly in the planting of the seed of industrial unionism in some factories, the industrial workers were mostly without union protection.

As a result, with profits high and wages low, the people who produced the goods increasingly found themselves unable to buy what their hands had made.

Purchasing power began to shrivel, although there were plenty of goods on store shelves.

The wheels of industry began to turn more slowly . . . and then stopped altogether.

New York demonstration for jobless relief.

As the depression grew worse, jobs became impossible to find.

On Tuesday, October 29, 1929, America suddenly ceased being the promised land and became, as far as most people were concerned, a disaster area. The boom and prosperity, except for a fortunate few, were over.

Six months after the stock-market crash, four million people were out of work. Industry unceremoniously discarded much of its company union trappings such as profit sharing, welfare plans, and recreational projects. Where there were jobs, wage cuts were inevitable. But there were mostly no jobs; no food; no money; and, worse, no understanding of what had happened.

Political and industrial leaders—and even some from the ranks of labor—insisted that the emergency would soon be over. Leaders pointed to the long history of panics and depressions—1819, 1837, 1867, 1873, 1884, 1893, 1907, 1921. "Never before," said Charles M. Schwab, head of Bethlehem Steel Corporation, "has American business been as firmly entrenched for

prosperity . . ." And later, "Just grin, keep on working."

"All evidences indicate," said President Herbert Hoover who had succeeded Calvin Coolidge, "that the worst effects of the crash upon unemployment will be passed during the next 60 days."

"So long as we live under a system of individual liberty," stated George Mitchell of the National City Bank, "we are bound to have fluctuations in business." It was difficult for those in authority to realize that there were people in the nation actually starving. But children did die of starvation as crops lay rotting in the fields for lack of buyers. "Have you ever heard a hungry child cry?" asked Lillian Wald, head of the Henry Street Settlement in New York City.

"The depression won't end until mass buying power is restored," insisted Sidney Hillman, president of the Amalgamated Clothing Workers of America.

With existing labor unions inadequate to the crisis, inevitably voices of protest were raised that promised cures for ailments that unions did not seem able to provide. People obviously needed leadership. And these were fertile times for those with theories on how human values could replace the reign of property. Included were the raucous voices of those preaching racism, anti-Semitism, and other forms of bigotry—programs to which a frustrated people might be attracted.

A United States senator went so far as to declare that "if this country ever needed a Mussolini, it needs one now." From Royal Oak, Michigan, came the eloquent voice of the Reverend Charles E. Coughlin preaching what the historian Carl N. Degler termed "soured Popularism."

From the Deep South, Governor Huey Long of Louisiana advocated his program of making "every man a king." Congressman Martin Dies of Texas,

Some jobless sold apples on street corners.

Ohio steelworkers launch a national hunger march.

Sharecroppers visit Washington, D.C., seeking assistance.

Farmers and workers of North Dakota discussed their conditions.

*The United Mine Workers' Journal* reported an incident that reflected conditions in Harlan County, Kentucky, mines in the 1930s.

We are six brothers, all six feet tall. Never been to school. We just know the strength of six feet of muscles. Our shoulders are bent, lurched forward as if trying to fend a blow. When we walk our long arms dangle down most to the knee. We are not as good to look at as we used to be. We mine coal. Miles back into the bowels of the mountain we burrow, like a wild animal clawing its hole for hibernation. Our days are lived in the dark, bent in a strained crouch like you've seen a football team before the kickoff. Our heads set well back between the shoulders; necks bend sort of like a goose-necked hoe. That makes a large Adam's apple. Our eyes curve upward as if we study the weather. The mine is full of treacherous horsebacks—slate flakes that drop without warning. They leave a hole the shape of a horse's back, and crush whatever they fall on. We're always looking upward . . .

But this is America! We are part of her. Our fathers hewed the wilderness and fought the revolution. Our fathers were dangerous men. They believed in right. They took their guns and went barefooted with Washington. They made a revolution. And there may come a time when we are dangerous men, even the one-armed brother. For every day we look up and say: "God, must our children follow our stumbling feet! Is there no

using the House Un-American Activities Committee as a forum, was soon to add his voice to the chorus of American demagoguery.

With the federal government following a policy of placing the balancing of the budget ahead of human needs, acts of protest spread from one end of the country to the other. While one newspaper described the attitude of A.F. of L. leaders as standing "patient and hopeful," many thousands of unemployed and dispossessed were finding ways to register their needs. There were tenant strikes, unemployed demonstrations, and demands for unemployment relief often organized and led by radicals and communists. Hungry auto workers marched on a closed River Rouge automobile plant in Dearborn. There was hardly a city without its hunger marches.

Speaking before a congressional committee in 1932, Oscar Ameringer of Oklahoma City, a radical editor, stated: "In Oregon I saw thousands of bushels of apples rotting in the orchards. . . . The last thing I saw on the night I left Seattle was . . . women searching for scraps of food in the refuse piles . . ."

Protest march of miners' wives to Springfield, Illinois.

One section of the "bonus army" of World War I veterans demonstrates in the nation's capital.

sunshine of new life, of intelligent learning, ideas that will penetrate even the dismal depths of Dark Hollow?"

Our kids, they're all that matter now.

The economic upheaval of the 1930s was by no means the first panic or depression to devastate the nation. However, lacking in such historical informa-tion, many victims of the 1930s depression tended to blame themselves for their plight.

It was to require further years and far greater perspective on history for people to realize, in greater numbers, that the cause of such misfortunes were nothing for which they, as individuals, could be held responsible. Contributing to this awareness were events immediately in the offing.

Contrasting billboards.

THIRTEEN

## 1932-1938

# INDUSTRIAL UNIONISM
# AND THE NEW DEAL

*"I pledge you;
I pledge myself, a
new deal for the American people."*

The nation was overready for drastic social change. But there were those who feared its coming.

"The grass will grow in streets of one hundred cities, a thousand towns," predicted President Hoover, warning against a Democratic victory in 1932. "The weeds will over-run the fields of a million farms."

However, the Democratic candidate—Franklin D. Roosevelt, urbane, jaunty cousin of the former President—was about to help launch the most far-reaching social crusade in the nation's history. Responsive to the prevailing mood, he said: "I pledge you; I pledge myself, a new deal for the American people," ten million of whom were without jobs.

Times were so bad that corn was being burned for fuel because it was cheaper than coal. One out of every four farms was sold for debts and taxes. Cash income of farmers had fallen from $7 billion in 1929 to $2 billion in 1932. The nation's total income had dropped from $82 billion to $40 billion in the same period. Corporation income was reduced from $11 billion to $2 billion. Business failures rose from twenty thousand a year in 1929 to thirty-one thousand in 1932.

Taking office in March 1933, Roosevelt inaugurated three months of legislative action founded on a philosophy new to American political leadership; the

**250**

Franklin D. Roosevelt: He knew how to listen.

In addition to his humanitarianism, Roosevelt was at the time also a critic of financial greed. "Among us today," he said in his 1938 message to Congress, "a concentration of private power without equal in history is growing. This concentration is seriously impairing the economic effectiveness of private enterprise. . . . Private enterprise is ceasing to be free enterprise . . ."

Under Roosevelt, nobody should be allowed to starve. Such a concept had never gained political legitimacy in America where the rule of the strong and powerful had been king.

From the start of his administration, Roosevelt was sharply critical of "practices of the unscrupulous money changers," who, he said, "have fled from their high seats in the temple of our civilization. We may now restore that temple to the ancient truths. The measure of the restoration lies in the extent to which we apply social values more noble than mere monetary profit.

"I see millions of families trying to live on incomes so meager that the pall of family disaster hangs over them day by day," Roosevelt told the nation, ". . . I see one-third of a nation ill-housed, ill-clad, ill-nourished."

Our "greatest primary task," Roosevelt said, "is to put people to work." From this was launched a vast

President reflected a concern for people—"the forgotten man," "the man at the bottom," "the little man."

If the New Deal and its leader tended occasionally to lag, there was the swelling demand of millions of Americans to urge it on.

"We are going to make a country," Roosevelt declared, "in which no one is left out."

"And please don't let them sit down in my factory"

NRA MEMBER U.S.

WE DO OUR PART

series of work-relief programs in the hope that they would save the self-respect and preserve the morale of millions as well as prime the pump of economic recovery. The goal of the New Deal was to get purchasing power in the pockets of those who had nothing to spend.

Roosevelt did not set about to aid labor as a social reform but as a matter of absolute right, demanded by vast numbers of people. He had compassion. But he also shrewdly recognized an idea whose time had come. Previously, labor unions had been tolerated. They were now to be encouraged.

The New Deal gained support not so much for its eloquent words, but for its forthright deeds. In the early thirties one followed quickly upon the other from the reopening of the banks with safeguards in 1933 to ending Prohibition, extending credit to farmers, establishing unemployment relief and work projects, rural electrification, the Tennessee Valley Authority, investment reform, more housing for slum dwellers, tax bills "to tax the greedy, not the needy," and more. Vast programs were launched, such as the Work Progress Administration (WPA), to put the unemployed to work; and the Civilian Conservation Corps (CCC) to give constructive work to young people.

The New Deal thus established a system of work-relief projects—the most effective under the Work Progress Administration. This WPA was bitterly attacked by its opponents. Yet it supplied livelihoods for millions of workers and provided the nation with a network of permanent roads, bridges, viaducts, water lines, and public buildings.

The WPA provided an innovation by attempting to fit the job to the skill of the person. Much was patchwork; little was fully adequate; but government no longer remained an aloof spectator to the plight of the people.

THE THINKER

Putting jobless youth to work under the Civilian Conservation Corps, which launched the New Deal program in March 1933.

The National Recovery Administration (NRA), created by the National Industrial Recovery Act, announced its goal "the assurance of a reasonable profit to industry and living wages for labor." An effort was made to establish governmental codes or ground rules under which labor and management might work out their problems jointly. Included was a section, 7a, which guaranteed workers the right to organize and bargain collectively, later to be incorporated into the National Labor Relations Act. These were magic words destined to change the face of the nation.

As the administration sought to build a new relationship between labor and industry, workers who had been suffering from economic want through the depression and for years before found new hope. They flocked into available unions by the thousands to add their voices to the demand for a share of the new benefits promised. Unions that had watched their membership dwindle during the early days of the depression (A.F. of L. membership dropped to 2,608,-000) now were revitalized by militant workers, especially in mass-production industries.

"There was a virtual uprising of workers for union membership," reported the A.F. of L. executive council to its 1934 convention. "Workers held mass meetings and sent word they wanted to be organized."

Having been slow to organize such industries in the past, the craft-oriented A.F. of L. now established federal unions, or industrial local unions directly af-

Breadlines.

filitated with the A.F. of L. itself. In addition, some sixteen hundred volunteer A.F. of L. organizers were appointed.

However, the hopes of workers for amelioration of their problems often met rebuffs from employers and delays from the government. This disillusionment, backed up by hunger and insecurity, set off a series of strikes that spread like a tidal wave from one end of the country to the other.

Over one million working people went on strike in 1932–1934. More than thirty thousand workers in Pennsylvania stopped work; sixty thousand clothing workers in New York, Chicago, Boston, Saint Louis, and other centers; almost a thousand taxi drivers in Philadelphia; twelve thousand shoe workers in Massachusetts; five thousand steelworkers in West Virginia; nine thousand auto workers in Detroit, Flint, and other centers; three thousand shipbuilders in New Jersey; twenty thousand New York truck drivers.

There was a nationwide textile strike that involved communities from New England to the Deep South; strikes of farmers, often led by IWW veterans, took place in the Imperial Valley and other areas in the Far West; Mexican-Americans began to speak out concerning their special problems. In many of these strikes and demonstrations, violence against labor protestors occurred as in the past, with strikebreakers, tear gas, troops, and often violent death involved.

On the West Coast, longshoremen went on strike—starting in the spring of 1934—a long-festering revolt against ten-dollar-a-week wages, dangerous working conditions, and the discharge of workers by shipowners for talking union.

The strike, winning support from other maritime unions, shut down the waterfront all along the Pacific Coast. In San Francisco itself, the strike developed into an outright battle between police and striking longshoremen.

For a time hysteria was widespread. Such newspaper headlines as "Red Army Marching on City" prompted the president of the Chamber of Commerce to declare the strike no longer a struggle "between capital and labor—it is a conflict . . . between American principles and un-American radicalism . . . the welfare . . . of the entire public is at stake . . ."

Police action resulted in the death of two longshoremen and injury to many more. Other unions in the city, shocked and angry, issued a call for a protest general strike. Although troops were called in, the entire city was paralyzed. "San Francisco was a ghost," one writer reported. Not even restaurant waiters reported for work.

In mid-July the general strike ended. So did the violence against the longshoremen. About two weeks later their strike terminated with the winning of a six-hour workday, a thirty-hour week, time and a half for overtime, wage increases, the basis for a new system of hiring, and recognition of the union.

The West Coast maritime strike was a harbinger of

Textile workers in Gastonia, North Carolina.

things to come in other industries: steel, auto, rubber. "It set an example of labor solidarity," one commentator wrote, "that proved unbeatable."

"There are two major ways of dealing with great national problems," one United States senator declared. "When an army of unemployed marched upon Washington five years ago, one way of meeting them was with bayonets and tear gas. The other way . . . [is] to search for the underlying causes of nation-wide unemployment and to seek to remove those causes . . ."

The strike wave of the early 1930s served as a dramatic incentive to propelling New Deal legislators into action. In addition to vast programs of work relief for the unemployed, a proposal was drawn up for a system of unemployment insurance. In 1935, a Social Security Act was passed establishing for the first time a system of insurance payments to cushion workers against the disaster of loss of jobs. The new proposal also established a pension system for the elderly as well as aid to dependents.

The funeral of longshoremen who lost their lives in the 1934 West Coast strike.

The Act did not protect everyone; farm workers, domestic workers, teachers, and many others were excluded. However, the bill encountered strong opposition with one congressman predicting, if approved, an "end to progress," and another warning of destruction of the "integrity of our institutions."

Traditionally, the idea of social security had not only been opposed by such spokesmen but by A.F. of L. leaders as well. "Voluntarism," as Samuel Gompers's program was called, stressed self-help. He resented ideas and plans that, he felt, might weaken trade-union bargaining or obscure the need for labor organization. After Gompers's death, other A.F. of L. leaders inherited this point of view.

In 1937, Congress passed a National Apprenticeship Law under which written agreements could be made between an employer and an apprentice to learn a craft, trade, or job. It included two or more years of on-the-job training under the guidance of an experienced craftsman and a few classroom hours each week.

Another legislative landmark was passage of the Fair Labor Standards Act of 1938, the culmination of many years of effort to establish a ceiling on hours and a floor on wages. "It should be possible," commented President Roosevelt, "to put some floor below which the wage ought not to fall." This the new law did by establishing a twenty-five-cent-an-hour minimum wage that progressively increased as the years passed. In addition, a maximum work week was established for employees in interstate industry; time-and-a-half rates were put into effect for overtime work, and the abolition of child labor—for so long a demand on the part of so many people—was officially made the law of the land.

The new law set a minimum age for general employment at sixteen, including farm work during school hours and employment in hazardous farm work at any time. For employment in hazardous nonfarm occupations, the minimum age was set at eighteen. Minors fourteen and fifteen years of age could be employed outside school hours in a variety of non-hazardous, nonmanufacturing, and nonmining jobs for limited hours and under specific conditions.

The Fair Labor Standards Act, which was called "a step in the direction of Communism" by the National Association of Manufacturers, did provide greatly needed benefits for many working people. During its first two years of operation, nearly a million men and women received wage increases under its provision, and over three million had their hours of work shortened.

In the 1930s one means of stimulating the economy, the administration believed, was to raise wage levels and thus increase buying power. The logic of the situation called for a healthy, aggressive labor movement. However, the era of the open shop had not only weakened many existing unions but helped prevent organization of the unorganized.

Now the need was to change all this. "Trade un-

President Franklin D. Roosevelt signs the Social Security Act in 1935. To his right is Senator Robert F. Wagner, from New York, co-author of the bill; to the President's left is Representative Daniel J. Lewis of Maryland, co-author of the bill; directly behind FDR is Mrs. Frances Perkins, secretary of labor and first woman Cabinet member; to the right of Mrs. Perkins is Senator Robert M. La Follette, chairman of the La Follette Civil Liberties Committee.

ionism has helped to give every one who toils the portion of dignity which is his due," said President Roosevelt, adding later, "If I went to work in a factory, the first thing I'd do would be to join a union."

Of all New Deal legislation, the most meaningful to organized labor was the law that established the right of working people to join unions of their own choosing. Prior to this law, while unionization was not against the law, efforts to organize—especially industrially—were surrounded with difficulties, not the least of which were reprisals from the company being unionized. In setting forth the National Labor Relations Act, the statement of policy declared in part: "It is hereby declared to be the policy of the

United States to . . . eliminate . . . obstructions . . . by encouraging . . . collective bargaining and by protecting the exercise by workers of full freedom of association, self-organization, and designation of representatives of their own choosing . . ."

What came to be known as the Wagner Labor Relations Act, passed in July 1935, was, in a manner, an extension of the ruling of Chief Justice Lemuel Shaw just a century before. The Wagner Act declared that workers "shall have the right to self-organization, to form, join or assist labor organizations, to bargain collectively by representatives of their own choosing, and to engage in concerted activities for the purpose of collective bargaining or other mutual aid or protection."

The act outlawed certain unfair labor practices, which included interfering with the right to join a union; interfering with or dominating any labor organization; discriminating in hiring or firing workers; discharging a worker for giving testimony before the National Labor Relations Board provided for in the act; refusing to bargain collectively with elected representatives; and so on.

"The isolated worker today is a mere connection link in an impersonalized and heartless machine," stated Senator Robert F. Wagner to the United States Senate.

He is powerless to defend himself . . .

Effective contact between the two [worker and industry] is physically impossible. That is why the right to bargain collectively is a necessary implement not only to social justice for the worker, but equally to the wise and rational conduct of business affairs.

The Wagner Act opened the way for a renaissance in collective bargaining: negotiations between an employer and employees through their union to reach an agreement on terms and conditions of employment. Until the mid-1830s, this collective bargaining had been considered a "criminal conspiracy" by the courts and, later, was resisted in the name of defense of the open shop.

Industrial unionism, sometimes called "vertical unionism," was the organizational form under which millions of hitherto unorganized workers now joined labor unions. Of course, industrial unionism was not a new idea.

In the 1830s, the New England Association of Farmers, Mechanics and Other Workingmen made a first attempt at industrial unionism. Later the National Labor Union and the Knights of Labor had embraced all workers (and many nonworkers as well) regardless of skill, color, or sex, and promoted the idea of an industrial form of organization. The United Mine Workers of America and the Western Federation of Miners both adopted industrial unionism in the 1890s as did the IWW, founded on the basis of "one big union" in

The Wagner Labor Relations Act encouraged unions to launch organizing campaigns.

# INDUSTRIAL UNIONISM

## The Vital Problem of Organized Labor

**Committee for Industrial Organization**
Washington, D. C.

Lewis as a young leader of the United Mine Workers. To his right is Philip Murray, vice-president, UMW, to become chairman of the CIO Steel Workers Organizing Committee (SWOC).

the early twentieth century. Such unions as those in men's and women's garment production and the typographical trades functioned on an industrial basis within the existing labor movement.

But industrial unionism was not generally representative of the organized labor movement, which was mostly based on trade or craft. Samuel Gompers had for long been an opponent of industrial unionism, claiming "industrial organization runs counter to the best conception of the toiler's interest." By 1935, of the 109 national and international A.F. of L. unions, only 16 were industrial in makeup. Most working people were concentrated in the huge factories of the nation, but there were few if any unions for them.

There were, however, labor spokesmen in the 1930s, both within and outside A.F. of L. ranks, who championed the principle of industrial unionism. One of these was Charles P. Howard of the International Typographical Union. Another was Sidney Hillman, president of the Amalgamated Clothing Workers, who believed "the working class must accept the principle of industrial unionism or it is doomed to impotence." Still another was John L. Lewis, ninth president of the United Mine Workers of America.

On October 16, 1935, Lewis addressed the fifty-fifth A.F. of L. convention in Atlantic City. Considered by some to be the best rough-and-tumble debater in America, Lewis spoke with a rugged eloquence that compelled attention. "Great combinations of capital have assembled great industrial plants," rumbled Lewis before the listening delegates, "and they are almost 100% effective in opposing organization of the workers under the policies of the American Federation of Labor. What are we going to do about it?

It was said that John L. Lewis, CIO chairman and founder, "made a noise like the whole labor movement."

". . . prepare yourself by making a contribution to your less fortunate brethren, heed this cry from Macedonia that comes from the hearts of men. Organize the unorganized . . ."

Lewis and the miners were eager to organize industrial workers for a special reason of their own. The unorganized steel industry was moving into the mining business, threatening the United Mine Workers itself. "Miners on strike in the captive mines of the Tennessee Coal & Iron Company," declared Lewis, "are suffering tonight by the fact that the A.F. of L. had failed, after all these years, to organize the iron and steel workers."

But the A.F. of L. convention voted against the proposal for organizing industrial workers. Said Matthew Woll, A.F. of L. vice-president: "This proposal . . . will spell ruination for the labor movement . . ."

Without delay, Lewis convened a private meeting of a small number of presidents of A.F. of L. international unions in such industries as typographical, men and women's clothing, textile, oil, cap and millinery, and metal mining.

Shortly thereafter an announcement was made of the formation of a Committee for Industrial Organization (CIO). In resigning from the A.F. of L. executive council, Lewis stated: "I have neither the time nor the inclination to follow the peregrinations of the Council from the Jersey beaches in the summer to the golden sands of Florida in the winter."

With the announcement of the formation of the CIO, what amounted to a labor crusade swept the nation, entering the mines, mills, foundries, and workshops of the country from coast to coast. Almost overnight, as Edward Levinson recalled it, "millions of CIO buttons sprouted on overalls, shirtwaists and workers' hats and caps. They became badges of a new independence."

A new spirit was in the land. The initials CIO became the symbol and slogan of twentieth-century labor. "CIO! CIO!" became a chant of working people inside the shop and on the picket lines as well. From black menhaden fishermen on the Chesapeake Bay,

the slogan spread to warehousemen on the San Francisco Embarcadero, to shoe workers in Lynn, Massachusetts, to oil drillers in Oklahoma, and to woodworkers in Tacoma, Washington.

The A.F. of L. resisted, claiming the new organization was a "dual union" and urging the CIO to return to "the house of labor." But, growled Lewis, "He is a madman or a fool who believes that this river of human sentiment . . . can be dammed."

A CIO recruiting poster.

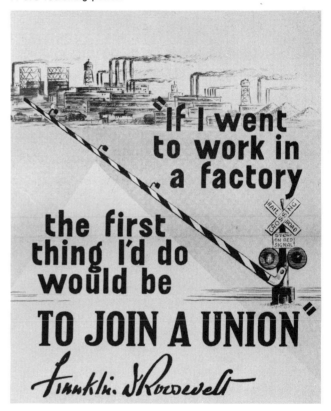

The new unionists were recruited from industries and groups not before believed organizable.

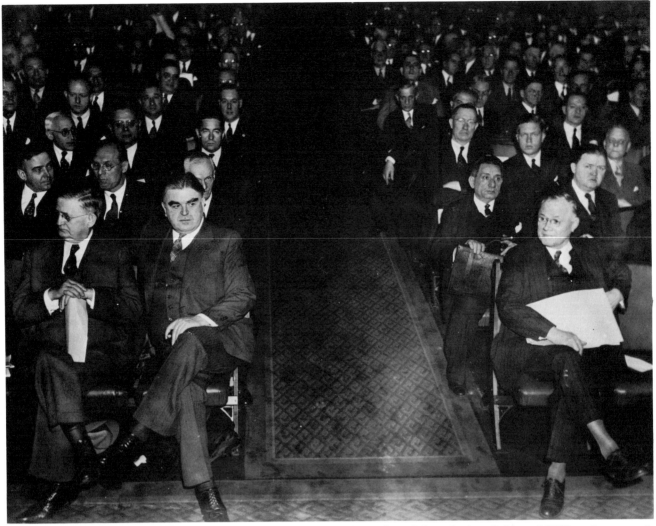

More than an aisle separated John L. Lewis, chairman of the Committee for Industrial Organization *(left)*, and William Green, president of the American Federation of Labor.

The CIO's constitution expressed the organization's aim "to achieve and extend industrial and political democracy . . . to bring about the effective organization of the working men and women of America regardless of race, creed, color or nationality, and to unite them for common action into labor unions for their common aid and protection."

The appeal of the new unions was to the very bottom of the economic pyramid—to working people hitherto considered either unorganizable or unwanted or both. Black workers responded in large numbers to the crusade. The CIO offered union membership on terms of equality; a new dignity for black workers who most often were assigned the most dangerous, hottest, dirtiest, heaviest, most insecure employment—the last hired and the first fired.

The National Association for the Advancement of Colored People was to state that the "CIO has proved that it stands for our people within the unions and outside the unions . . . every attack on labor is an attack on the Negro, for the Negro is largely a worker . . . organized labor is now our national ally."

Women workers, never before considered eligible for unionization, joined the new unions along with the men. Not only did they join unions, but they played leading roles in their management and administration. While many women joined women's auxiliaries, especially nonworking wives of union men, it was to the unions themselves that women flocked, demanding "equal pay for equal work."

The first test of the CIO came at Akron, Ohio, in the winter of 1936 when John L. Lewis personally opened the campaign to organize rubber workers. And it was here for the first time that workers spontaneously introduced a new labor tactic: the sit-down strike. Instead of leaving their place of employment, workers merely sat down at their benches and refused to go home at closing time.

It was a momentous development. Newspaper edi-

Women and black workers joined the new industrial unions.

On the other hand, Lewis told the sit-downers: "You men are undoubtedly carrying on through one of the most heroic battles that has ever been undertaken by strikers in an industrial dispute."

In less than a year, drives were under way to organize workers in other mass-production industries. Most prominent among these was the automotive industry and, within this, the world's largest corporation, General Motors.

General Motors employees had been subject to intolerable working conditions for many years. "The speed of the industry," wrote Mary Heaton Vorse, "left them gutted at 40. The complicated pace system was unsatisfactory. Men had no say whatsoever as to how they should work; no way of airing their griev-

torials, radio commentators, and corporate spokesmen condemned the sit-down as a direct threat to the principle of private property. "Give way to this," it was declared, "and we give way to socialism."

However, the sit-down proved to be more of a strike tactic than an attempt to alter the nation's form of government. For the strikers it had one powerful virtue: the sit-down strike lessened the threat of strikebreakers and the accompanying violence that often accompanied their use.

The outcome of the Akron strike was union recognition from the big rubber corporations' hitherto open shops. A wave of sit-downs now spread throughout the nation. "Sit down! Sit down! Sit down!" became the rallying cry.

Among those who opposed the sit-down strikes was A.F. of L. president William Green: "Both personally and officially, I disavow the sit-down strike as a part of the economic and organizational policy of the A.F. of L."

A picket line of industrial workers.

Greensboro, Georgia, textile strikers.

A CIO early cartoon on industrial unionism.

Auto workers sit down in Dodge plant in Detroit.

ances. Men were fired for any union activity . . .
there was no job security . . ." But said Alfred P.
Sloan, Jr., General Motors president, in a report to
stockholders in April 1937: "The automobile worker
stands as the most favored of all workers in American
industry . . ."

"The real issue," declared General Motors, "is will a
labor organization run the plants of General Motors
Corporation or will the management continue to do
so."

Early in the winter of 1936, officials of CIO's
United Automobile Workers dispatched a letter to the
company requesting a national collective-bargaining
conference. They were referred to local plant managers. It was but another in a long series of frustrated
efforts in what was to develop, as one writer put it,
into "the most significant industrial battle since labor's
defeat at Homestead."

In protest, workers began to walk out of various of
the sixty-five GM plants—Cleveland, Detroit, Ander-
son, Junesville, Norwood, Saint Louis, Kansas City,
Toledo, and others. However, in Flint, Michigan,
where the company made its important dies, the
workers acted differently. Instead of walking out, they
sat down, singing:

> "These 4,000 union boys
> Oh, they sure made lots of noise.
> They decided then and there to
> shut down tight.
> In the office they got snooty,
> So we started picket duty,
> Now the Fisher body shop
> is on a strike."

"What more sacred property rights are there," asked
the UAW, "than the right of a man to his job." Said
the writer Upton Sinclair: "For 75 years big business
has been sitting down on the American people."

Leaflets—the CIO method of communication.

"The corporation's position was that the union had
'seized' its property and they would not discuss a settlement until we had returned that property to its
rightful owners," recalls Wyndham Mortimer, United
Automobile Workers' vice-president.

I replied by saying, "We have not seized anything. Every man sitting down in these plants
entered onto company property with the company's knowledge and consent. All the strikers
can be accused of is that they have not yet gone
home. The property is still the corporation's, and
is being better cared for now than it has ever
been."

Governor Frank Murphy took exception to
this line of reasoning.

"But, Mr. Mortimer, you are fully aware of the
fact that your remaining in their plants is illegal,
are you not?"

"Governor," I replied, "is it not true that the
Supreme Court of the State of Michigan has

Women oppose violence.

A Ford worker and his family. "These Americans are afraid of
Henry Ford," said the New York newspaper *PM*.

Workers picketing Ford's River Rouge plant—part of over seventy thousand on strike.

As a determination after forty-four days of the strike, General Motors finally agreed to recognize the UAW-CIO with no discrimination against strikers and the establishment of a grievance procedure. The sit-down was declared over and, led by a brass band, the workers marched from the buildings. There had been no violence; no liquor; no vandalism. There had been utmost discipline. "Until that moment," a General Motors worker reported to the writer Studs Terkel, "we were non-people, we didn't exist."

The General Motors victory was a turning point in the CIO drive. In the years that followed, corporation after corporation—some with struggle and some without—approved collective-bargaining contracts with the new industrial unions. The Ford Motor Corporation, long a holdout against unionism, signed. The CIO crusade brought unionism to electrical workers at General Electric and Westinghouse corporations; packinghouse workers organized Armour and Swift; textile workers unionized American Woolen and other textile mills north and south; maritime workers converted ships to union strongholds on almost every sea and river; white-collar workers, newspapermen, government workers—all joined the crusade.

Perhaps the most dramatic campaign was the one to organize steel mills—the first since the 1919 strike defeat. The Steel Workers' Organizing Committee headed by Philip Murray, a United Mine Workers vice-president, astonished the nation by signing a contract with Carnegie-Illinois Steel, a subsidiary of the United States Steel Corporation, granting a forty-hour week, wage increases, and union recognition. The most important defender of the open shop had recognized the new union.

The last holdout in the steel industry was described by Murray as an "unholy alliance of the independent steel companies." A strike was called against these companies when union workers were discharged. It

ruled that there is no such thing as peaceful picketing, and therefore whatever we do would be illegal?"

The Governor nodded, "Yes, that unfortunately is true."

"Well, then, Governor," I said, "since there isn't anything legal we can do, we are forced to do the one illegal thing that is most effective."

The Governor did not carry the matter further.

Police administering a beating to UAW-CIO organizers in 1937 at Ford River Rouge plant, the largest industrial unit in the world.

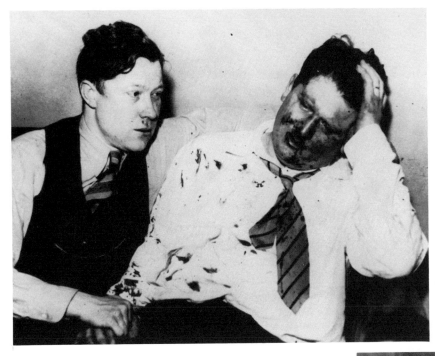

Walter P. Reuther and Richard T. Frankensteen, UAW organizers, after the encounter.

soon spread to seven states and twelve cities, involving over eighty thousand working people. Tom M. Girdler, president of Republic Steel, became the spokesman for management. "I have never seen John L. Lewis except at a distance," stated Girdler, "and I hope to God I never do." In a letter to his employees, Girdler asked: "Must Republic and its men submit to the communist dictates and terrorism of the CIO? If America is to remain a free country, the answer is no."

The strike was to reach a dramatic and tragic climax on Memorial Day, 1937, when strikers and their families demonstrated before the Republic Steel plant in Chicago. An attack was launched by police in which four working people were killed and more than eighty injured, many seriously. While at first the incident was not reported widely, a motion-picture film—at first repressed—was finally made public.

"On Memorial Day, about a thousand union sympathizers, including many women and children, marched in peaceful fashion. . . . They were unarmed," one report stated. "They were several blocks from the gate of the plant . . . when the Chicago police . . . fired, threw tear gas bombs, then attacked with clubs. Not a single policeman was shot."

A Senate committee found that "the sole objective of the meeting and the parade was to march past the plant gate or establish a mass picket line in front of it. . . . Had the police let the parade proceed as planned, the day would have passed without violence or disorder . . ."

The La Follette Committee was to find later as the CIO reported that "many of the best known and respected companies employed agents to spy on labor and stored up tear gas to be used against labor. . . . Many organizers were beaten up, and peaceful pickets . . . killed in cold blood . . ."

UAW-CIO signs the first Chrysler Corporation collective-bargaining agreement on April 6, 1937. Included are John L. Lewis, Governor Frank Murphy of Michigan, and Walter P. Chrysler.

"Little Steel," including Girdler and Republic Steel, eventually signed with the CIO.

The main endeavor on the part of foes of the developing unions both in industry and the older craft unions was to attempt to encourage division in CIO ranks, to destroy labor unity. A detailed analysis of

The Memorial Day tragedy of 1937, in which seventeen people were killed and more than 150 injured.

such tactics was made in a well-publicized senatorial investigation conducted by Senator Robert M. La Follette, Jr., son of the onetime Presidential candidate.

There were many proposals opposed by labor. One that was strongly opposed by the CIO was the move to provide cooling-off periods by legislative action—a time during which unions could not take strike action. "On the face of it," said the CIO, "this cooling off plan is made to look reasonable . . . actually . . . the basic idea . . . is to put the blame for strikes entirely on the workers. It is designed to make a strike look like the work of hotheaded union leaders. . . . It completely ignores . . . real grievances over a long period of time. It ignores the fact that CIO unions

spend weeks and months in negotiations before they even take a strike vote." A decade later it was to become the law of the land.

The very right to strike itself was a point in controversy. Some congressmen, agitated by the breadth of labor's crusade, made proposals to limit the right to strike, even including, in extreme instances, the suggestion that twenty years in prison or the electric chair be punishment for strikers.

"The right to organize and bargain collectively," responded the CIO, "implies the right to strike, since strike action is frequently the only way organized workers have of enforcing collective bargaining. . . ."

Despite these and other reactions, the CIO con-

A Detroit billboard.

Packinghouse workers in Chicago demonstrate for higher wages.

A Michigan protest against police action.

tinued to grow as did the A.F. of L. By 1938, almost four million workers were organized in some thirty-two CIO national and international unions. A billion dollars in wage increases had been won by CIO unions as well as a shorter workday for two million workers, vacations with pay, and other benefits included in some thirty thousand signed agreements.

John L. Lewis continued to give aggressive leadership to the CIO movement throughout this period. "I have pleaded your case . . . not in the quavering tones of a mendicant asking alms," Lewis informed union members, "but in the thundering voice of the captain of a mighty host, demanding the rights to which free men are entitled."

A group of CIO officers: John L. Lewis (center); to his left are Homer Martin, first UAW-CIO president, and David Dubinsky, president of the International Ladies' Garment Workers' Union.

Collective bargaining in the transit industry *(left to right)*: Allan S. Haywood, CIO official; Walter P. Reuther, UAW-CIO president; Michael Quill, president, Transport Workers' Union; Mayor Joseph A. Clark, Jr., of Philadelphia; Albert M. Greenfield and Charles Ekert, Philadelphia transit officials.

A newspaper report of the United States Supreme Court upholding the constitutionality of the Wagner Labor Relations Act, April 12, 1937.

A CIO leaflet on production speedup.

Workers organized in maritime industries, rubber, steel, and many other industries.

# FOURTEEN

# 1938-1960

# LABOR

# IN WAR AND PEACE

*"Labor . . . must have
an increasing participation
in . . . government . . ."*

For millions of factory workers, the new unionism was more than a labor organization. It was a new way of life. One union summarized changed conditions now affecting many CIO and A.F. of L. unions:

Before the CIO, a factory worker was more or less on his own. There was usually nobody to solve his problems. After the CIO, representatives negotiated with the company on the terms and conditions of employment for all workers. Before the CIO, a worker in a factory could only join the union of his craft. For most unskilled workers, there was no union. After the CIO,

workers—skilled and unskilled—could join a union.

Before the CIO, a worker's troubles on the job often went unsettled. While grumbling was common, most feared to complain individually. Before the CIO, unions set up "grievance machinery," a system of elected union representatives in each department of a factory. These representatives or "stewards" could call grievances of workers to the attention of management. Before the CIO, most industrial workers could be laid off, shifted about, speeded up, or wages cut—without explanation or warning. After the CIO, working people gained a measure of security in terms of the collective bargaining contract. People could not be moved around, out of seniority, without agreement. Before the CIO, especially in maritime industries, workers were hired by "shaping up." They would stand about and the hiring official would point out the workers he wanted. Bribery was not unknown to get work. After the CIO, the "hiring hall" replaced the shape-up. Workers were more often hired by seniority and qualifications to do the job.

Before the CIO, many workers received no remuneration when they were away on vacation or holidays. In some factories workers did not dare be absent at all. After the CIO, unions won the right to paid vacations, the number of weeks usually depending upon length of service. Workers could also take off for holidays and be paid. Before the CIO, industrial employee pension systems were infrequent. Often veteran workers would be laid off because of their years. After the CIO, many unions negotiated pensions, sickness and accident benefits, hospitalization, etc.

Before the CIO, most industrial workers had little opportunity to be involved in the democratic process. After the CIO, the union helped give its members dignity and self-respect. Members could elect their own representatives. They could speak out at meetings. They voted on whether the union should strike or not; and whether to accept a contract or not.

Important, too, was the entrance of the new industrial unions—with their millions of votes—into political and legislative activity.

Labor elected its first congressman in the early 1830s. The National Labor Union, the Knights of Labor, the Populists and the Farmer-Labor activity of the Midwest—all demonstrated labor's political aspirations.

But political activity that was more than legislative maneuvering was frowned upon by Samuel Gompers. The A.F. of L. tended to avoid partisan politics, content to "reward labor's friends and punish labor's enemies." It was not until industrial unionism became a massive reality that organized labor returned to its early political commitment. Both CIO and A.F. of L. organizations participated increasingly in political activity.

A specialized CIO political arm—Labor's Non-Partisan League—was established in the summer of 1936 in an effort to unite all of labor in support of President Roosevelt's electoral campaign. The CIO's early LNPL leaders included John L. Lewis, Sidney Hillman, and George L. Berry, president of the Printing Pressmen's Union.

In answer to those who feared political action would cause disunity in labor's ranks, a labor spokesman replied that "we are not thinking in terms of

Oil worker

Machinist

Technician

Philip Murray

promoting chaos within the ranks of labor by creating differences of opinion as to what kind of a political party labor should affiliate itself with, but, rather, concentrating labor's mind and thinking processes upon the enactment of constructive measures to promote the best interests of labor and electing to public office men and women who will serve labor. That is the primary function of Labor's Non-Partisan League."

The CIO's first constitutional convention, held in Pittsburgh in the winter of 1938, changed the organization's name to the Congress of Industrial Organizations. In addition, the convention emphasized that "labor . . . must have an increasing participation in the functions of government . . ." However, by the 1940 Presidential campaign a rift appeared in CIO's more or less united political aims. Although John L. Lewis was opposed—at least in his CIO days—to the Gompers's tradition of "business unionism," he did retain some of the Gompers's dislike of labor dependence on government.

Lewis's estrangement from the CIO began when he questioned the interest of both the Democratic or the

Change of shift at Aliquippa, Pa., steel plant

Republican parties in matters of most concern to working people. In addition, sharp personality clashes developed between Lewis and the President.

Despite certain warnings, on October 25, 1940, Lewis made news in a radio address in which he said that if President Roosevelt were to be reelected, he "will accept the result as being the equivalent to a vote of no confidence and will retire as president of the Congress of Industrial Organizations . . ."

Roosevelt was reelected. True to his word, Lewis resigned from the CIO and was succeeded by Philip Murray, a gentle-voiced aide who for many years was in both the CIO and United Mine Workers. As president of the miners, Lewis was to remain a power in labor and the nation. During World War II he claimed coal operators were seeking to use the war effort to weaken the union contract. The series of stoppages that took place in 1943 as a protest—at a critical juncture in the war—brought down on Lewis the wrath of President Roosevelt and Congress. But the miners gained their desired agreement.

While American labor was organizing its new millions, politically and economically, German labor was being attacked and its unions outlawed under nazism, the German manifestation of fascism, a system of government characterized by forcible suppression of the opposition. As early as 1938, John L. Lewis had reflected his organization's opposition to "the brutal system of Fascism," which, he said, was hostile to "the organization of workers into strong unions . . ."

As the menace of fascism and its leader, Adolph Hitler, spread, so did the threat of a new world war. Labor had, from the start, opposed the fascist ideology. "One of the most important changes Fascism brings about," stated a United States government study, "is the abolition of free collective bargaining and of self-governing labor organizations. Labor policy under Fascism first of all takes away from the worker all means of self-defense. It renders all militant labor action impossible." For many, the entrance of the United States in the war against spreading fascism was inevitable—once it spread itself over a large part of the world. Shortly after the United States declaration of war, on December 8, 1941, President Roosevelt called a conference of union and industry officials. At the end of the meeting, a voluntary no strike pledge was announced. In addition, management representatives pledged not to permit lockouts. These pledges were part of an overall agreement that evolved into the establishment of a National War Labor Board to consider all labor management disputes affecting the war, and to provide for peaceful settlements where possible.

Time lost in strikes during the conflict was estimated at a mere one-seventh of 1 percent of available work time. "Labor never failed the Army or the nation," stated General Douglas MacArthur, allied commander in the Southwest Pacific. General Dwight D. Eisenhower expressed similar thoughts when he said:

The production award for excellence.

"Thank God for American industry—labor and management—which has given us the weapons and equipment . . ."

During the war, union membership—A.F. of L., CIO and independents—steadily rose with the greatest gains being in steel, shipbuilding, aircraft, automotive, and similar war industries. Hourly wages increased during World War II. In addition, there was much overtime. When the government's stabilization policy, during the war and after, forbade wage raises, working people tried to keep up with rising living costs by winning such fringe benefits as paid vacations, paid holidays, shift differentials, and insurance and pension plans.

By 1944, members of the A.F. of L. numbered some 6,800,000. CIO membership was at 6,000,000. There were some 3,500,000 women in unions of the 18,600,000 in industry as a whole. Before World War II there were relatively few women workers, contrasted with the number of working men. With many of these men entering the armed services, and with production of war goods essential, an increasing number of women found job openings in industry. By early summer, 1943, there were more than four hundred thousand women at work in arms factories and offices. Even more women continued to enter the factory production force, learning skills they had never been given the opportunity to learn before. "Rosie, the riveter" was a popular tune of the day as women became expert operators of lathes, band saws, and rivet guns.

"The skill and ease with which women adjusted themselves to the drill operations in these plants,"

REICHSGESETZBLATT (GERMAN BULLETIN OF LAWS), 1933, PART I, PAGE 83

DECREE OF THE REICH'S PRESIDENT.
FOR THE PROTECTION OF THE PEOPLE AND STATE
February 28, 1933

In virtue of paragraph 2, § 48, of the German Constitution, the following is decreed as a defensive measure against Communist acts of violence, endangering the state:

§ 1

Sections 114, 115, 117, 118, 123, 124, and 153 of the Constitution of the German Reich are suspended until further notice. Thus, restrictions on personal liberty, on the right of free expression of opinion, including freedom of the press, on the right of assembly and the right of association, and violations of the privacy of postal, telegraphic, and telephonic communications, and warrants for house-searches, orders for confiscations as well as restrictions on property, are also permissible beyond the legal limits otherwise prescribed.

.    .    .    .    .

§ 6

This decree enters in force on the day of its promulgation.

BERLIN. *February 28, 1933*

Reich's President VON HINDENBURG
Reich's Chancelor ADOLF HITLER
Reich's Minister of the Interior FRICK
Reich's Minister of Justice GÜRTNER

Labor leaders meet with Donald Wilson *(center)*, chairman of the War Production Board. On Wilson's right is William Green, A.F. of L. president, on his left is Philip Murray, CIO president.

states Elizabeth Faulkner Baker in her study of technology in women's work, "were often commented upon by personnel administrators or supervisors. Foremen could point with pride to a young girl who as a spot welder had more than doubled the previous record of boys, or to a woman operating a sensitive drill who maintained daily output double that of the man for whom she substituted . . ."

Black workers in industry also increased during the war. By 1944, there were 850,000 black unionists. Of these men and women, 350,000 were in the A.F. of L., and 425,000 in the CIO.

For a number of years, an effort had been made by the Roosevelt administration to achieve a more equitable hiring policy. In 1941, a Presidential executive order established the Fair Employment Practice Committee (FEPC), founded on the principle that

"there shall be no discrimination in the employment of workers in defense industries or government because of race, creed, color or national origin." A bill to establish this organization as a permanent agency was defeated by a filibuster in Congress. However, in the war years a number of states passed their own FEPC laws forbidding racial or religious discrimination.

As the war progressed, CIO leaders expressed the need for a new organization to rally political support for victory—at home and abroad. "I have an idea that I would like to form a political action committee in the CIO," Philip Murray said to Sidney Hillman at a luncheon meeting one day, "and I would like you to head the committee."

Under Hillman's leadership, the CIO Political Action Committee (PAC) became a force in the mid-

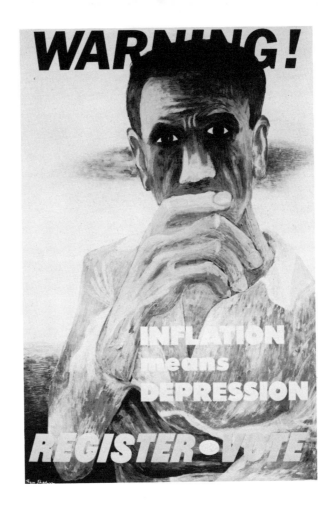

Campaign posters designed by artist Ben Shahn, issued by the CIO Political Action Committee in the 1940s.

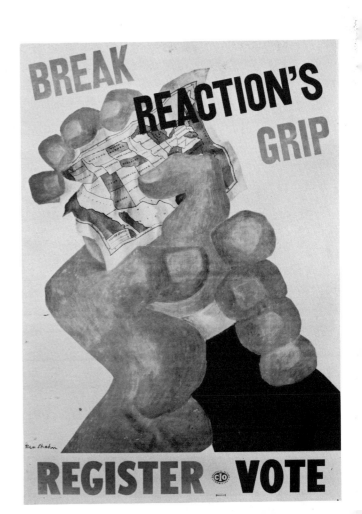

At the coffee docks on the river front in New Orleans.

## WHAT EVERY CANVASSER SHOULD KNOW

A CIO POLITICAL ACTION COMMITTEE PAMPHLET

1940s, rallying political support for Roosevelt. It was consequently the object of attack by opponents of FDR. Such attacks even included an investigation by the Un-American Activities Committee. "The nation was declared to be in constant peril of capture by 'Sidney Hillman, the pants presser,'" says Matthew Josephson in his biography of Hillman. "President Roosevelt and Mrs. Roosevelt were pictured in our yellow press as surrounded by gangsters . . ."

Hillman replied to his critics at one point: "Neither the CIO nor the PAC nor its chairman, is an issue in this election. But the right of workers and other common men and women . . . to organize for full . . . participation in politics is an issue . . ." Later, Hillman, claiming that anti-Semitism was on the increase, said that certain newspapers "rarely miss an opportunity . . . to drag in the fact that I am a Jew . . . I don't apologize to anybody for it."

The increasing effectiveness of CIO-PAC was explained: "One thing we know in the labor movement is organization." In the 1944 campaign, PAC issued

Producing the armaments for victory.

The "most priceless thing in the world."

A group of West Coast drydock workers at a win-the-war rally.

Learning new skills.

Billboard attack on Sidney Hillman, CIO-PAC chairman and Amalgamated Clothing Workers official.

Sewell Avery, president of Montgomery Ward, being removed by troops from his office on April 26, 1944, for refusal to obey an order of the War Labor Board to recognize the union of his employees.

JOBS FOR ALL AFTER THE WAR

CIO POLITICAL ACTION COMMITTEE

With the war nearing an end, the CIO and A.F. of L. proposed a program for the transition to a peacetime economy.

over eighty million pieces of printed material; wrote and took part in radio programs, meetings, interviews, canvassing, and other political activities. On election day President Roosevelt was reelected. More than forty-five million people had voted. There were those who claimed that labor had been the decisive force.

"I can think of nothing more important in the years to come," President Roosevelt wrote Hillman shortly after the election, "than the continuing political education and political energy of the people who do the jobs in this land . . ."

As an end to the war appeared in sight, President Roosevelt took the opportunity to present his views on what he considered the future of the American people. In a Chicago speech in 1944, he stated that "America must remain the land of high wages and efficient production. Every full-time job in America must provide enough for a decent living, and that goes for jobs in mines, or offices, or factories, stores, canneries,—and everywhere where men and women are employed."

In January, Roosevelt had presented to the nation his most carefully conceived program for the future, which he referred to as "a second Bill of Rights, under which a new basis for security and prosperity can be established for all—regardless of station, race, or creed." This economic Bill of Rights included: "The right to a useful and remunerative job . . . the right to earn enough to provide adequate food and clothing and recreation; the right of every farmer to raise and sell his products at a return which will give him and his family a decent living."

# The Rights we Fight for

## THE BILL OF RIGHTS, *December 15, 1791*

CONGRESS shall make no law respecting an establishment of religion, or prohibiting the free exercise thereof; or abridging the freedom of speech, or of the press; or the right of the people peaceably to assemble, and to petition the Government for a redress of grievances.

A well regulated Militia, being necessary to the security of a free State, the right of the people to keep and bear Arms, shall not be infringed.

No Soldier shall, in time of peace be quartered in any house, without the consent of the Owner, nor in time of war, but in a manner to be prescribed by law.

The right of the people to be secure in their persons, houses, papers, and effects, against unreasonable searches and seizures, shall not be violated, and no Warrants shall issue, but upon probable cause, supported by Oath or affirmation, and particularly describing the place to be searched, and the persons or things to be seized.

No person shall be held to answer for a capital, or otherwise infamous crime, unless on a presentment or indictment of a Grand Jury, except in cases arising in the land or naval forces, or in the Militia, when in actual service in time of War or public danger; nor shall any person be subject for the same offence to be twice put in jeopardy of life or limb; nor shall be compelled in any criminal case to be a witness against him-self, nor be deprived of life, liberty, or property, without due process of law; nor shall private property be taken for public use, without just compensation.

In all criminal prosecutions, the accused shall enjoy the right to a speedy and public trial, by an impartial jury of the State and district wherein the crime shall have been committed, which district shall have been previously ascertained by law, and to be informed of the nature and cause of the accusation; to be confronted with the witnesses against him; to have compulsory process for obtaining witnesses in his favor, and to have the Assistance of Counsel for his defence.

In suits at common law, where the value in controversy shall exceed twenty dollars, the right of trial by jury shall be preserved, and no fact tried by a jury, shall be otherwise re-examined in any Court of the United States, than according to the rules of the common law.

Excessive bail shall not be required, nor excessive fines imposed, nor cruel and unusual punishments inflicted.

The enumeration in the Constitution of certain rights, shall not be construed to deny or disparage others retained by the people.

The powers not delegated to the United States by the Constitution, nor prohibited by it to the States, are reserved to the States respectively or the people.

## MESSAGE FROM THE PRESIDENT OF THE UNITED STATES ON THE STATE OF THE UNION, *January 11, 1944*

IN OUR DAY these economic truths have become accepted as self-evident. We have accepted, so to speak, a second Bill of Rights under which a new basis of security and prosperity can be established for all—regardless of station, race, or creed.

Among these are:

The right to a useful and remunerative job in the industries, or shops or farms or mines of the Nation;

The right to earn enough to provide adequate food and clothing and recreation;

The right of every farmer to raise and sell his products at a return which will give him and his family a decent living;

The right of every businessman, large and small, to trade in an atmosphere of freedom from unfair competition and domination by monopolies at home or abroad;

The right of every family to a decent home;

The right to adequate medical care and the opportunity to achieve and enjoy good health;

The right to adequate protection from the economic fears of old age, sickness, accident, and unemployment;

The right to a good education.

All of these rights spell security. And after this war is won, we must be prepared to move forward, in the implementation of these rights, to new goals of human happiness and well-being.

America's own rightful place in the world depends in large part upon how fully these and similar rights have been carried into practice for our citizens. For unless there is security here at home there cannot be lasting peace in the world.

## NATIONAL POLITICAL ACTION COMMITTEE CIO

Franklin D. Roosevelt's Economic Bill of Rights.

On April 12, 1945, Franklin D. Roosevelt died. Labor, together with other segments of the nation, sought to pick up where he left off in seeking a tranquil transition from war to peacetime economy. In a proposal for reemployment, Philip Murray stated in 1944 that labor is "deeply interested in the security and prosperity of every section of the nation . . . farmers . . . independent businessmen and progressive people . . . veterans. We champion the cause of all racial and national minorities . . . health, education and economic security are vital . . . for democracy . . .

"Unless jobs are available," Murray warned, "the second World War would be lost. . . . And the seeds of World War III would be planted and cultivated for another bloody harvest when the infants of 1944 reached manhood."

Various other unions, both CIO and A.F. of L., put forward their ideas for the future. One union declared that "one-third of all the homes are in need of repair; one-third of all homes have no bath; one-third of all homes are still without electricity; 95,000,000 people have a poor diet. Almost 40 percent of all draftees are rejected for physical reasons." During this period the A.F. of L. departed from tradition and established its Labor's Educational and Political League, formed to encourage the A.F. of L. into greater legislative and political activity.

As more than ten million servicemen and women were demobilized, there was a need for massive programs of employment. However, thousands of factories were involved in the process of retooling for a civilian economy. Many cut their working hours. Some shut down completely. Workers faced losses in their take-home pay.

In the face of this, prices remained high and there were disquieting reports of the huge profits that were being made by industry. Tom M. Girdler, president of Republic Steel, who had combatted the coming of unionism so strongly, was reported to be making an annual salary of $275,000. Another foe of unionism,

James H. Rand, Jr., was reported to be making more than $255,000 a year.

In the transitional period, organized labor expressed its unwillingness to cut back on gains won during the war years. On the contrary, the feeling of working men and women was to extend their gains rather than reduce them. One union stated: "We had warned of a need for a planned approach to problems of reconversion, but instead of planning, the reconversion process shows increasing signs of chaos." The demand of organized labor for wage increases resulted in a series of major postwar strikes, particularly in the steel, electrical, and automobile industries.

★ Final Edition  **The Detroit News**  Part One

**FORD AND CHRYSLER SIGN**

**Settlement Reached in GE Strike**
**Union Gets 18½ Cents an Hr. Hike**
**STEEL WORKERS STRIKE!**

**General Motors, General Electric**
**Strikes End in 18½c Hourly Rise;**

Postwar inflation was a cause of economic struggles on the home front.

Campaign for control of prices.

Some of the strikes lasted as long as a hundred days. Wage increases were won and, more important, according to union claims, the attempt of industry to weaken the union movement, which had achieved such gains and recognition during the war years, had been set back.

With labor's wartime strength reinforced by postwar victories, its membership and public prestige steadily increased. However, a new struggle was at hand. Two opposing points of view were coming into open conflict: "The future of labor is the future of America," John L. Lewis had declared in 1938. Now, years later, Charles Wilson, president of General Motors, was to enunciate a different philosophy: "What is good for General Motors is good for the United States."

Contributing to domestic uncertainty and tension was the development internationally of a cold war atmosphere. As such a state of mind increased, labor militancy became suspect, at least in the eyes of those hostile to unionism. Although it was a psychological rather than a military struggle, the implications for the American labor movement were profound. "Gone were the memories of labor's war time loyalties," stated the monthly journal of the International Association of Machinists. "Capitalizing upon the wave of post-war industrial unrest inspired largely by recalcitrant management, a labor-hostile Congress sought to shackle unionism . . ."

The most prominent target of those concerned over the rise of labor was the Wagner Labor Relations Act, passed under the New Deal, which guaranteed to working people the right to join unions and bargain collectively through them. In 1947, the United States

Typical labor cartoons of the 1950s.

*The dispensary's straight ahead . . .*

Chamber of Commerce stated its belief that "it is probable that the 80th Congress will modify the Wagner Act so that employers can work more effectively, and without fear of law violation." The prediction proved correct because in a few months, on June 23, 1947, the Labor Management Relations Act —better known as the Taft-Hartley Act—was passed over a Presidential veto. The new law had as its stated purpose the reestablishment of a balance between labor and industry, "which the Wagner Act

had upset." Labor claimed the new law, rather than establishing a balance, was an attempt to return industry to the open shop.

An analysis by the United States Department of Labor of the Taft-Hartley legislation stated:

> Certain agreement provisions, such as the closed shop, were banned under the revised law, while others, such as the union shop, check-off, welfare funds, grievance procedure, and contract termination provisions, were restricted or regulated. A list of "unfair labor practices"—actions which the unions might not undertake without violating the law—was added to counterbalance, according to its advocates, the unfair labor practices prohibited employers under the Wagner Act.
>
> The Labor Management Relations Act also imposed certain limitations on strikes and lock-

The Taft-Hartley Act was passed over a Presidential veto.

outs. Secondary boycotts, for example, became "unfair labor practices" and stoppages over such issues might be penalized by court action and law suits for damages.

Special rules were written into the law governing controversies or strikes which imperil the national health or safety. In any such dispute or strike, the President of the United States may appoint a "board of inquiry" to investigate the facts. Thereafter, an injunction forbidding the occurrence or continuance of a stoppage for a period of 80 days can be obtained. During this "cooling-off" or "waiting" period, further efforts are made to settle the dispute. If no voluntary agreement is reached within 60 days, the employees are given the opportunity to vote by secret ballot as to whether they accept the "final offer" of their employer. After all these steps are taken, however, the law requires that the injunction be dissolved.

Special opposition was voiced to what are called "right-to-work" laws, which extend Taft-Hartley by banning not only the closed shop (agreement to hire union workers only) but also the union shop (agreement requiring newly hired workers to join a union after a given interval) and related forms of union security.

William F. Schnitzler, an A.F. of L. officer, testified before a senatorial committee that "the Taft-Hartley Act actually furnishes the tools by which those blind to human rights can effectively undermine the workers' efforts to attain a more complete enjoyment of their fundamental rights." The CIO executive board went on record that "we would not merit the name of free Americans, if we acquiesced in a law which makes it a crime to exercise rights of freedom of speech, freedom of press, and freedom of assembly."

From John L. Lewis came a blast at the new law as "the first ugly, savage thrust of fascism in America."

Others were also concerned. "Given an administration in Washington which was not pro-union," said *Business Week*, ". . . the Taft-Hartley Act could conceivably wreck the labor movement."

The effects of the new legislation were not to be fully felt for many years. Labor had been unable to mobilize sufficient support to defeat the law largely because in an atmosphere of cold war, militant advocacy of almost any issue was at a minimum. There was the increasing danger that strong convictions on controversial matters could be equated with subversion. The new law, proposing as it did anticommunist affidavits from union officials, tended to intimidate leaders who did not desire to be accused of pro-communist leanings. While President Harry Truman, successor to FDR, had spoken against the law (which was passed over his veto) as a "dangerous intrusion on free speech," he made use of it on a number of occasions after its passage.

Taft-Hartley was not the only repressive legislation passed in this era. The Immigration and Nationality Act of 1952 (McCarran-Walter Act), most of which was strongly opposed by labor, was passed, in which foreign-born people were threatened with denaturalization or deportation for vaguely defined offenses.

The Landrum-Griffin bill was approved in 1959, markedly increasing the severity of the Taft-Hartley Act's provisions governing union-activities.

Such influences had their inevitable effects on organized labor. Almost a quarter of a century later one union officer was to declare that "no one can estimate how much American workers have lost in wages, in conditions and hours, because of the crippling of unions . . ."

Militant labor voices, often raucous in their impatience with the status quo, were largely silenced in the repressive atmosphere. Few wanted to raise issues that might be viewed as controversial at best, and traitorous at worst.

A further step in this direction came in 1949 with the expulsion of eleven CIO international unions "masquerading as labor unions," according to the CIO, which charged them with "communist domination." Actually, CIO differences were more over foreign policy and union autonomy than Marxian concepts. But the expulsion of approximately one million members not only reduced the CIO numerically but contributed further to shutting off voices of dissent in labor's ranks.

Twenty-two years later, in 1971, Leonard Woodcock, president of the United Auto Workers, expressed doubts as to the wisdom of the expulsions when he told a convention of one of the banished unions, the United Electrical Workers, that labor needs "to pull together as we have never pulled together before. Possibly we should never have been split asunder, and we in my union helped cause that splitting asunder."

With labor divided, the repressive trend reached its climax in the early 1950s with the rise and brief reign of Senator Joseph McCarthy. His biographer, Richard H. Rovere, said that McCarthy "drilled communism and saw it come up a gusher." The senator conducted investigations into government, schools and unions—seeking "communists," but gaining mostly headlines. The "Red hunt" ranged from the young investigators for the New Deal La Follette Committee to the high brass of the military establishment. The fact that no one appeared safe created a form of national hysteria.

Organized labor was generally opposed to McCarthy. Among the voices raised was that of Frank Rosenblum, secretary-treasurer of the Amalgamated Clothing Workers, who stated:

The McCarthys . . . have a field day. Protected by Senatorial immunity, they snipe ceaselessly at men better than themselves and slowly are destroying the faith of our people in our Government, our Constitution and the American way of life. . . . Our civil rights are insidiously being impaired, restricted and curbed. A wave of legislation, beginning with the Taft-Hartley Act . . . has created, in effect, a parallel legal system superceding the Bill of Rights, the constitution and our traditional body of law.

But McCarthyism had its effect on organized labor, particularly many of its leaders. These labor spokesmen, one writer said, "many up from the mines or mills, could not but value their image of respectability and statesmanship even from anti-labor sources. When condemned for not acting against 'communism' or militancy in CIO ranks, it cut deep."

McCarthyism outlasted McCarthy. The senator died shortly after he was officially reprimanded by action of the United States Senate.

In November 1952, eleven days apart, Philip Murray and William Green both died. With them passed an era in the history of American labor. Walter P. Reuther, forty-five-year-old president of the United Automobile Workers, succeeded Murray to the CIO presidency. George Meany, fifty-eight-year-old A.F. of L. secretary-treasurer, succeeded Green to the presidency of the older federation.

The American Federation of Labor suffered its most drastic division in the 1930s when the CIO came into existence to give expression to the economic and political needs of millions of unorganized working people. Two decades later, the labor movement, suffering from post-World War II repressions, decided to unite its forces against a common enemy.

Signatories to the AFL-CIO merger.

CONCLUSION

The members of the Joint AFL-CIO Unity Committee proudly and unanimously submit and recommend the foregoing xxx agreement to both federations. The xxxxx adoption of the agreement will bring about honorable, organic labor unity. It will contribute to the strength and effectiveness of the trade union movement and to the economic well being of working men and women throughout the land. It will materially benefit the entire nation. It will add strength to the free trade union movement of the world. It will realize a long cherished goal.

for the CIO    and    for the AFL

In December 1955, the A.F. of L. and CIO combined forces and established a single organization. George Meany, A.F. of L. president, and Walter P. Reuther, CIO president, consummate the merger.

Taft-Hartleyism and McCarthyism had splintered away many of the differences that separated the two organizations. Militancy was scarcely the issue any longer. Of the approximately sixty million eligible men and women who made up the nation's work force, the labor movement accounted for only fifteen million. Of these, ten million were in the amazingly durable A.F. of L. and five million in the CIO.

In December 1955, the two federations voted to merge. It had not been an easy consummation.

In 1950, John L. Lewis had proposed a series of joint CIO-AFL actions. CIO president Murray shortly thereafter made additional suggestions for the beginning of unity talks. Further developments included the appointment by the A.F. of L. in May 1950 of a "merger committee." In the summer of

Rival unions of electrical workers unions joined forces on the picket line in 1969.

In 1969, four railroad unions—locomotive firemen, trainmen, conductors, brakemen and switchmen—announced a merger, forming the United Transportation Union, AFL-CIO. *Left to right:* union officers Clyde F. Lane, Neil P. Speirs, H. E. Gilbert, and Charles Luna.

Union officials examine referendum vote of membership approving graphic arts merger combining unions of bookbinders, lithographers, and photoengravers.

Collective bargaining in the garment industry.

1950, a formal A.F. of L.-CIO merger talk took place. In a joint statement, the two federations observed that because of "the disturbed world conditions and the march of communism," the "necessity for organic unity is virtually a must." Following this, differences developed and merger talks were dropped. However, the leaders of both federations subsequently died and their successors renewed the merger discussions during the winter of 1952–1953.

By the winter of 1955, final details had been worked out for the "organic" merger. Arthur J. Goldberg, former CIO legal counsel and future secretary of labor, was credited by *The New York Times* as being a "principal architect of labor unity."

As the result of the merger of the A.F. of L. and CIO, *Life* magazine stated that "United States labor stands more powerful and more united than it has ever been before . . . in contrast to the bitter anti-capitalism in the past, most union leaders now espouse and play a role as partners in capitalism."

The *United States News & World Report* commented: "The most powerful labor force in the United States history has been created . . ." The *Nation* stated: "Today the CIO, according to its own . . . figure, is only 5,000,000 strong. Its elan is gone . . ."

The much publicized CIO Political Action Committee (PAC) now merged into the A.F. of L. to become the Committee on Political Education (COPE). The unification of the two major labor federations thus established the difficult task of organic unification. But it did not by any means end the myriad of difficulties facing working people.

The handshake that ends a collective-bargaining session.

# FIFTEEN

## 1960-1970s

# TODAY'S PROBLEMS —
# AND PROMISE

*". . . what has gone wrong
with the Dream Machine?"*

The era of the 1960s was one of promise for greater security for American working people—for "a new frontier" and "a great society" where men and women could respond to the challenge of building a better future for all. There was hope that war could be restricted to one waged against poverty; and an end could be made to racial bias.

While the promise of the period was realized mostly in words, as far as many working people were concerned, there were specific areas of social progress. In 1961, the Fair Labor Standards Act, passed under the New Deal, was amended to raise the minimum wage to $1.25 an hour and expand its coverage to 3,600,000 additional workers. In 1966, this minimum was again raised to $1.40 an hour; and, in 1968, to $1.60. Included among employees covered were those working in schools, laundries, hospitals, restaurants, and hotels.

Public works appropriations were increased, including $900 million for distressed areas. Urban regions were assisted and an expanded public and private housing program launched. There was an extension, too, of the Social Security Act to provide increased benefits for the temporarily unemployed and the elderly. Congress approved Medicare, a program, strongly supported by organized labor, providing sick-

Walter P. Reuther at the Washington, D.C., civil rights rally in 1963.

ness benefits to those over sixty-five years of age.

Legislation was passed giving aid to public education, more assistance to cities, and an Economic Opportunity Act, which appropriated almost $1 billion for a jobs corps for young people, work assistance projects, and other socially useful programs. Legislative action to increase protection of the civil rights of minorities had been proposed by President John F. Kennedy to the 88th Congress. It was not, however, until the Lyndon B. Johnson administration in 1964 that the Civil Rights Act became law. Hailed by

President Johnson as a "major step towards equal opportunity," the legislation set penalties for discriminatory activities in education, voting, and employment. After the passage of the act for which it had worked, the AFL-CIO declared its passage "so long awaited, marked the beginning of a new struggle to translate the rights thus confirmed by Congress into living reality . . ."

There also had been progress toward extending the boundaries of worker security through collective bargaining. In 1955, the automobile workers' union had negotiated a precedent-making agreement with General Motors providing for special jobless benefits supplementing those paid by state funds. This was considered a first step toward the union's goal of what it called a "guaranteed annual wage" for its members. Nine years later, the union negotiated new contracts with several companies providing earlier retirement arrangements, larger pensions, improved wage payments, and other benefits. The settlements, requiring a series of strikes before they were gained, influenced numerous other unions in their contract negotiations.

However, despite such progress during the decade, there was an increasing sense of insecurity among working people. The new technology and mechanization was not only bringing about what some called a "second industrial revolution," but also loss of many jobs.

New automated machines and techniques were rapidly replacing the old. In 1961, one company an-

nounced methods by which electronic tape would henceforth replace human workers in the making of airplane parts in its plant, which produced, it announced, "the nation's first all electronically controlled line of machine tools." One machine was able, on short runs, to increase productivity as much as 420 percent!

Another device, "the pushbutton miner," was described in an AFL-CIO discussion of automation as "a mechanical giant standing three stories high and weighing more than 1½ million pounds. It cuts and loads as much as 266 tons of coal an hour in one continuous operation, without drilling or blasting and with very little human intervention . . ."

Inroads of sophisticated mechanization of the 1960s were not confined to mass-production industries. At one of the nation's huge electrical companies, orders were received from district officers throughout the country by teletype at its Pittsburgh office. Upon receipt of an order, a computer typed out an invoice

Machines outnumber men.

The anonymous worker.

containing the list price, the discount, the state sales tax, and other information. It then automatically wired the information to the warehouse nearest to the customer. There, the order came off the teletype machine with a bill of lading, addressed carton labels, and data concerning the stock bin in which the product was located. Meanwhile, back at the central office, the computer adjusted its inventory record and, if needed, instructed one of the company's manufacturing plants to replenish the house stock. What once took three to five days and the services of scores of people now was completed in less than five minutes!

Still another contrivance, an intricate "plow," laid miles of telephone cable virtually unaided. Pulled by tractors, the machine dug the trench, laid the cable, covered it, all in a single operation. It was capable of laying some sixty miles of cable in a single day, attended by only a handful of workers.

Such mechanized and automated marvels influenced the working practices of virtually every occupation—from gas-station attendants to coal miners. Production of almost everything rose beyond a point ever thought possible—and with declining work force and work hours. "Productivity has nearly tripled in the synthetic fibers industry," a labor spokesman told a congressional hearing in the 1960s: "It has more than doubled in cigar manufacturing; it almost doubled in bituminous coal mining and in agriculture; and it increased two-thirds in such diverse industries as railroad transportation, canning, preserving and freezing, and cement manufacturing."

But what of the human consequence of all this mechanization? "Every big corporation in America," stated AFL-CIO President George Meany, "is in a mad race to produce more and more with less and less labor, without any feeling as to what it may mean to the whole national economy."

An automatic plow lays telephone cable

A statement by a group of economists, labor leaders, and educators, addressed to the President of the United States in 1968, warned that—unless new planning and policies were devised to distribute the machine-made wealth—poverty, joblessness, and social disorder must certainly increase. Labor more and more complained of the variety of human problems developing. "While this is highly profitable for management," one labor spokesman stated, "it is a menace to the nation and its working people, unless planned and controlled."

"Though society cannot smash the machines," commented an AFL-CIO official in this period, "we must take whatever steps are needed to insure that the machines do not smash society."

Such voices demanded action to help working people over the transition interval. Nor was new technology the only major cause of increasing job insecurity. Among other contributing conditions were a growing number of imports from abroad, and not necessarily the products of other nations themselves. A large proportion of imported products—from chil-

dren's shoes to industrial steel—were made by American multinational corporations that established factories in foreign lands where labor costs were much lower than at home. Building or buying facilities in nations around the world, corporations took advantage of low wage rates.

Products, thus inexpensively manufactured, were transported to American markets, and often sold at prices below American-made goods. The jobs of countless American workers melted away—seemingly with permanence. One congressman declared that such products appear to be bargains but are not. "Imported goods," he stated, "cost more because their real cost is the destruction of the economy. American jobs which go unfilled because of imports mean a growing number of American consumers who are unable to consume. In other words, they are diminishing the buying power of our citizens, and buying power is the very cornerstone of our economy."

A onetime auto workers' union official, Wyndham Mortimer, added a further point of view on the problem:

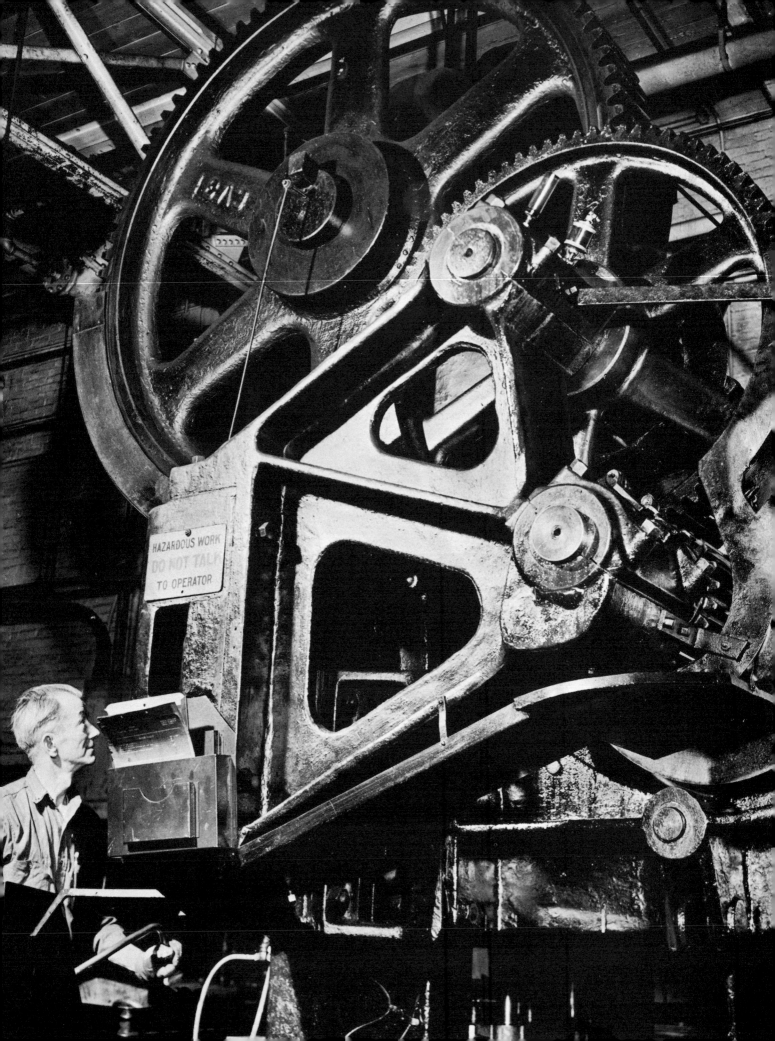

Railroad workers

The machine towers over its operator.

**More Than 100 Escape**

## 24 Men Dead In Blaze In Idaho Silver Mine

KELLOGG, Idaho (AP) — A least 24 miners died in the nation's richest silver mine after fire swept through mineshafts more than half a mile underground, authorities said today.

Shoshone County Sheriff Lou Gardner said 19 bodies were being brought to the surface in addition to the five mine officials said were removed from the murky shafts Tuesday.

The fire was believed to have broken out among timbers between the 3,400 and 3,700-foot levels of the Sunshine Mining Co. operation in this mineral rich area of northern Idaho.

More than 100 men escaped. Families and co-workers of miners reported missing huddled over warming stoves on the surface while rescue crews sealed off shafts they had checked but found empty.

First reports said 77 miners were unaccounted for. It was not immediately clear whether the death toll of 23 cited by the sheriff included some of the 77 missing miners.

About 100 rescue personnel were charting areas sealed behind bulkheads to keep flames from spreading into new portions of the mine. The rescuers were working their way smokefilled mine tried to locate

**Signal Ignored**

## Fatal Darien Train Wreck Blamed On Dead Engineer

A federal agency blamed a dead engineer for Penn Central train wreck Darien last year, which kil four persons and injured 44 ers.

The National Tra Safety Bo

### Factory Injury Rate Jumps to 18-Year High

The rate of disabling injuries in manufacturing industries has risen to its highest point in 18 years, according to Dept

Problems of the era were reflected in newspaper headlines.

DAY MORNING, DECEMBER 31, 1970    40 CENTS A WEEK Carrier Delivered    10¢

*Gas Slows Rescue Attempt*

## Toll Of 39 Feared In Kentucky Blast

*3 Bodies Found; Dust Is Blamed*

HYDEN, Ky. (AP) — An explosion rumbled through a coal mine under a Southeastern Kentucky mountain Wednesday and 39 miners were feared dead. Another near the mouth of th

"When I tried to get up, I couldn't stand. I kept falling down."

He said the coming

To an increasing extent the standard of life in America will be determined by the standard of life elsewhere. The American auto worker will not earn comparatively high wages for very long when the British, German, and Italian auto worker is making seventy cents an hour. The American metal miner cannot maintain his wage levels and compete with the copper miners of Peru who earn seventy cents a day . . .

While job opportunities decreased, corporate earnings—from such developments as automated production and imports from American multinational operations—grew dramatically.

Even though only a fragment of the population was enjoying such affluence, prosperity of a kind was by no means restricted to them. Working people shared in some of the opulence. New automobiles (often two to a family) were a commonplace. Many workers were able to purchase their own homes, which were equipped with the latest electrical appliances from refrigerators to color televisions.

But underneath it all, the uneasy realization existed

that such possessions were usually purchased at the cost of going deeply into debt. According to a survey conducted by the Research Center of the University of Michigan, released in 1971, approximately half of all American families had outstanding installment debts . . . 60 percent of all homeowners were burdened by mortgages . . . Two-thirds of all new car purchases were on credit, which, the Associated Press reported, "is the American way . . ."

To keep up with such obligations, many working people tried to fill two jobs—one by day and the other at night. About four million people held two jobs in the winter of 1971, according to the United States Bureau of Labor Statistics. Debts needed paying and the cost of living seemed forever advancing.

In 1970, the average nonagricultural worker in the United States, according to governmental figures, made less than $6,000 a year *before* deductions for tax and other purposes. Farm workers earned less, often much less.

Examination of the status of construction workers—painters, plumbers, ironworkers, bricklayers, carpen-ters—provided a significant index not only to working conditions but also to the variation of the appraisals of these conditions. "The fantastic climb of wage rates in the construction industry," stated *Fortune* in October 1970, "has become so routine that it hardly makes the papers any more. . . . 'It's the American way, Sonny,' one avuncular $8-an-hour plumber cheerfully explains. 'Three years from now, I'll be knocking down close to $12 an hour.'"

Representatives of construction workers put forward a different point of view. Hourly rates paid construction workers, they say, are an unreliable index to total income. "The claim that building trades wages are an important factor in causing inflation is as phony as a $7 bill," stated the president of the International Brotherhood of Carpenters. "At least half of all building trades workers make less than $9,000 per year—even at today's wage rates . . ."

"Construction workers average less than 1,300 hours. . . per year," according to the carpenters' union. ". . . In other words, four months out of the year without work. . . . Also . . . the unemploy-

Construction workers have a high incidence of accidents.

Dock worker

Basketball player

Actress

ment rate in construction nearly doubles the rate of non-agricultural workers in industry as a whole."

The composite picture of the average construction worker was drawn by labor as a man who found mechanical devices cutting down his working hours.

If he is a painter, the paint roller and sprayer create greater efficiency but reduce available work. If he is a carpenter, the electric saw provides valuable efficiencies but cuts away at work hours. Bad weather for the iron worker means loss of work hours as it does for the bricklayer and the roofer. . . .

Injuries are a constant cause of loss of work time in the construction trades. The iron worker

faces the hazard of falls; the painter faces the menace of fumes from new, sometimes toxic preparations; the carpenter is in danger from both cuts and falls.

In 1966, there were 2,800 building-trades workers killed on the job. Another 240,000 were seriously injured. The following year the Associated Press reported: "The four million men who make their living building the nation's projects earn the highest workmen's wages. Their job is also the deadliest."

There was some belief that service industries—gasstation attendants, TV repairmen, waiters, government employees, nurses, insurance agents, telephone

Chemical tester

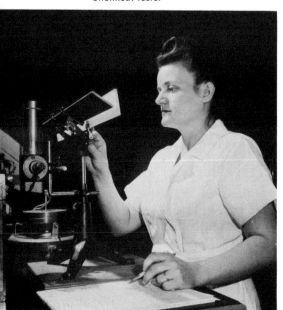

Bricklayer

Garment workers

Grinder

Schoolteachers

Laborer

operators, sales help, hospital workers—would absorb production workers displaced by automation or the movement of factories to nations overseas. And, indeed, in the 1960s the service industries boomed. If it were possible to cut back on those producing the machines and materials American consumers desired, it was not possible to do without *services* for these contrivances. The garage mechanic became almost as important as the physician; and the entire family waited anxiously until the TV repairman arrived. If machines replaced people in many areas of activity,

there was still the need of the service of a fireman in the event of fire; a policeman when in trouble; or a nurse when ill.

However, mechanization and modernization reached even into these services. Many of the nation's 1,600,000 salesmen found their traditional method of earning a living challenged by direct selling techniques of print advertising or television commercials. The new breed of salesmen had to provide more than traditional salesmanship. In addition to selling, they often had to learn the technology of their prod-

Auto worker

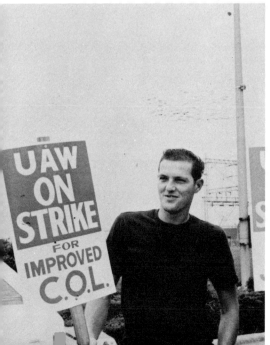

Baseball umpire

Railroad operator

Garageman

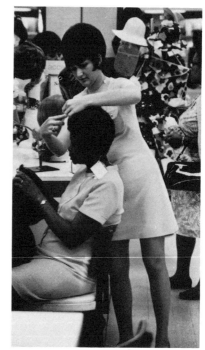

Store clerk

Public employee

Airline employee

Restaurant employee

Supermarket employee

Telephone operator

Service employees are increasing in number.

ucts in order to add service to selling. "You have to make yourself of indispensable value to your customers," one salesman of the 1960s said.

For many working people—especially the less skilled, the poorly educated blacks, Puerto Ricans, Chicanos, and others—jobs had never been easily available. Dispatches from the United States Labor Department in 1970 indicated that when the nation's total unemployment rate fluctuated around the 6 percent mark, the jobless total for nonwhites was 10.7 percent or, in many urban areas, much higher.

The thin line between chronic unemployment and poverty began to be obliterated. A seemingly permanent body of destitute and semidestitute people came into existence. In 1971, the Bureau of the Census reported a sharp increase in the number of poor people. The figures indicated 25,500,000 people officially classified as living below the "poverty line." Presenting what it called a "focus on poverty," a *Wall Street Journal* report described typical victims of poverty:

> A 35 year old Negro mother of four, who is being treated for a psychotic fear of rats at a Harlem Clinic . . . a jobless east Kentucky coal miner, who buries potatoes from his garden each fall and then digs them up to eat in winter when food is scarce . . . a migrant worker in California catching some sleep in a battered car before the pre-dawn hiring starts for the next day's fruit picking. . . . The other America has somewhere between 20,000,000 and 40,000,000 inhabitants . . . about one out of five . . .

Michael Harrington, the author of *The Other America,* has pointed to constrast between the poor of generations ago and today.

> The economy is so different. . . . In absolute terms and objective indices, the impoverished today are better off than their predecessors in misery; but relatively speaking, in terms of hope and economic opportunity, their plight is much

The Reverend Martin Luther King, Jr., on a union picket line.

worse. . . . The new poor have fewer internal resources with which to combat their degradation. . . . The new poor do not even have the economic hope which existed in 1936 and 1937, when the CIO emerged . . .

By the 1970s family-operated farms were disappearing at the rate of nearly one hundred thousand a year.

Poor housing, North.

For a mounting number of working people, thus, joblessness became chronic. For others, wages were inadequate to keep up with expenses. They were, although employed, part of a growing army of the "working poor."

Problems of the cities particularly affected working people since most wage earners lived in urban areas. The crumbling urban centers—with congestion, substandard housing, pollution, drug abuse, crime, and racism—were faced with problems that were among the most serious in the nation. Between the years 1941 and 1971, more than thirty million people left the nation's farms and small towns for urban life. Many moved to cities to become factory workers; others became service employees. Others, finding themselves without skills or good luck, became migrant workers—shuttling their families from farm to farm or cannery to cannery, depending on the season.

Farming in America had changed. A trend from small scale to large scale farming had been under way for decades. Many workers who came to the cities were actually small farm owners who had found it impossible to compete against the larger farm holders. From 1910 to 1940, the number of farms of one thousand acres or more increased from some fifty thousand to more than one hundred thousand. Simultaneously, smaller farms decreased in number. This trend continued through the ensuing decades. The family-sized farm gradually gave way to vast agricultural holdings. The gulping down of the small farm caused the Department of Agriculture to advise men thinking about taking to farming to consider that "measured in dollars and cents, the odds are against your making more than modest returns."

By 1959, there were 4,105,000 farms in the nation. In 1969, that number had declined to 2,970,000, while the average acreage per farm had increased from 288 to 377 acres.

When the farm worker moved to the city, he was influenced, as the National Advisory Committee on Child Labor pointed out in 1963, by "poverty and endemic unemployment, with their attendant conditions of poor health and housing, child labor and meager education. . . . All the problems of farm workers are related to the fact that they have the lowest wage rates and total earnings and the highest unemployment rate of any group in the United States working force . . ."

A contributing factor to the problems of the cities has been the reduction in the number of unskilled and

Poor housing, South.

A government housing project is named after a labor pioneer.

Child labor today.

ment of Health as the nation's number one health problem—was increasing in shops and factories.

Beyond the factory, the farm worker faced special health hazards, including those from toxic anti-insect sprays. A report in the autumn of 1971 revealed how low-flying planes spray insecticide on plants and

AFL-CIO president George Meany was news in the 1970s.

semiskilled jobs—that require little or no education or training. These types of jobs had helped previous generations of immigrants adjust to urban living. Now mechanization and automation reduced the number of such job opportunities. "Trapped by a history of degradation and the recent impact of automation," stated the AFL-CIO in 1967, ". . . new immigrants to the city are also trapped by the unavailability of low and moderate cost housing, as well as by discrimination."

No group had been victimized in greater numbers by such entrapment than black workers who migrated from rural southern areas in the post-World War II decades. Because they were condemned, almost exclusively, to manual labor from the earliest days of slavery, black workers contributed the hardest, hottest, dreariest, most dangerous, most rigorous toil to the making of America. And now even these jobs were disappearing.

The number of problems confronting the nation and its working people—of which about nineteen million of a forty million potential were organized into labor unions—by no means stopped here. Describing drug abuse by workers in Detroit automobile factories, *The New York Times* in 1971 observed that "some suggest that the tedium of the job drives workers to drugs. In a single day, a worker performs the same 'one cycle' operation—twisting the same bolt, setting the same screw—400 times in seven hours, ten minutes, with 46 minutes for lunch and breaks . . ." However, while the drug problem was causing concern, alcoholism—described by the United States Depart-

A turn of a knob does the work of many.

workers alike in some rural areas. "We have to lay flat down on the ground to keep from getting hit," one worker in a migrant worker's camp stated. "By the time it's over you, it's too late and you're too tired to run." Five years after federal minimum wage legislation was extended to include agriculture in 1971, thousands of farm workers still worked for wages well below the legal $1.30 an hour minimum.

Children, too, worked in the fields in increasing numbers, when they should have been in school. "Over 800,000 child farm laborers, at least 300,000 of them migrants, working under conditions that break their bodies and spirit, are virtually excluded from regular schooling," stated one newspaper editorial in 1971. "Non-enforcement of attendance laws combined with hostility on the part of local communities often condemn them to educational retardation."

Adding to the general atmosphere of insecurity among people were other causes of uneasiness. Labor unions and many of their leaders were under attack as at no time since the 1930s. A percentage of such criticism was clearly warranted. There were flagrant instances of union leaders undemocratically controlling their unions. In one union, brought before the courts, there had been no election for thirty years. In another, the international president was "elected" for a life term. In a number of instances, unions developed deliberate techniques to prevent rank-and-file participation.

Then there was the often discussed evil of union racketeering. A recent New York Grand Jury found that "most of the rackets in this city are based on systematic extortion of money from business by the criminal underworld, through pretended trade and protective associations, labor union racketeers, or plain intimidation. . . . We have found that many labor unions and their helpless members are being mercilessly exploited by corrupt leaders and gangsters who run the unions for their own profits . . ."

These and other charges, leveled against organized labor, contributed to uneasiness in the minds of numerous people.

Yet the record of criminal convictions showed no evidence that union leaders are more prone to corrupt practices than any other segment of society. "The percentage of union officers who violate their trust," stated the historian Philip Taft, "was never large and may even be smaller today than in former years. Racketeering in labor unions appears to flow from a general slackness in American society . . ."

But, no matter the source of such tendencies, they contributed to a certain stagnation in labor's economic progress. The great labor surge of the 1930s and after had, as one national magazine put it, "slowed to a standstill." The AFL-CIO merger, while realizing a cherished dream of "labor unity," had not met the expectations of some of those who had helped bring the two labor groups together. Among these was Walter P. Reuther, president of the United Automobile Workers, one of the largest labor unions with well over a million members. Reuther and the UAW International Executive Board sent a letter to the AFL-CIO Executive Council early in 1967, which criticized it for "lack of social vision." A year later the UAW withdrew from the AFL-CIO, and, together with the International Brotherhood of Teamsters and a few other independent unions, established an "Alliance for Labor Action," which, it seems, never evolved into an effective labor body.

Contributing to the uncertainty of the era was the series of assassinations that shocked the nation: President Kennedy in 1963; Senator Robert Kennedy in 1968; Dr. Martin Luther King, Jr., the same year. Violence seemed to be everywhere: in the upheavals in the city ghettos; crime on the streets; on the college campus. And most upsetting of all, the war in Vietnam which, as *Time* reported in 1971, "entered most Americans' consciousness almost surreptitiously, until in the later 1960s, they found themselves fighting . . . to their own bewilderment, the longest war of their national history . . ."

According to the United States Bureau of Labor Statistics, one million civilian jobs were created by the war that started in late 1955. About 70 percent of these were in manufacturing—the largest number in aircraft production. As such job opportunities fluctuated with the waging of the Vietnam conflict, fear and insecurity became the prevailing mood of many working people. The demand of labor for greater se-

The right to strike has been a labor issue throughout American history.

curity was reflected in a mounting number of demands for higher wages and approval of strike action to reinforce such demands. Adding to the uncertainty was the threat of antiunion legislation proposed as a means of solving the developing economic crisis. One college professor wrote at length to support the thesis, not restricted to him, that "collective bargaining is becoming an ever more questionable idea."

At the beginning of the 1970s, there were some five hundred thousand collective-bargaining contracts in the nation. To remove or weaken the collective-bargaining function, labor unions maintained, would be an introduction to chaos. There was some evidence to support this argument. The United States Department of Labor pointed out that "over 95% of the agreements that are re-negotiated in a year are settled without resort to a work stoppage." According to *The New York Times:* "Lost in the turmoil is the fact that daily contract negotiations covering hundreds of different occupations result more often in handshakes than headlines . . ."

There was also a movement to outlaw labor's right to strike. "The strike is an out-dated weapon," stated the governor of Connecticut in 1971. "Rather than liberalizing . . . we should be restricting the right to strike . . ." But there were other views. "Any broad prohibition of strike freedom," warned Professor Thomas Kennedy of the Harvard Business School, "would prove to be very costly in itself and also lead

to major government controls over other parts of the economy."

To some, the right to strike was connected with the use of force and violence. They claimed that labor's progress over the centuries had depended on use of violent tactics. "We in the UAW," responded the late Walter P. Reuther, "know something about violence. We have tasted its bitter fruits from our early beginnings. Some of us have been shot at. We have been beaten up. We have had our offices blown up. We have had our homes threatened and we know that violence solves no problems. It just intensifies old problems and creates new ones."

Confronted with loss of jobs to war, violence, a polluted atmosphere, decaying educational facilities, and threats of repressive legislation, working people responded with increased demands for a solution to their immediate problems.

In the wave of strike actions affecting the nation, many groups of workers participated, a large number from industries and crafts not previously associated with militant labor action. Among those were schoolteachers, newspaper employees, sanitation workers, airplane pilots, baseball players, policemen, postal employees, telephone workers, social workers, college janitors, subway and bus workers . . . The immediate issue was almost invariably the inflationary cost of living.

The work stoppages included farm laborers—largely

Cesar Chavez provided leadership for the Agricultural Workers Organizing Committee, AFL-CIO.

dustry. The effort of these workers developed into a major farm labor struggle. "La Causa" and "Huelga" (strike) became workers' rallying cries.

The struggle merged with an effort of the National Farm Workers' Association in Delano, California, to gain decent housing at reasonable rents. Workers of the association, under the leadership of Cesar Chavez, an Arizona-born Mexican-American farm worker, joined the Farm Workers' Organizing Committee, which was made up largely of Filipino workers. The strike action against the largest West Coast ranches was nonviolent and united. Under the leadership of Chavez, an appeal was issued to the consumers of the nation to boycott table grapes.

The strike received strong community support, attracted national sympathy, and was climaxed in 1966 when the workers marched from Delano to Sacramento, the state capital three hundred miles away. It took twenty-five days to reach their destination, the marchers, varying from forty to a few hundred until they reached the capitol building steps, when they numbered over eight thousand.

Such demonstrations of unity and national support helped win the struggle for the strikers. In the summer of 1967, victory was declared with the workers receiving collective-bargaining rights, wage increases, and other benefits. The strike helped improve the farm labor situation throughout the nation.

Another dramatic struggle of the 1960s took place among traditionally underpaid and unorganized black hospital workers of Charleston, South Carolina. In 1969, under the leadership of the Drug and Hospital Workers' Union, and with support from the national labor movement, the working man and woman were united behind the slogan: "Union Power Plus Soul Power Equals Victory." There were hundreds of arrests; the National Guard was summoned. Never before had the community seen low paid minority

Spanish-speaking men, women, and even children—among the most exploited of all working people. In 1965, members of the Agricultural Workers Organizing Committee, AFL-CIO, went on strike in California's rich Coachella Valley, seeking to increase their wages from $1.20 to $1.40 an hour and to also win piecework increases from the grape-growing in-

Boilermaker

A union organizing drive among hospital workers in Charleston, South Carolina.

A Navajo utility worker

workers in such an effort. After 113 days, the strike ended with the strikers winning most of their demands. One worker said: "It helped me to realize how important I am as a person, which I am afraid I didn't quite realize before." Another expressed a prevailing sentiment:

> *Where is the Union now, friend,*
> *at the Strike's end?*
> *Inside my heart, friend.*

Yet another of many influential labor protests took place in September 1970, against General Motors when four hundred thousand members of the United Auto Workers went on strike for wage increases, larger pensions, and a national agreement. "I am helping my children," one thirty-five-year-old Detroit paint sprayer said. "I'm striking now so they won't have to do it when they work." The strike lasted until late November when it was settled with a three-year contract and wage increases.

It was not only through such strikes that union labor sought to keep up with inflationary costs. A trend toward unification was discernible throughout the era. While auto workers did leave the AFL-CIO in the early 1970s, there were signs of a rapproche-

The participation of women in labor and community affairs is increasing.

ment in the form of united action. Unions in the electrical industry, long rivals, reunited on picket lines and at collective-bargaining tables. The United Transportation Union was founded in 1969, a merger of four railroad unions. The American Postal Workers' Union was founded in 1971, the result of unification of four postal unions. Discussions for joint relationships took place in 1971 between onetime rival longshore unions on the East and West Coasts.

Also signs of working relationships were shown between black and whites in the Deep South. In Mississippi, in the fall of 1971, striking white pulpwood workers applied to local black leaders for aid. One worker declared: "The only way . . . is for all the poor people to get together, no matter what their color of skin is. Black and white is brothers." Charles Evers of Fayette, the first black mayor in Mississippi

history, replied: "I've always known that the poor black and poor white would some day get together. Thank God it's beginning to happen here in Jones County."

Of all working people, minority groups—those most exploited—acted most militantly for change. Black power advocates, organized within unions and especially among the youth, operated with varying strength and visibility. Black caucuses and independent black unions succeeded in forcing on some labor union leaders the task of eliminating discrepancies between rhetoric and performance in the treatment of minority workers. Martin Luther King, Jr., lost his life to an assassin's bullet while in Memphis, Tennessee, assisting black sanitation workers in getting union recognition.

Working women—black and white—spoke out increasingly for equality—on the job, in the home, and in public life. "We women won the right to vote," one factory worker said. "Now we're fighting for our full economic rights. We want to be paid properly for what we do . . ." In response one union declared: "Fighting the exploitation of women is men's business, too, as more and more men workers are faced with rate cuts and speed up . . ."

The desire for cooperation among working people with similar problems and goals became increasingly apparent at the start of the 1970s. The Brotherhood of Carpenters, one of the largest unions in the country, declared: "The need for solidarity is unprecedented."

This trend to greater unification of labor was accelerated by common problems resulting from the wage freeze in late 1971. There were those who accused unions of being largely responsible for the inflation of the economy. When anti-inflationary wage and price limitations were put into effect under the administration of President Richard M. Nixon, labor found itself restricted in negotiating monetary increases of substance. This prompted the accusation by the AFL-CIO Executive Council that the wage freeze was designed to "destroy the basic American concept of free collective bargaining."

"If one sector of the economy is asked to sacrifice, then all must sacrifice," the AFL-CIO stated.

As the twentieth century's three-quarter mark approached—as well as the two hundredth anniversary of the country itself—working people were playing a significant role in the turbulent affairs of the nation. Simultaneously, there were those in labor's ranks who expressed views that America had lost its way—was at a dead end—was baffled by a multitude of choices.

"We are stunned by sky-rocketing prices for things

"The challenge of environmental degradation," states Leonard Woodcock, auto workers' president, "is too important to be left to the environmentalists . . ."

The young people of today are picking up the threads of labor history.

we buy," said one labor affiliate. "We worry over unemployment in the cities and hard times on the farm. We cannot help but wonder what has gone wrong with the Dream Machine?"

The problems of our era—war, pollution, mechanization versus the human spirit, joblessness, racial antagonisms, urban blight—require new attitudes and solutions. *There is an unprecedented requirement for change. The monumental question is whether organizational forms—corporate and labor alike—can meet this requirement. And in time.*

Answers to such problems are being sought in many quarters. But no segment of our nation's past holds such promise for providing clues to the answers we seek than the history of America's working people.

Such study shows that Americans are not descendants of timid or cowardly or selfish people. Rather, their heritage is that of service and self-sacrifice for the common good. "The strongest bond of human sympathy outside the family relation," said Abraham Lincoln, "should be one uniting all working people, of all nations, and tongues and kindreds."

That bond today—uniting all people of goodwill—can be labor's most productive contribution to peace, security, and justice in the world. In more ways than are often recognized, efforts of working people to better their own conditions reinforce the democratic process as a whole and contribute to general economic well-being.

A study of labor history reveals the common people's tenacity to survive and progress—despite adversity. We may have to learn from them lessons for the survival and progress of us all.

# CHAPTER NOTES

In addition to thousands of newspapers, brochures, governmental proceedings, broadsides, speeches, magazines, notebooks, poems, plays, interviews, as well as personal experiences, that went to make up this work, there were countless books—some easily available and others rare—that contributed importantly. These notes are provided, in addition to a lengthy bibliography, for those interested in further readings. There are available a number of labor histories that present useful information from varied points of view, including works by John Bach McMaster, John R. Commons and Associates, Foster Rhea Dulles, Philip S. Foner, Philip Taft, Joseph G. Rayback. In addition, the following suggested readings may possibly whet the appetite of the reader who wishes more than this volume can provide.

### CHAPTERS I AND II

## A NATION IS FOUNDED ON HARD WORK
## BUILDING A DEMOCRATIC FOUNDATION

Reading suggestions: *Government and Labor in Early America*, by Richard B. Morris; *Out of Our Past*, by Carl N. Degler; *The Story of Manual Labor*, by Simonds and McEnnis; Works of Charles and Mary Beard; *Freedom of Speech and Press in Early American History*, by Leonard W. Levy; *The American Labor Movement*, by Leo Litwack; *Life in America* by Marshall B. Davidson.

### CHAPTER III

## LABOR FACES AN INDUSTRIAL REVOLUTION

Reading suggestions: Works of John R. Commons and Associates; *The Golden Threads*, by Hannah Josephson; *Samuel Slater*, by E. H. Cameron; *A New England Girlhood*, by Lucy Larcom; *Lucy Larcom*, by Daniel Dulany Addison; *The Industrial Worker, 1840–1860*, by Norman Ware; *The Story of Textiles*, by Perry Walton; *One Hundred Years Progress of the United States*; *The Great Industries of the United States*, by Horace Greeley.

### CHAPTER IV

## EARLY EFFORTS AT LABOR ORGANIZATION

Reading suggestions: *Poles in American History and Tradition*, by Joseph A. Wytrwal; Works of Commons and Morris; *American Labor*, by Henry Pelling; *Organized Labor in American History*, by Philip Taft; *"An Address to the Working Men of New England,"* by Seth Luther; *History of Great American Fortunes*, by Gustavus Myers; *The Age of Jackson*, by Arthur M. Schlesinger, Jr.; *Most Uncommon Jacksonians*, by Edward Pessen.

### CHAPTER V

## WORKING PEOPLE IN THE CIVIL WAR ERA

Reading suggestions: *Frederick Douglass*, by Benjamin Quarles; *A Pictorial History of the Negro in America*, by Langston N. Hughes and Milton Meltzer; *Abraham Lincoln*, by Carl Sandburg; *Abolition and Labor*, by Walliston H. Lofton (*Journal of Negro History*, July 1948); *The Underground Railroad Records*, by William Still; *North of Slavery*, by Leon Litwack; *Labor: Free and Slave*, by Bernard Mandel; *Labor—Champion of Public Education* (AFL-CIO); *Labor and Politics* (AFL-CIO); *The Life of Billy Yank*, by Bell Irvin Wiley.

### CHAPTER VI

## REBUILDING AFTER THE WAR

Reading suggestions: *Black Reconstruction in America, 1860–1880*, by W. E. B. Du Bois; *Beyond Equality*, by David Montgomery; *Journey to America*, by Alexis de Tocqueville; *William H. Sylvis and the National Labor Union*, by Charlotte Todes; *Sylvis Said*, published by the Industrial Molders Union; *Thirty Years of Labor*, by Terence V. Powderly; *The Path I Trod*, by Terence V. Powderly; *Century of Struggle*, by Eleanor Flexner; *Tom Watson, Agrarian Rebel*, by C. Vann Woodward.

### CHAPTER VII

## THE FOUNDING OF THE AMERICAN FEDERATION OF LABOR

Reading suggestions: *The Molly Maguires*, by Anthony Bimba; *The Molly Maguires*, by Wayne G. Broehl, Jr.; *A Brief History of the United Mine Workers of America*, by Justin McCarthy; *1877: Year of Violence*, by Robert V. Bruce; *Seventy Years of Life and Labor*, by Samuel Gompers; *American Labor Struggles*, by Samuel Yellen; *Gompers*, edited by Gerald Emanuel Stearn; *History of the United Mine Workers* (*United Mine Workers' Journal*), by George Korson.

### CHAPTER VIII

## THE LABOR STRUGGLE AGAINST HUMAN EXPLOITATION

Reading suggestions: *The History of the Haymarket Affair*, by Henry David; *Famous Speeches of the Eight Chicago Anarchists*, by Lucy Parsons; *Altgeld's America*, by Ray Ginger; *Eagle Forgotten*, by Harry Barnard; *Looking Backward*, by Edward Bellamy; *Wealth Against Commonwealth*, by Henry Demarest Lloyd; *Trusts, Pools and Corporations*, by William Z. Ripley; *The Black Worker*, by Spero and Harris.

CHAPTER IX

## THE CONFLICTS AT HOMESTEAD AND PULLMAN

Reading suggestions: *Lockout*, by Leon Wolff; *Incredible Carnegie*, by John K. Winkler; *A Momentous Question*, by John Swinton; *Writings and Speeches*, by Eugene V. Debs; *The Bending Cross*, by Ray Ginger; *Debs*, edited by Ronald Radosh; *The Pullman Strike*, by Reverend William H. Carwardine; *American Labor Struggles*, by Samuel Yellen.

CHAPTER X

## AMERICA ENTERS THE TWENTIETH CENTURY

Reading suggestions: *The Jungle*, by Upton Sinclair; *The Triangle Fire*, by Leon Stein; *Our Times*, by Mark Sullivan; *Bill Haywood's Book*, by William Haywood; *The Women's Garment Workers*, by Louis Levine; *The Children of the Poor*, by Jacob A. Riis; *Organized Labor*, by John Mitchell; *Autobiography*, by Lincoln Steffens; *Crusade for the Children*, by Walter I. Trattner; *The Bitter Cry of the Children*, by John Spargo; *Florence Kelley*, by Dorothy Rose Blumberg; *Rebel Voices*, by Joyce L. Kornbluh; *The Wobblies*, by Patrick Renshaw; *Out of Our Past*, by Carl N. Degler.

CHAPTER XI

## LABOR IN THE WORLD WAR I ERA

Reading suggestions: *Only Yesterday*, by Frederick Lewis Allen; *Bill Haywood's Book*, by William Haywood; *American Labor Struggles*, by Samuel Yellen; *Dynamite*, by Louis Adamic; *Out of the Depths*, by Barron B. Beshoar; *Violence in America*, by Graham and Gurr; *The Story of My Life*, by Clarence Darrow; *Frame-up*, by Curt Gentry; *The Man Who Never Died*, by Barrie Stavis; *Joe Hill*, by Gibbs M. Smith; *The Bending Cross*, by Ray Ginger; *The Case of Sacco and Vanzetti*, by Felix Frankfurter; *The Letters of Sacco and Vanzetti*, edited by Marion Denman Frankfurter and Gardner Jackson; *Steel, the Diary of a Furnace Worker*, by Charles Rumford Walker; *The Great Steel Strike and Its Lessons*, by William Z. Foster; *Labor in Crisis*, by David Brody.

CHAPTER XII

## THE POSTWAR "PROSPERITY"

Reading suggestions: *Our Times*, by Mark Sullivan; *The Jazz Age*, by Marvin Barrett and William Cahn; *The Big Change*, by Frederick Lewis Allen; *The Perils of Prosperity*, by William E. Leuchtenburg; *I Break Strikes*, by Edward Levinson; *Critics and Crusaders*, by Charles A. Madison; *The American Automobile*, by John B. Rae; *The Hungry Years*, by Adrian

A. Paradis; *The Great Depression*, by Robert Goldston; *The Great Depression*, edited by David A. Shannon; *The Lean Years*, by Irving Bernstein; *Seven Lean Years*, by Woofter and Winston; *From the Depths*, by Robert H. Bremner; *American Labor in the 20th Century*, by Jerold S. Auerbach.

CHAPTER XIII

## INDUSTRIAL UNIONISM AND THE NEW DEAL

Suggested readings: *Labor's New Millions*, by Mary Heaton Vorse; *Labor on the March*, by Edward Levinson; *The Labor Spy Racket*, by Leo Huberman; *The Many and the Few*, by Henry Kraus; *Labor Radical*, by Len De Caux; *John L. Lewis*, by Saul Alinsky; *Walter Reuther, Building the House of Labor*, by Fred J. Cook; *Labor and Liberty*, by Jerold S. Auerbach; *Men Who Lead Labor*, by Minton and Stuart; *Labor*, by Richard A. Lester; *American Labor*, by Herbert Harris; *Toil and Trouble*, by Thomas R. Brooks; *American Labor in the Twentieth Century*, by Jerold S. Auerbach.

CHAPTER XIV

## LABOR IN WAR AND PEACE

Suggested readings: *The Development of the Social Security Act*, by Edwin E. Witte; *The Crisis of the Old Order*, by Arthur M. Schlesinger, Jr.; *The History of the New Deal*, by Basil Rauch; *The First Round*, by Joseph Gaer; *The New Age of Franklin Roosevelt*, by Dexter Perkins; *Sidney Hillman*, by Matthew Josephson; *Senator Joe McCarthy*, by Richard H. Rovere.

CHAPTER XV

## TODAY'S PROBLEMS—AND PROMISE

Suggested readings: *Automation and Society*, by Jacobson and Roucek, *Automation*, by William Francois; *The Black Worker*, by Spero and Harris; *La Causa*, by Fusco and Horwitz; *Delano*, by John Gregory Dunne; *The Labor Revolution*, by Gus Tyler; *Labor in Learning*, by Will Scoggins: *The Other America*, by Michael Harrington.

CHILDREN'S BOOKS

The number of books for children specifically on the subject of labor is not numerous. A few of those available include: *Bread and Roses*, by Milton Meltzer; *This Union Cause*, by Katherine B. Shippen; *Labor's Defiant Lady, the Story of Mother Jones*, by Irving Werstein; *No Time for School, No Time for Play—The Story of Child Labor in America*, by Rhoda and William Cahn; *Wandering Workers*, by Willard A. Heaps.

# BIBLIOGRAPHY

While a monumental number of resources were consulted other than this bibliography, the following books were particularly helpful in whole or in part. A representative bibliography of American labor history has been compiled by Professor Maurice F. Neufeld and published by the New York State School of Industrial and Labor Relations for those seeking additional sources.

ADAMIC, LOUIS. *Dynamite, The Story of Class Violence in America.* New York: Chelsea House Publishers, 1958.

ADDAMS, JANE. *A Centennial Reader.* New York: The Macmillan Company, 1960.

ADDISON, DANIEL DULANY. *Lucy Larcom—Life, Letters and Diary.* Boston: Houghton Mifflin Company, 1895.

ALINSKY, SAUL. *John L. Lewis, an unauthorized biography.* New York: G. P. Putnam's Sons, 1949.

ALLEN, FREDERICK LEWIS. *The Big Change, America Transforms Itself, 1900–1950.* New York: Harper & Brothers, 1952.

———. *Only Yesterday, an Informal History of the 1920s.* New York: Harper & Brothers, 1931.

*American Federationist,* official monthly magazine of the AFL–CIO, 1881–1972, Washington, D.C.

*American Story of Industrial and Labor Relations, The.* New York State Joint Legislative Committee on Industrial and Labor Conditions, 1943.

APTHEKER, HERBERT. *The Labor Movement in the South During Slavery.* New York: International Publishers Co., Inc., n.d.

ASHTON, T. S. *The Industrial Revolution, 1760–1830.* New York: Oxford University Press, 1964.

AUERBACH, JEROLD S. *American Labor in the Twentieth Century.* Indianapolis: The Bobbs-Merrill Co., Inc., 1969.

———. *Labor and Liberty, The La Follette Committee and the New Deal.* Indianapolis: The Bobbs-Merrill Co., Inc., 1966.

AUSTIN, ALEINE. *The Labor Story, a Popular History of American Labor.* New York: Coward-McCann, Inc., 1949.

*Authentic History of the Lawrence Calamity Embracing a Description of the Pemberton Mill, An.* Boston: John J. Dyer & Co., 1860.

BAGDIKIAN, BEN H. *In the Midst of Plenty—the Poor in America.* New York: The New American Library, Inc., 1964.

BAKER, ELIZABETH FAULKNER. *Technology in Woman's Work.* New York: Columbia University Press, 1964.

BARNARD, HARRY. *Eagle Forgotten, the Life of John Peter Altgeld.* Indianapolis: The Bobbs-Merrill Co., Inc., 1962.

BARNARD, J. LYNN. *Factory Legislation in Pennsylvania: Its History and Administration.* Philadelphia: University of Pennsylvania Press, 1907.

BARRETT, MARVIN, and CAHN, WILLIAM. *The Jazz Age.* New York: G. P. Putnam's Sons, 1959.

BEARD, CHARLES A. and MARY R. *The Rise of American Civilization.* New York: The Macmillan Company, 1930.

BEARD, MARY RITTER. *The American Labor Movement, a Short History.* New York: The Macmillan Company, 1942.

BECKER, CARL L. *The Declaration of Independence.* New York: Vintage Books, 1942.

BEDFORD, HENRY F. *Socialism and the Workers in Massachusetts, 1886–1912.* Amherst, Massachusetts: University of Massachusetts Press, 1966.

BELLAMY, EDWARD. *Looking Backward—2000–1887.* New York: The New American Library, Inc., 1962.

BENNETT, LERONE, JR. *Before the Mayflower: A History of the Negro in America 1619–1962.* Chicago: Johnson Publishing Co., 1962.

BERNSTEIN, IRVING. *The Lean Years, a History of the American Worker—1920–1933.* Baltimore: Penguin Books, Inc., 1970.

BESHOAR, BARRON B. *Out of the Depths, the Story of John R. Lawson, a Labor Leader.* The Colorado Labor Historical Committee of the Denver Trades and Labor Assembly, 1957.

BIMBA, ANTHONY. *The History of the American Working Class.* New York: International Publishers Co., Inc., 1927.

———. *The Molly Maguires.* New York: International Publishers Co., Inc., 1932.

BLUMBERG, DOROTHY ROSE. *Florence Kelley: The Making of a Social Pioneer.* New York: Augustus M. Kelley, 1966.

BOK, DEREK C., and DUNLOP, JOHN T. *Labor and the American Community.* New York: Simon and Schuster, Inc., 1970.

BOYER, RICHARD O., and MORAIS, HERBERT M. *Labor's Untold Story.* New York: United Electrical Workers, 1971.

BRAMSON, ROY T. *American Mass Production.* Detroit: The Bramson Publishing Co., 1945.

BREMNER, ROBERT H. *From the Depths—the Discovery of Poverty in the United States.* New York: New York University Press, 1964.

*Brief History of the American Labor Movement, A.* Washington, D.C.: United States Department of Labor, n.d.

BRODY, DAVID. *Labor in Crisis, the Steel Strike of 1919.* Philadelphia: J. B. Lippincott Co., 1965.
——. *Steel Workers in America, the Non-Union Era.* New York: Harper & Row, Publishers, 1969.

BROEHL, WAYNE G., JR. *The Molly Maguires.* New York: Vantage/Chelsea House Publishers, 1968.

BROOKS, THOMAS R. *Toil and Trouble, a History of American Labor.* New York: Dell Publishing Co., Inc., 1964.

BROTSLAW, IRVING. *The Struggle to Unite: A Brief History of the American Labor Movement.* Madison, Wisconsin: University of Wisconsin Press, 1964.

BRUCE, ROBERT V. *1877: Year of Violence.* Chicago: Quadrangle Books, Inc., 1970.

BURLINGAME, ROGER. *March of the Iron Men, a Social History of Union Through Invention.* New York: Grosset & Dunlap, Inc., 1938.

BURNS, WILLIAM J. *The Masked War.* New York: Hodder and Stoughton, 1913.

BUTLER, BENJAMIN F. *Butler's Book.* Boston: A. M. Thayer & Co., 1892.

CAMERON, E. H. *Samuel Slater, Father of American Manufactures.* Portland, Maine: The Bond Wheelwright Company, 1960.

CARLTON, FRANK TRACY. *Organized Labor in American History.* New York: D. Appleton & Company, 1920.

CARSON, GERALD. *The Old Country Store.* New York: Oxford University Press, 1954.

CARWARDINE, REVEREND WILLIAM H. *The Pullman Strike.* Chicago: Illinois Labor History Society, 1971.

CHAFEE, ZECHARIAH, JR. *35 Years With Freedom of Speech.* New York: Civil Liberties Foundation, 1952.

CHALMERS, DAVID MARK. *The Social and Political Ideas of the Muckrakers.* New York: Citadel Press, 1964.

CHAPLIN, RALPH. *Wobbly.* Chicago: University of Chicago Press, 1948.

CHILDS, MARQUIS. *The Farmer Takes a Hand.* New York: Doubleday & Company, Inc., 1952.

*CIO—1935-55. Industrial Democracy in Action.* Washington, D.C.: Congress of Industrial Organizations, 1955.

CLEWS, HENRY. *Twenty Eight Years in Wall Street.* New York: Irving Publishing Company, 1888.

COBEN, STANLEY. Article, *Political Science Quarterly,* March 1964.

COLE, DONALD B. *Immigrant City, Lawrence, Massachusetts, 1845 and 1921.* Chapel Hill, North Carolina: University of North Carolina Press, 1963.

COLE, MARGARET. *Robert Owen of New Lenark.* New York: Oxford University Press, 1953.

COLLIER, JOHN. *Indians of the Americas, the Long Hope.* New York: The New American Library, Inc., 1947.

COLTON, SAMUEL. *Sagas of Struggle, a Labor Anthology.* New York: Claridge Publishing Corp., 1951.

COMMAGER, HENRY STEELE. *The Era of Reform 1830-1860.* Princeton, New Jersey: D. Van Nostrand Co., Inc., 1960.
——. and Nevins, Allan. *The Heritage of America.* Boston: Little, Brown and Company, 1939.

COMMONS, JOHN R. *A Documentary History of American Industrial Society.* Glendale, California: Arthur H. Clark Company, 1910.
——. *History of Labour in the United States.* Vols. I and II. New York: The Macmillan Company, 1926.
——. *Myself, The Autobiography of John R. Commons.* Madison, Wisconsin: University of Wisconsin Press, 1964.

COOK, FRED J. *Walter Reuther, Building the House of Labor.* Chicago: Encyclopaedia Britannica, Inc., 1963.

DACUS, J. A. *Annals of the Great Strikes in the United States.* Saint Louis: Scammell and Comby, 1877.

DANISH, MAX D. *William Green.* New York: Inter-Allied Pub., 1952.
——. *The World of David Dubinsky.* Cleveland: The World Publishing Company, 1957.

DARROW, CLARENCE. *The Story of My Life.* New York: Grosset & Dunlap, Inc., 1932.

DAVID, HENRY. *The History of the Haymarket Affair.* New York: Collier Books, 1963.

DAVIDSON, MARSHALL B. *Life in America.* Vols. I and II. Boston: Houghton Mifflin Company, 1951.

DAVIS, HORACE B. *Shoes, the Workers and the Industry.* New York: International Publishers Co., Inc., 1940.

DAWSON, HENRY B. *The Sons of Liberty in New York.* Poughkeepsie: Platt & Schram, 1859.

DEBO, ANGIE. *A History of the Indians of the United States.* Norman: University of Oklahoma Press, 1970.

DEBS, EUGENE V. *Writings and Speeches.* New York: Hermitage Press, Inc., 1948.

DE CAUX, LEN. *Labor Radical, From the Wobblies to the CIO.* Boston: Beacon Press, 1970.

DEGLER, CARL N. *Out of Our Past, the Forces that Shaped Modern America.* New York: Harper & Row Publishers, 1959.

DENNIS, R. ETHEL. *The Black People of America, an Illustrated History.* New Haven: Readers Press, Inc., 1970.

DICKENS, CHARLES. *American Notes.* Greenwich, Connecticut: Fawcett Publications, Inc., 1961.

DIDEROT, DENIS. *Pictorial Encyclopedia of Trades and Industry.* New York: Dover Publications, 1959.

DONNER, FRANK J. *The Un-Americans.* New York: Ballantine Books, Inc., 1961.

DORR, RHETA CHILDE. *What Eight Million Women Want.* Boston, 1910.

DREIER, MARY E. *Margaret Dreier Robins.* New York: Island Press Cooperative, Inc., 1950.

Du Bois, W. E. B. *Black Reconstruction in America, 1860–1880.* Cleveland: The World Publishing Company, 1964.

Dulles, Foster Rhea. *Labor in America.* New York: Thomas Y. Crowell Company, 1955.

Dunn, Robert W., and Hardy, Jack. *Labor and Textiles.* New York: International Publishers Co., Inc., 1931.

Dunne, John Gregory. *Delano, the Story of the California Grape Strike.* New York: Farrar, Straus & Giroux, Inc., 1969.

*Eighty Years Progress of the U.S.* Hartford: L. Stebbins, 1869.

*Eleventh Annual Meeting, The National Civic Federation.* New York: The National Civic Federation, 1911.

Eskew, Garnett Laidlaw. *Salt, the Fifth Element.* Chicago: J. G. Ferguson & Associates, 1948.

*Farm Labor Organizing—1905–1967, a Brief History.* New York: National Advisory Committee on Farm Labor, 1967.

*Fascism in Action, a Documented Study and Analysis of Fascism in Europe.* Washington, D.C.: Government Printing Office, 1947.

Faulkner, Harold U., and Starr, Mark. *Labor in America.* New York: Oxford Book Co., Inc., 1955.

Filler, Louis. *Crusaders for American Liberalism.* New York: Collier Books, 1961.

——. *Late 19th Century American Liberalism.* Indianapolis: The Bobbs-Merrill Co., Inc., 1962.

Flexner, Eleanor. *Century of Struggle—The Women's Rights Movement in the United States.* New York: Atheneum Publishers, 1970.

Flower, B. I. *Progressive Men, Women and Movements of the Past Twenty-Five Years.* Boston: The New Arena, 1914.

Foner, Philip S. *History of the Labor Movement in the United States.* Vols. 1–4. New York: International Publishers Co., Inc., 1947.

——. *The Letters of Joe Hill.* New York: Oak Publications, Inc., 1965.

Ford, Henry. *Great Lives Observed.* Edited by John B. Rae. Englewood Cliffs, New Jersey: Prentice-Hall, Inc., 1969.

Fortune, Timothy Thomas. *Black and White, Land, Labor and Politics in the South.* Chicago: Johnson Publishing Co., 1970.

Foster, William Z. *The Great Steel Strike and Its Lessons.* New York: B. W. Heubsch, Inc., 1920.

——. *Pages from a Worker's Life.* New York: International Press Co., Inc., 1939.

Fraenkel, Osmond K. *The Supreme Court in Civil Liberties.* New York: American Civil Liberties Union, 1949.

Francois, William. *Automation, Industrialization Comes of Age.* New York: Collier Books, 1964.

Frankfurter, Felix. *The Case of Sacco and Vanzetti.* New York: Grosset & Dunlap, Inc., 1961.

Frankfurter, Marion Denman, and Jackson,

Gardner, eds. *The Letters of Sacco and Vanzetti.* New York: E. P. Dutton & Co., Inc., 1960.

Fusco, Paul, and Horwitz, George D. *La Causa: The California Grape Strike.* New York: Collier Books, 1970.

Gabriel, Ralph Henry. *Toilers of Land and Sea.* New Haven: Yale University Press, 1926.

Gaer, Joseph. *The First Round.* New York: Duell, Sloan & Pearce, 1944.

Gambs, John S. *The Decline of the IWW.* New York: Russell & Russell Publishers, 1966.

Gentry, Curt. *Frame-up, The Incredible Case of Tom Mooney and Warren Billings.* New York: W. W. Norton & Company, Inc., 1967.

Ginger, Ray. *Altgeld's America.* Chicago: Quadrangle Books, Inc., 1965.

——. *The Bending Cross—A Biography of Eugene Victor Debs.* New Brunswick, New Jersey: Rutgers University Press, 1949.

Giovanetti, Arturo. *Arrows in the Gale.* Riverside, Connecticut: Hillacre Bookhouse, 1914.

Goldberg, Harvey. *American Radicals: Some Problems and Personalities.* New York: Modern Reader Paperbacks, 1957.

Goldbloom, Maurice; Herling, John; Seidman, Joel; and Yard, Elizabeth. *Strikes Under the New Deal.* New York: League for Industrial Democracy, 1935.

Goldstein, Abraham S. *Conspiracy to Defraud the United States.* New Haven: Yale Law Journal, vol. 68, no. 3, January 1959.

Goldston, Robert. *The Great Depression, the United States in the Thirties.* Greenwich, Connecticut: Fawcett Publications, Inc., 1968.

Gompers, Samuel. *Seventy Years of Life and Labor, an autobiography.* New York: E. P. Dutton & Co., Inc., 1925.

Graham, Hugh Davis, and Gurr, Ted Robert. *Violence in America.* New York: Bantam Books, Inc., 1969.

Greeley, Horace. *The Autobiography of Horace Greeley.* New York: E. B. Treat, 1872.

——. *The Great Industries of the United States.* Hartford: J. B. Burr & Hyde, 1872

Greenslet, Ferris. *The Lowells and Their Seven Worlds.* Boston: Houghton Mifflin Company, 1946.

*Growth of Industrial Art, The,* arranged under the supervision of the Honorable Benjamin Butterworth. Washington, D.C.: Government Printing Office, 1892.

*Growth of Labor Law in the United States,* United States Department of Labor. Washington, D.C.: Government Printing Office, 1967.

Harrington, Michael. *The Other America, Poverty in the United States.* Baltimore: Penguin Books, Inc., 1971.

Harris, Herbert. *American Labor.* New Haven: Yale University Press, 1941.

HARTLEY, FRED A., JR. *Our New National Labor Policy.* New York: Funk & Wagnalls, 1948.

HAYS, ARTHUR GARFIELD. *Let Freedom Ring.* New York: Boni & Liveright, 1928.

——. *Trial by Prejudice.* New York: Covici, Friede, Publishers, 1935.

HAYWOOD, WILLIAM. *Bill Haywood's Book.* New York: International Publishers Co., Inc., 1929.

——. *Testimony Before Industrial Relations Commission.* Chicago: IWW Publishing Bureau, 1920.

*Hearings Before the Committee on Rules of the House of Representatives. The Strike at Lawrence, Mass.* Washington, D.C.: Government Printing Office, 1912.

HERZOG, ELIZABETH. *About the Poor, Some Facts and Some Fictions.* Washington, D.C.: U.S. Department of Health, Education and Welfare, 1967.

HILLQUIT, MORRIS. *History of Socialism in the United States.* New York: Funk & Wagnalls, 1910.

HOFSTADTER, RICHARD. *The Progressive Movement, 1900–1915.* Englewood Cliffs, New Jersey: Prentice-Hall, Inc., 1963.

HOLBROOK, STEWARD A. *Dreamers of the American Dream.* Garden City, N.Y.: Doubleday & Company, Inc., 1957.

HORAN, JAMES D. *The Pinkertons, the Detective Dynasty That Made History.* New York: Crown Publishers, Inc., 1967.

HOURWICH, ANDRIA TAYLOR, and PALMER, GLADYS L. *I Am a Woman Worker, a Scrapbook of Autobiographies.* New York: The Affiliated Schools for Workers, Inc., 1936.

HOWARD, ROBERT WEST. *This Is the West.* New York: Signet Books, 1957.

HUBERMAN, LEO. *The Great Bus Strike.* New York: Modern Age Books, Inc., 1941.

——. *The Truth About Unions.* New York: Reynal and Hitchcock, Inc., 1946.

——. *We, the People.* New York: Harper & Brothers, 1947.

HUGHES, LANGSTON N., and MELTZER, MILTON. *A Pictorial History of the Negro in America.* New York: Crown Publishers, Inc., 1956.

HUTCHINS, GRACE. *Women Who Work.* New York: International Publishers Co., Inc., 1934.

*ILWU Story, The.* San Francisco: International Longshoremen's and Warehouse Men's Union, 1955.

JACOBSON, HOWARD BOONE, and ROUCEK, JOSEPH S. *Automation and Society.* New York: Philosophical Library, Inc., 1959.

JACOBSON, JULIUS. *The Negro and the American Labor Movement.* New York: Doubleday & Company, Inc., 1968.

JOHNSON, OAKLEY C. *Robert Owen in the United States.* New York: Humanities Press, Inc., 1970.

JONES, MALDWYN ALLEN. *American Immigration.* Chicago: University of Chicago Press, 1960.

JOSEPHSON, HANNAH. *The Golden Threads, New England's Mill Girls and Magnates.* New York: Duell, Sloan & Pearce, 1949.

JOSEPHSON, MATTHEW. *The Robber Barons, the Great American Capitalists, 1861–1901.* New York: Harcourt, Brace & World, Inc., 1962.

——. *Sidney Hillman, Statesman of American Labor.* New York: Doubleday & Company, Inc., 1952.

JOUGHIN, LOUIS, and MORGAN, EDMUND M. *The Legacy of Sacco and Vanzetti.* Chicago: Quadrangle Books, Inc., 1964.

KARSNER, DAVID. *Debs, His Authorized Life and Letters.* New York: Boni & Liveright, 1919.

KARSON, MARC. *American Labor Unions and Politics.* Boston: Beacon Press, 1965.

KEFAUVER, ESTES. *In a Few Hands, Monopoly Power in America.* New York: Pantheon Books, Inc., 1965.

KEIR, MALCOLM. *The Epic of Industry.* New Haven: Yale University Press, 1926.

——. *Labor's Search for More.* New York: The Ronald Press Company, 1937.

KORNBLUH, JOYCE L. *Rebel Voices, an IWW Anthology.* Ann Arbor: The University of Michigan Press, 1964.

KORSON, GEORGE. *History of the United Mine Workers.* Washington, D.C.: The United Mine Workers Journal, 1965–1967.

——. *Minstrels of the Mine Patch.* Hatboro, Pennsylvania: Folklore Associates, 1964.

KRAUS, HENRY. *The Many and the Few.* Los Angeles: The Planter Press, 1947.

KUCZYNSKI, JURGEN. *The Rise of the Working Class.* New York: McGraw-Hill Book Company, 1967.

*Labor—Champion of Public Education.* Washington, D.C.: American Federation of Labor and Congress of Industrial Organization, 1970.

*Labor History* (a magazine). New York: The Tamiment Institute, 1960–1972.

*Labor and Politics.* Washington, D.C.: American Federation of Labor and Congress of Industrial Organization, 1970.

LANGDON, MRS. EMMA F. *The Cripple Creek Strike.* Victor Daily Record Press, 1903–1904.

LARCOM, LUCY. *A New England Girlhood.* Boston: Houghton Mifflin Company, 1889.

LASKY, VICTOR. *Arthur J. Goldberg, the Old and the New.* New Rochelle: Arlington House, Inc., 1970.

LENS, SIDNEY. *Radicalism in America.* New York: Thomas Y. Crowell Company, 1969.

LEONARD, EUGENIE ANDRUSS. *The Dear-Bought Heritage.* Philadelphia: University of Pennsylvania Press, 1965.

LePRADE, RUTH. *Debs and the Poets.* Pasadena, California: Upton Sinclair, 1920.

LESTER, RICHARD A. *Labor, Readings on Major Issues.* New York: Random House, Inc., 1965.

LEUCHTENBURG, WILLIAM E. *The Perils of Prosperity, 1914–1932.* Chicago: University of Chicago Press, 1958.

LEVINE, LOUIS. *The Women's Garment Workers.* New

York: B. W. Heubsch, Inc., 1924.

LEVINSON, EDWARD. *I Break Strikes.* New York: Robert M. McBride & Co., 1935.

——. *Labor on the March.* New York: Harper & Brothers, 1938.

LEVY, LEONARD W. *Freedom of Speech and Press in Early American History, Legacy of Supression.* New York: Harper & Row, Publishers, 1963.

——. *The Law of the Commonwealth and Chief Justice Shaw.* 32 Colum. L. Rev. 1128 (1932).

LITWACK, LEON. *The American Labor Movement.* Englewood Cliffs, New Jersey: Prentice-Hall, Inc., 1962.

——. *North of Slavery, the Negro in the Free States, 1790–1860.* Chicago: University of Chicago Press, 1969.

LLOYD, HENRY DEMAREST. *Wealth Against Commonwealth.* New York: Harper & Brothers, 1903.

LUNDBERG, FERDINAND. *America's Sixty Families.* New York: Citadel Press, 1960.

——. *The Rich and the Super Rich.* New York: Bantam Books, Inc., 1968.

LUTHER, SETH. "An Address to the Working Men of New England." In *The Working Man's Advocate,* by George H. Evans, New York, 1833.

LYND, ROBERT S., and MERRELL, HELEN. *Middletown, a Study in Contemporary American Culture.* New York: Harcourt, Brace and Company, Inc., 1929.

LYND, STOUGHTON. *Non-Violence in America.* Indianapolis: The Bobbs-Merrill Co., Inc., 1966.

LYON, PETER. *To Hell in a Day Coach.* Philadelphia: J. B. Lippincott Co., 1968.

MADISON, CHARLES A. *American Labor Leaders.* New York: Frederick Ungar Publishing Co., Inc., 1962.

——. *Critics and Crusaders.* New York: Henry Holt & Co., 1947–1948.

MANDEL, BERNARD. *Labor: Free and Slave.* New York: Associated Authors. 1955.

MARKOFF, SOL. *The Changing Years, 1904–1954.* New York: ·The National Child Labor Committee, 1954.

MASON, LUCY RANDOLPH. *To Win These Rights, a Personal Story of the CIO in the South.* New York: Harper & Brothers, 1952.

McCARTHY, JUSTIN. *A Brief History of the United Mine Workers of America.* Washington, D.C.: United Mine Workers Journal, n.d.

McDONALD, DAVID J. and LYNCH, EDWARD A. *Coal and Unionism, a History of the American Coal Miner's Union.* Silver Springs, Maryland: Cornelius Printing Company, 1939.

McGOVERN, GEORGE S., and GUTTREDGE, LEONARD F. *The Great Coalfield War.* Boston: Houghton Mifflin Co., 1972.

McMASTER, JOHN BACH. *The Acquisition of Political, Social and Industrial Rights of Man in America.* New York: Frederick Ungar Publishing Co., Inc., 1961.

——. *The Political Depravity of the Feuding Fathers.*

New York: The Noonday Press, 1964.

MELTZER, MILTON. *Bread and Roses, The Struggle of American Labor, 1865–1915.* New York: Alfred A. Knopf, Inc., 1967.

——. *A History of the American Negro.* New York: Thomas Y. Crowell Company, 1967.

MIERNYK, WILLIAM H. *Trade Unions in the Age of Affluence.* New York: Random House, Inc., 1964.

MILES, REVEREND HENRY A. *Lowell, As It Was and It Is.* Lowell: Powers and Bagley, 1845.

MINTON, BRUCE, and STUART, JOHN. *Men Who Lead Labor.* New York: Modern Age Books, Inc., 1937.

MINTON, LEE W. *Flame and Heart, a History of the Glass Bottle Blower Association.* Philadelphia: Merkle Press, Inc., 1961.

MIRSKY, JEANNETTE, and NEVINS, ALLAN. *The World of Eli Whitney.* New York: The Macmillan Company, 1952.

MITCHELL, JOHN. *Organized Labor.* Philadelphia, Pennsylvania: American Book and Bible House, 1903.

MONTGOMERY, DAVID. *Beyond Equality, Labor and the Radical Republicans, 1862–1872.* New York: Alfred A. Knopf, Inc., 1967.

*Mooney-Billings Report, The, Suppressed by the Wickersham Commission.* New York: Gotham House, Inc., 1932.

MORAIS, HERBERT M. *The Struggle for American Freedom—The First 200 Years.* New York: International Publishers Co., Inc., 1944.

MORISON, SAMUEL ELIOT. *The Maritime History of Massachusetts—1783–1860.* Boston: Houghton Mifflin Company, 1961.

MORRIS, RICHARD B. *Government and Labor in Early America.* New York: Harper & Row, Publishers, 1965.

MORTIMER, WYNDHAM. *Organize: My Life as a Union Man.* Boston: Beacon Press, 1971.

MOWRY, ARTHUR MAY. *The Dorr War, the Constitutional Struggle for Rhode Island.* New York: Chelsea House Publishers, 1970.

MYERS, GUSTAVUS. *America Strikes Back, a Record of Contrasts.* New York: Ives Washburn, Inc., 1935.

——. *History of Great American Fortunes.* Chicago: Charles H. Kerr & Company, 1917.

NEILL, CHARLES P. *Report on Conditions of Women and Children Wage Earners in the U.S. 19 vols.* Washington, D.C.: Government Printing Office, Senate Docate 645, 61st Congress, 2nd Session, 1910.

NYE, RUSSEL B. *Filtered Freedom—Civil Liberties and the Slavery Controversy, 1830–1860.* East Lansing: Michigan State College Press, 1949.

O'CONNOR, HARVEY. *Steel Dictator.* New York: The Job Day Co., 1935.

OLMSTED, FREDERICK LAW. *The Slave States.* New York: Capricorn Books, 1959.

*One Hundred Years Progress of the United States* (by eminent library men). Hartford, Connecticut: L.

Stebbens, 1870.

PARADIS, ADRIAN A. *The Hungry Years.* Philadelphia: Chilton Book Company, 1967.

——. *Labor in Action, The Story of the American Labor Movement.* New York: Julian Messner, 1963.

PARSONS, LUCY. *Famous Speeches of the Eight Chicago Anarchists.* New York: Arno Press, 1969.

PARTON, JAMES. *The Life of Horace Greeley.* Boston: James R. Osgood & Company, 1872 .

PELLING, HENRY. *American Labor.* Chicago: University of Chicago Press, 1968.

PERKINS, DEXTER. *The New Age of Franklin Roosevelt, 1932–45.* Chicago: University of Chicago Press, 1957.

PERKINS, FRANCES. *The Roosevelt I Knew.* New York: The Viking Press, Inc., 1946.

PERLMAN, SELIG. *A History of Trade Unionism in the United States.* New York: Augustus M. Kelley, Inc., 1950.

PESSEN, EDWARD. *Most Uncommon Jacksonians, The Radical Leaders of the Early Labor Movement.* Albany, New York: State University of New York Press, 1967.

PHELPS, F. WESLEY. *Seven Nights Debates on Closed Shop and Open Shop.* Seattle: The School of Utilitarian Economics, 1922.

PHILLIPS, WENDELL. *Speeches, Lectures and Letters.* Boston: Lee and Shepard, 1894.

PIERSON, FRANK C. *Unions in Post-war America.* New York: Random House, Inc., 1967.

POWDERLY, TERENCE V. *The Path I Trod.* New York: Columbia University Press, 1940.

——. *Thirty Years of Labor, 1859–1889.* Columbus: Excelsior Publishing House, 1889.

PRINGLE, HENRY F. *The Life and Times of William Howard Taft.* Vol. 1. New York: Farrar & Rinehart, Inc., 1939.

PROCEEDINGS *of the First Convention of the Industrial Workers of the World.* New York: The New York Labor News Co., 1905.

QUARLES, BENJAMIN. *Frederick Douglass.* New York: Atheneum Publishers, 1969.

——. *The Negro in the Civil War.* Boston: Little, Brown and Company, 1953.

QUIN, MIKE. *The Big Strike.* Olema, California: Olema Publishing Co., 1949.

RADDOCK, MAXWELL C. *A Portrait of an American Labor Leader: William L. Hutcheson.* New York: American Institute of Social Science, 1955.

RADOSH, RONALD. *American Labor and United States Foreign Policy.* New York: Random House, Inc., 1969. ,

——. ed. *Debs.* Englewood Cliffs, New Jersey: Prentice-Hall, Inc., 1971.

RAE, JOHN B. *The American Automobile, A Brief History.* Chicago: University of Chicago Press, 1965.

RAUCH, BASIL. *The History of the New Deal, 1933–38.* New York: Capricorn Books, 1963.

RAYBACK, JOSEPH G. *A History of American Labor.* New York: The Free Press, 1966.

RENSHAW, PATRICK. *The Wobblies, the Story of Syndicalism in the U.S.* New York: Doubleday & Company, Inc., 1967.

*Report of the First Annual Session of the Federation of Organized Trades and Labor Unions of the United States and Canada.* Cincinnati: Robert Clark & Co., 1882.

*Report of the Lawrence Survey, The.* Studies in relation to Lawrence, Massachusetts, made in 1911. Andover, Massachusetts: The Andover Press, 1912.

*Report on the Steel Strike of 1919 by the Commission of Inquiry, the Interchurch World Movement.* New York: Harcourt, Brace & Howe, 1920.

*Report on the Strike of Textile Workers in Lawrence, Massachusetts, in 1912.* Washington, D.C.: Government Printing Office, state documents 62nd Congress, second session.

REUTHER, WALTER P. *Selected Papers.* New York: The Macmillan Company, 1961.

RIIS, JACOB A. *The Children of the Poor.* New York: Charles Scribner's Sons, 1892.

——. *How the Other Half Lives.* New York: Charles Scribner's Sons, 1902.

RIPLEY, WILLIAM Z. *Trusts, Pools and Corporations.* Boston: Ginn & Co., 1916.

ROBINSON, DONALD B. *Spotlight on a Union, the Story of the United Hatters Cap and Millinery Workers International Union.* New York: The Dial Press, Inc., 1948.

ROCHESTER, ANNA. *Labor and Coal.* New York: International Publishers Co., Inc., 1931.

——. *The Populist Movement in the United States.* New York: International Publishers Co., Inc., 1943.

ROSE, THOMAS. *Violence in America.* New York: Random House, Inc., 1969.

ROVERE, RICHARD H. *Senator Joe McCarthy.* New York: Harcourt, Brace & Company, Inc., 1959.

RUCHANES, LOUIS. *The Abolitionists, a Collection of Their Writings.* New York: Capricorn Books, 1963.

RUHEYSER, MERRYLE STANLEY. *Collective Bargaining: The Power to Destroy.* New York: Dell Publishing Co., Inc., 1968.

RUTTENBER, E. M. *Obstructions to the Navigation of Hudson's River.* Albany: J. Munsell, 1860.

SALZMAN, JACK. *Years of Protest.* New York: Pegasus, 1967.

SANDBURG, CARL. *Abraham Lincoln.* Vols. 1–4. New York: Harcourt, Brace & Company, Inc., 1939.

——. *The People, Yes.* New York: Harcourt, Brace & Company, Inc., 1936.

SCHLESINGER, ARTHUR M., JR. *The Age of Jackson.* Boston: Little, Brown and Company, 1945.

——. *The Crisis of the Old Order—The Age of Roosevelt, 1919–1933.* Boston: Houghton Mifflin Company, 1957.

SCHLUTER, HERMAN. *Lincoln, Labor and Slavery.* New York: Socialist Literature Co., 1913.

SCHWAB, CHARLES M. *Succeeding with What You Have.* New York: The Century Co., 1917.

SCOGGINS, WILL. *Labor in Learning, Public School Treatment of the World of Work.* Los Angeles: University of California (Institute of Industrial Relations), 1966.

SCONESBY, REVEREND WILLIAM. *American Factories and Their Female Operatives.* Boston: William D. Ticknor & Co., 1845.

SHANNON, DAVID A., ed. *The Great Depression.* Englewood Cliffs, New Jersey: Prentice-Hall, Inc., 1960.

*Signature of 450,000.* New York: International Ladies' Garment Workers' Union, 1964.

SIMONDS, JOHN CAMERON, and McENNIS, JOHN T. *The Story of Manual Labor.* Chicago: R. S. Peale & Co., 1887.

SINCLAIR, UPTON. *The Jungle.* New York: The Viking Press, Inc., 1946.

——. ed. *The Cry for Justice,* an anthology of social protest. Philadelphia: The John C. Winston Company, 1915.

SMITH, GIBBS M. *Joe Hill.* Salt Lake City: University of Utah Press, 1969.

SPARGO, JOHN. *The Bitter Cry of the Children.* Chicago: Quadrangle Books, Inc., 1968.

SPERO, STERLING, and HARRIS, ABRAM L. *The Black Worker, the Negro and the Labor Movement.* New York: Atheneum Publishers, 1968.

STAFFORD, WENDELL PHILLIPS. *Wendell Phillips Centenary, 1911.* New York: National Association for the Advancement of Colored People, 1911.

STANDARD, WILLIAM L. *Seamen, a Short History of Their Struggles.* New York: International Publishers Co., Inc., 1947.

STANTON, ELIZABETH CADY. *Eighty Years and More (1815–1897).* New York: European Publishing Company, 1898.

STAVIS, BARRIE. *The Man Who Never Died, a Play About Joe Hill.* New York: Haven Press, 1954.

STEARN, GERALD EMANUEL. *Gompers.* Englewood Cliffs, New Jersey: Prentice-Hall, Inc., 1971.

STEFFENS, LINCOLN. *Autobiography.* New York: Harcourt, Brace & Company, Inc., 1931.

STEIN, LEON. *The Triangle Fire.* Philadelphia: J. B. Lippincott Co., 1962.

——. and TAFT, PHILIP. *American Labor—From Conspiracy to Collective Bargaining.* New York: Arno Press, 1969. 60 vols.

STEVENS, GEORGE A. *New York Typographical Union No. 6.* Albany: J. B. Lyon Co., 1913.

STILL, WILLIAM. *The Underground Railroad Records.* Hartford: Belts & Co., 1886.

STONE, ORVAL. *The History of Massachusetts Industries.* Boston: The S. J. Clarke Co., 1930.

SULLIVAN, MARK. *Our Times.* Vols. 1–6. New York: Charles Scribner's Sons, 1927.

SULZBERGER, C. L. *Sit Down with John L. Lewis.* New York: Random House, Inc., 1938.

SWADOS, HARVEY. *Years of Conscience: The Muckrakers.* Cleveland: The World Publishing Company, 1962.

SWEENEY, VINCENT D. *The United Steelworkers of America.* Pittsburgh: The United Steelworkers, CIO, 1946.

SWINTON, JOHN. *A Momentous Question.* Philadelphia: Keller Publishing Company, 1895.

*Sylvis Said.* Cincinnati: Industrial Molders Union, 1971.

*Symposium on Andrew Furuseth, A.* New Bedford, Massachusetts: The Darwin Press, n.d.

TAFT, PHILIP. *Corruption and Racketeering in the Labor Movement.* New York School of Industrial and Labor Relations, 1970.

——. *Organized Labor in American History.* New York: Harper & Row, Publishers, 1964.

——. and Ross, Philip. "*American Labor Violence: Its Causes, Character and Outcome.*" In *History of Violence in America.* New York: Bantam Books, Inc., 1969.

TERKEL, STUDS. *Hard Times, an Oral History of the Great Depression.* New York: Pantheon Books, Inc., 1970.

THOMPSON, FRED. *The IWW, Its First 50 Years.* Chicago: Industrial Workers of the World, 1955.

TODES, CHARLOTTE. *Labor and Lumber.* New York: International Publishers Co., Inc., 1931.

——. *William H. Sylvis and the National Labor Union.* New York: International Publishers Co., Inc., 1942.

TRACY, GEORGE A. *History of the Typographical Union.* Indianapolis: International Typographical Union, 1913.

TRATTNER, WALTER I. *Crusade for the Children.* Chicago: Quadrangle Books, Inc., 1970.

TURNER, ERNEST S. *What the Butler Saw: Two Hundred and Fifty Years of the Servant Problem.* New York: St. Martin's Press, Inc., 1963.

TYLER, GUS. *The Labor Revolution.* New York: The Viking Press, Inc., 1967.

UNGER, IRWIN. *Beyond Liberalism: The New Left Views American History.* Waltham, Massachusetts: Xerox College Publishing, 1971.

UPHOFF, WALTER H. *Kohler on Strike, Thirty Years of Conflict.* Boston: Beacon Press, 1966.

*U.S. Immigration Commission Report on Steerage Conditions, The.* Washington, D.C.: Government Printing Office, 1909.

VAN VORST, MARIE. *The Woman Who Toils.* New York: Doubleday, Page, and Company, 1903.

VORSE, MARY HEATON. *Labor's New Millions.* New York: Modern Age Books, Inc., 1938.

WALKER, CHARLES RUMFORD. *Steel, the Diary of a Furnace Worker.* Boston: The Atlantic Monthly Press, 1922.

WALLACE, MICHAEL. "The Uses of Violence in American History." *The American Scholar*, Winter, 1970.

WALTON, PERRY. *The Story of Textiles*. New York: Tudor Publishing Co., 1925.

WARE, NORMAN. *The Industrial Worker, 1840–1860*. Chicago: Quadrangle Books, Inc., 1964.

WAXMAN, CHAIM ISAAC. *Poverty: Power and Politics*. New York: Grosset & Dunlap, Inc., 1968.

WEEKS, LYMAN HORACE. *The History of Paper Manufacturing in the United States, 1690–1916*. New York: Lockwood Trade Journal Company, 1916.

WEEKS, ROBERT P. *Commonwealth vs. Sacco and Vanzetti*. Englewood Cliffs, New Jersey: Prentice-Hall, Inc., 1962.

WERSTEIN, IRVING. *Labor's Defiant Lady—The Story of Mother Jones*. New York: Thomas Y. Crowell Company, 1969.

WEST, GEORGE P. *United States Commission on Industrial Relations Report on the Colorado Strike*. Washington, D.C.: Government Printing Office, 1915.

WHITE, GEORGE S. *Memoirs of Samuel Slater, Father of American Manufactures*. Philadelphia: Printed at No. 46 Carpenter St., 1836.

WILEY, BELL IRVIN. *The Life of Billy Yank*. Indianapolis: The Bobbs-Merrill Co., Inc., 1966.

WILLEY, FREEMAN OTIS. *The Laborer and the Capitalist*. New York: The National Economic League, 1896.

WILSON, MITCHELL. *American Science and Invention*. New York: Simon and Schuster, Inc., 1954.

WINKLER, JOHN K. *Incredible Carnegie*. New York: Vanguard Press, Inc., 1931.

WISSLER, CLARK. *Indians in the United States*. New York: Doubleday and Co., 1966.

WITTE, EDWIN E. *The Development of the Social Security Act*. Madison: University of Wisconsin Press, 1962.

WOLFF, LEON. *Lockout, The Story of the Homestead Strike of 1892*. New York: Harper & Row, Publishers, 1965.

WOODHAM-SMITH, CECIL. *The Great Hunger*. New York: The New American Library, Inc., 1962.

WOODWARD, C. VANN. *Tom Watson, Agrarian Rebel*. New York: Oxford University Press, 1969.

WOOFTER, T. J., JR., and WINSTON, ELLEN. *Seven Lean Years*. Chapel Hill, North Carolina: University of North Carolina Press, 1939.

*Workers' Story—1913–1953, The*. Washington, D.C.: Labor Year Book II, United States Department of Labor, 1953.

WRIGHT, MORRIS. *"Takes More Than Guns," a Brief History of the International Union of Mine, Hull and Smelter Workers*. Denver, n.d.

WYTRWAL, JOSEPH A. *Poles in American History and Tradition*. Detroit: Endurance Press, 1969.

YELLEN, SAMUEL. *American Labor Struggles*. New York: Harcourt, Brace and Company, Inc., 1936.

*Your Civil Rights*, A Handbook for Trade Union Members and Organizers. Congress of Industrial Organizations, 1946.

# SOURCES
# AND ACKNOWLEDGMENTS

To even begin to extend acknowledgments for a book of this scope is difficult.

Those who helped through their superior access to information were credited in the text where possible, without interrupting the book's readability. Most, we hope, are included in the acknowledgments or bibliography.

For specific written or pictorial contributions, as well as information, patience, and suggestions, we owe thanks to many people including: James Barnett, Millen Brand, Professor Robert V. Bruce, Hope M. Cinquegrana, Stephen C. Clark, Harry Collins, Dr. Jack Foster, Horace Goodson, John A. Goodwin, Richard Jackson, Ann Koburger, Dr. Martin Krieger, Ann Huber Maurer, Gilbert R. Merrill, Marsha Peters, Vianna Ramirez, Eilleen Reilly, Professor Leo Ribuffo, Judith A. Schiff, Steven Schultz, Ruth Smerechniak, and Moreau B. C. Chambers.

The selection of pictures followed the review of many thousands of photographs, drawings, woodcuts, engravings, letters, diaries, cartoons, archives. In a sense, the visual materials appearing in these pages are a graphic arts honor roll, for both meaning and quality. It is unfortunate that their source is not always known.

Institutions and organizations that assisted in small ways or large with information or materials include the following. Picture contributions are indicated by page number designations. Pictorial material appearing without page designation is from the author's collection. The positions of pictures on pages are indicated by abbreviations: L (left); C (center); R (right); T (top); M (middle); B (bottom).

Abbot Public Library, Marblehead, Massachusetts
Alderman Library, University of Virginia, Charlottesville, Virginia—9(B), 18(B), 19, 60(TR)
Aluminum Company of America
Amalgamated Clothing Workers of America (AFL–CIO)—238(B), 240(B), 263(T), 303(B)
Amalgamated Meat Cutters and Butcher Workmen of North America (AFL–CIO)
American Federation of Labor and Congress of Industrial Organizations—2(TR), 137(TL), 138(B), 163(BR), 209(TR), 242(TR), 283(B), 285, 286, 290
American Hoist & Derrick Company, St. Paul, Minnesota
American Iron and Steel Institute, Washington, D.C.
American Philosophical Society, Philadelphia—11
American Telephone and Telegraph Photograph Service—293
Andover (Massachusetts) Historical Society

Anheuser-Busch, Inc.
Armco Steel Corporation
The Art Institute of Chicago—96(T), Collection of Mr. and Mrs. Martin A. Ryerson
Association of American Railroads—295(B), 299(BR)
Bakery and Confectionery Workers' International Union of America
Bethlehem Steel Corporation, Inc.—233(T)
BIF, General Signal Corporation
Boot and Shoe Workers (AFL–CIO)
Boston Public Library, Government Documents Division—48
Brockton (Massachusetts) Public Library
Brown Brothers, New York—154, 161(BL), 164, 178(B), 184(MR), 189(B), 200(BL), 201(TL), 213, 220, 226(MR), 227(BR), 235(TL), 241(B), 269(T), 274
Bureau of Indian Affairs—297(BL), 309
Cahn, Daniel—295(T)
Carnegie Library of Pittsburgh
Catholic University of America, Washington, D.C.
Chicago Historical Society—95, 118, 136(T)
Cincinnati Historical Society—91(L)
City of Concord, New Hampshire
City Library, Lawrence, Massachusetts
City Library, Lowell, Massachusetts
Cleveland Museum of Art
Colorado Department of State—204(BL)
Congress of Industrial Organizations—257(B), 259(MR), 262(TR), 272(BR), 279, 280, 283(M)
Connecticut Historical Society—51(TL), 52, 61(TL), 68(MR), 82(B)
Connecticut State Department of Health
Connecticut State Library
Corcoran Gallery of Art, Washington, D.C.—176
Dartmouth College Library, Hanover, New Hampshire—vii
Debs, Eugene V. Foundation, Terre Haute, Indiana
Detroit Public Library—38(TR)
Detroit *Times*—264(TL)
Drug and Hospital Union, Local 1199 (AFL–CIO)—275(TR)(B), 301(T), 308
du Pont de Nemours, E. I. & Company, Wilmington, Delaware
Eleutherian Mills Historical Library, Wilmington, Delaware
Enoch Pratt Free Library, Baltimore
Farm Workers of America (AFL–CIO)
Federal Security Agency, Public Health Service—299(TL)
Ford Motor Company—238(TL), 239
Franklin D. Roosevelt Library, Hyde Park, New York

Free Library of Philadelphia

Free Public Library of Rowley, Massachusetts

General Motors Corporation

George Eastman House, Rochester, New York—184(TR), 193(ML), 198(BR)

Goodyear Tire & Rubber Company

Granite Cutters' International Association of America (AFL–CIO)

Gulf Oil Corporation

Hall of Records, Annapolis, Maryland

Harvard University, Baker Library, Graduate School of Business Administration—49(T)

Haverhill (Massachusetts) Public Library

Illinois Labor History Society

Industrial Union Department (AFL–CIO)

Industrial Workers of the World—203(TR)(MR), 225

International Association of Machinists and Aerospace Workers (AFL–CIO)—140

International Brotherhood of Teamsters, Chauffeurs, Warehousemen and Helpers

International Business Machines Corporation

International Ladies' Garment Workers' Union (AFL–CIO)—298(BR)

International Longshoremen's and Warehousemen's Union (ILWU)—255

International Maritime Union of America (AFL–CIO)

International Molders and Allied Workers Union (AFL–CIO)—114

International Salt Company

International Typographical Union—67(TC)(TR)(BR), 68(TR), 70(TR), 121(MR)

International Union, United Automobile, Aerospace & Agricultural Implement Workers of America—299(BR)

Jones and Laughlin Steel Corporation

Journeymen Tailors' Union (ACWA, AFL–CIO)

Kaiser Aluminum, Inc.—291

Kelley, Augustus M.—198(BC)

*Labor* (a newspaper)

Lackawanna Historical Society

Lawrence (Massachusetts) Public Library—50(MC)

Library, Boston Athenaeum

Library of Congress, Manuscript Division, Washington, D.C.

Library of Congress, Prints and Photograph Division—ii, x, 1(R), 6(B), 7(T), 17, 22(MR), 36(B), 69(MR), 70(B), 89(T), 99(BR), 101, 108(T), 119, 120, 121(TR)(ML), 134(TR), 135(B), 162, 167(TL), 168(TR), 169, 170, 175(T)(ML)(BL), 179, 180(B), 182, 183(TL), 185(T), 192(BR), 193(TR)(BR), 196, 199(TR), 208(TR), 210(TL), 234(BL), 237, 244(B), 245(TL), 248(T), 298(TL)

Lincoln National Life Foundation, Fort Wayne, Indiana —90(TL)

Lithographers and Photo Engravers International Union (AFL–CIO)—287(ML)

Maine Historical Society

Major League Baseball Players Association, New York City

Maryland Hall of Records—159

Maryland Historical Society

Massachusetts Historical Society

Massachusetts State House, Boston—7(L)

Merrimack Valley Textile Museum, North Andover, Massachusetts—53(TL)

Metropolitan Museum of Art—74(T) Morris K. Jessup Fund; 109 The Harris Brisbane Dick Fund

Missouri State Historical Society

Mount Vernon Ladies' Association of the Union, Mount Vernon, Virginia

Museum of Art, Carnegie Institute, Pittsburgh

Museum of the City of New York—41(B)

Museum of Fine Arts, Boston—38(B)

Museum of Modern Art, Film Library—249(BR)

National Archives

National Association for the Advancement of Colored People

National Basketball Association—298(TC)

National Broadcasting Company—231(T), 238(MR), 240(T)

National Maritime Union of America

National Safety Council

National Sharecroppers Fund—3(BR), 247(BR), 301(BL), 304(T) (George Ballis)

Nebraska State Historical Society

New Hampshire Historical Society

New Haven Colony Historical Society

New York City Central Labor Council (AFL–CIO)—208(MR), 314 (Archer photo)

New-York Historical Society

New York Public Library—62, 64(MR), 65

New York Public Library, Art and Architecture Division

New York Public Library, Picture Collection—vi, 6(T), 10(T), 15, 21, 30(B), 31, 32, 34(TL), 59, 66(BR), 71(TC), 76, 79, 81, 82(T), 83(T), 84(T), 102, 109, 112, 129(TL), 167(TL), 187(B), 252(B)

New York Public Library, Schomberg Collection—116(TM), 278(T)

New York State Department of Labor—192(T), 215(T)(BR)

New York State Library

New York State School of Industrial and Labor Relations, Cornell University, Ithaca, New York

New York Telephone Company—245(TR)

Oil, Chemical and Atomic Workers, International Union (AFL–CIO)—271(T)

Pawtucket (Rhode Island) Public Library

Pennsylvania State University Library—117(T)

Photoworld, New York City—2(BR), 26(R), 139(L), 180(T), 191, 192(MR), 199(TL), 199(BR), 205(T), 206, 208(MR), 215(BL), 221, 222(T), 223(T), 227(TR), 230, 241(T), 242(TL), 243, 247(T), 249(T), 250, 253, 256, 257(T), 258(T)(BR), 259(BR), 260, 262(B), 265(MR), 268, 272(T), 279(T), 284

Providence Historical Society—61(MR)

Providence Public Library

Public Library of Cincinnati and Hamilton County

# INDEX

*Italic* figures refer to illustrations.

# ABOUT THE AUTHOR

William Cahn, a graduate of Dartmouth College, is the author of seventeen books and numerous articles on labor and corporate history. In all his writings he seeks to emphasize the importance of the human role in an industrialized society. As a newspaperman he covered the advance of industrial unionism in the thirties and over the years met such leading labor figures as John L. Lewis, William Green, Walter Reuther, David Dubinsky, Harry Bridges, Heywood Broun, Philip Murray, and others.

His research and writing on labor subjects received the unusual distinction of being cited by two American Presidents: Franklin D. Roosevelt and Lyndon B. Johnson.

Mr. Cahn's books include *Out of the Cracker Barrel*, the story of Nabisco; *A Matter of Life and Death*, the story of Connecticut Mutual; *The Story of Pitney-Bowes; Milltown*, the story of an industrial town; *The Story of Writing* (with Rhoda Cahn); and biographies of Albert Einstein, Harold Lloyd, Van Cliburn, and others.

Mr. Cahn lives with his family in New Haven, Connecticut. He has recently collaborated with his wife on *No Time for School, No Time for Play*, the story of child labor in America.